Contents

IMPERSONATIONS
Troubling the Person in Law and
Culture

Personhood is considered at once a sign of legal-political status and of socio-cultural agency, synonymous with the rational individual, subject, or citizen. Yet, in an era of life-extending technologies, genetic engineering, corporate social responsibility, and smart technology, the definition of the person is neither benign nor uncontested. Boundaries that previously worked to secure our place in the social order are blurring as never before. What does it mean, then, to be a person in the twenty-first century?

In *Impersonations*, Sheryl N. Hamilton uses five different kinds of persons – corporations, women, clones, computers, and celebrities – to discuss the instability of the concept of personhood and to examine some of the ways in which broader social anxieties are expressed in these case studies. She suggests that our investment in personhood is greater now than it has been for years, and that our ongoing struggle to define the term is evident in law and popular culture. Using a cultural studies of law approach, the author examines important issues such as whether the person is a gender-neutral concept based on individual rights, what the relationship is between personhood and the body, and whether persons can be property.

Impersonations is a highly original study that brings together legal, philosophical, and cultural expressions of personhood to enliven current debates about our place in the world.

SHERYL N. HAMILTON is Canada Research Chair in Communication, Law, and Governance and an associate professor in the School of Journalism and Communication and in the Department of Law at Carleton University.

SHERYL N. HAMILTON

Impersonations

Troubling the Person in Law and Culture

UNIVERSITY OF TORONTO PRESS
Toronto Buffalo London

© University of Toronto Press 2009
Toronto Buffalo London
www.utppublishing.com
Printed in the U.S.A.

Reprinted in paperback 2013
Reprinted 2014

ISBN 978-0-8020-9846-7 (cloth)
ISBN 978-1-4426-1606-6 (paper)

Printed on acid-free paper

Library and Archives Canada Cataloguing in Publication

Hamilton, Sheryl N., 1965–
    Impersonations : troubling the person in law and culture / Sheryl N. Hamilton.

    Includes bibliographical references and index.
    ISBN 978-0-8020-9846-7 (bound) ISBN 978-1-4426-1606-6 (pbk.)

    1. Persons.   2. Persons (Law).   3. Culture and law.   4. Technology – Social
    aspects.   5. Technology – Philosophy.   6. Philosophical anthropology.
    I. Title.

BD450.H253 2009   128   C2008-904591-2

University of Toronto Press acknowledges the financial assistance to
its publishing program of the Canada Council for the Arts and the
Ontario Arts Council.

This book has been published with the help of a grant from the Canadian
Federation for the Humanities and Social Sciences, through the Aid to
Scholarly Publications programme, using funds provided by the Social
Sciences and Humanities Research Council of Canada.

University of Toronto Press acknowledges the financial support of
the Government of Canada through the Canada Book Fund for its
publishing activities.

To my mother and father,
who taught me that I could do anything I put my mind to.
Thank you.

Acknowledgments

This project has been a long and challenging journey for me and I could not have done it without the friendship and assistance of numerous people and organizations.

My thanks to all my colleagues at both McGill University and Carleton University who have offered invaluable guidance and support. I couldn't have asked for more. The project could not have been completed without the generous financial support of both McGill and Carleton universities, the Social Sciences and Humanities Research Council of Canada, and the Fonds québécois de la recherche sur la société et la culture.

Without three graduate students, this book would never have been completed. To Elizabeth Wright, thank you for our shared pleasure in language and its playfulness. To Emily Truman, your intelligence, tenacity, and skill were repeatedly invaluable to me at many points in this project. What would I do without you? And to John Shiga – who managed to complete both an MA and a PhD in the time it has taken me to get this finished – after all your research, creative energy, and our shared interests in a number of the issues present in this book, all I can say is that I hope you like it!

Finally, saving the best for last, to the two most important people in my life. To my daughter, Brigitte, who is my reason to get up every morning: the journey of this book parallels the first few years of your life and I hope I have done justice to both. I hope you will be proud of your mom. To my husband, Neil Gerlach, you are the love of my life and without your support, intellectual camaraderie, love, and friendship, there would be no point in doing any of it.

IMPERSONATIONS:
TROUBLING THE PERSON IN LAW AND CULTURE

1 Introduction: Troubling the Person

It might turn out ... that the concept of person is only a free-floating honorific that we are all happy to apply to ourselves, and to others as the spirit moves us, guided by our emotions, aesthetic sensibilities, considerations of policy and the like.

(Dennett, 1976: 176)

Personalities have become surpassing legal fictions. In the name of an ogre twin, they threaten with oblivion the original embodiment of ourselves. ... Bluntly put, artificial persons, juristic personalities, and deceased personalities have been invested with greater presence than any indigenous embodied person. If such there be.

(Schwartz, 1996: 330–1)

On 25 February 1990, Theresa Marie Schiavo, subsequently known to the world as 'Terri' Schiavo, suffers a cardiac arrest apparently caused by a potassium imbalance. Her brain is deprived of oxygen for more than five minutes and severe brain damage results. Her husband, Michael, is appointed her guardian and various medical efforts are undertaken to rehabilitate her. Terri cannot speak or care for herself; she is fed through a feeding tube surgically implanted into her abdomen as she would aspirate any food or liquids placed in her mouth. Within three years of her cardiac arrest, she is pronounced by doctors to be in a 'persistent vegetative state' (PVS), a medical term to denote a lack of self-awareness, language comprehension, expression, and interactivity. These attributes exist despite periods where patients' eyes may be open, they exhibit some reflexes, and can even make some noises, words, and faces. In addition to finding Terri in a state of PVS, doctors note that she has no hope of recovery.[1]

After a 1992 medical malpractice suit results in an out-of-court settlement, including damages of $300,000 for Michael Schiavo and approximately $750,000 to be held in trust for Terri's care, Michael and Terri's parents, Robert and Mary Schindler, have a falling out regarding the preferred course of her therapeutic treatment. Terri's parents attempt to have Michael removed as her guardian in 1993, but the court refuses; further, a court-appointed guardian reports in 1994 that Michael has acted appropriately throughout. In 1998, Michael petitions a Florida court to have his wife's feeding tube removed, claiming that while she did not leave a 'living will,' she indicated to him verbally that she would not want to continue living in such a state. A second court-appointed guardian confirms that Terri is in a PVS, but also notes that Michael's decision-making may be influenced by his conflict of interest, as he stands to inherit her estate upon her death. Judge George Greer of the Pinellas-Pasco County Circuit Court finds Michael's testimony as to Terri's wishes credible and orders the removal of the feeding tube on 11 February 2000. Her death will result in approximately seven to fourteen days.[2] Her parents appeal that decision immediately, asserting that Terri is responsive and can recover with treatment. What follows is five further years of bitter legal wrangling over the status of Terri Schiavo and what should happen to her.[3]

Allegations of abuse and attempted murder are levelled against Michael Schiavo (who has a fiancée with whom he has two children); the conservative Christian Right, disability groups, and anti-abortionists launch protests, rally public opinion, and sit vigil outside Terri's hospice; and the judge in the case, who orders the removal of the feeding tube a total of three times, receives death threats. However, as almost any adult living in North America in 2005 remembers, the legal wrangling spilled out of the courts and into the halls of the Florida legislature, the Oval Office, the United States Congress, the Vatican, and the living rooms of a nation.

In 2003, Florida governor Jeb Bush mobilizes a discourse of 'a culture of life' in order to justify legislation hastily passed through the Florida legislature – 'Terri's law' – giving him the specific power to order a stay in 'certain cases.'[4] The legislation is denounced by experts and is subsequently held unconstitutional by the Florida Supreme Court. President Bush publicly commends his brother on how he has dealt with the case. Finally, after innumerable appeals and legal motions, the feeding tube is removed for the third and final time on 18 March 2005. The Florida legislature then makes a last-ditch effort to pass a bill which would have prohibited PVS patients from being denied food and water in the absence of their written intentions; however it fails by a Senate vote of 21–18. A Vatican Cardinal speaks to the Schiavo case in March 2005 on Vatican radio and Pope John Paul II himself issues a statement calling her death 'a violation of the sacred nature of life' that has 'shocked consciences' (in Goodnough, 2005: 1).[5] The American House of Representatives and the Senate each pass different legislation pertaining to the Schiavo case and then delay their respective recesses, working over the Easter weekend in 2005 to arrive at a joint bill which passes on 20 March, Palm Sunday. President George Bush returns early from his Easter holiday to sign the legislation that gives individual citizens an extraordinary right of action against the government for relief when other legal and administrative options have been exhausted. The United States Supreme Court repeatedly refuses to hear the case. Public opinion polls indicate that Americans generally favour Michael Schiavo's position, with even a small majority of those identifying themselves as evangelical Christians agreeing that the feeding tube should be removed.[6] Terri Schiavo dies of dehydration on 31 March 2005, thirteen days after food and water are withheld from her. A subsequent autopsy reveals that her brain had shrunk to half its normal size, that she was blind, and that there was no evidence of abuse by Michael Schiavo leading to her cardiac arrest (an allegation supported by Governor Jeb Bush). Polls after her death reveal a significant proportion of Americans disapproved of how President Bush, Governor Bush, and Congress handled the issue (Harris Poll, 2005, University of Miami, online).[7]

What is likely the most virulent and well-known debate over the conditions of personhood in recent years was mobilized, not by the request of Michael Schiavo to have his wife's feeding tube removed because of her diagnosis of PVS with no chance of recovery, but by six minutes of clandestine videotape footage of Terri Schiavo in which she appears to follow the movement of a balloon with her eyes, to smile at her mother, and to respond to her father's kiss. This footage was placed on the Internet and seems to have been the catalyst for the protests and supporters outside the hospice. The medical community's counterclaim that Terri's 'actions' in the video had to be random muscular responses, not directed by consciousness, and further, were highly selective moments, seems a weak rebuttal to the imagery which moved millions of viewers.

The combined terms of the diagnosis of a persistent vegetative state with no hope of recovery and the videotape imagery cause a nation to question how we characterize Terri Schiavo. Is she a person? A human being? A body? She is clearly not a person in the narrow, legal sense of the term, as she has neither the mental nor communicative capacities to represent herself legally. As a result, she has a legal guardian. But the legal answer does not resolve the broader issues of personhood playing out in the public imaginary. These include: what is the difference between a person and a human being? How do we make sense of the competing logics of ethics, religion, medicine, and law when each makes a different claim about the personhood of the same being? What should be the role of the state in determining our personhood? What is the relationship between the body and the person? Latent within many of these questions is a broader and even more difficult question: in what elements of human life is the essence of our personhood defined? For example, is our personhood constituted in our capacity to communicate with others? Is it in some notion of consciousness or self-awareness? Is it in our intellectual abilities or cognitive functions? Is it in our capacity to recognize and register a response to pain, physical or emotional, to interact with others, or to respond to our external environment? Is it a question of quality of life? Or, as one editorialist put it, is there 'a performance standard' of personhood (Hasbrouck, 2003: A27)?

Terri Schiavo's case elevated all of these questions to the forefront of the American legal, political, and social agenda. Yet more important, for my purposes, than absolute answers to any of the above questions is what else we see taking place in the case of Terri Schiavo. I suggest there are five key elements of our ongoing struggles with personality that are rendered visible in the Schiavo saga. First, we see that despite the fact that our human rights codes seemingly resolve many thorny issues of personality with which we have grappled historically, questions of personhood always lurk close by. They cannot be silenced or prevented by legislative action alone, however progressive or well-intentioned, nor is there a finite list of personhood claims that we have resolved over the course of the nineteenth and twentieth centuries. Who or what gets to be a person remains a very contested issue in the twenty-first century.

In many ways, with the simultaneous philosophical and scientific assaults on our modernist binaries of person and property, animal and object, nature and culture, human and machine, issues of personhood are engaging us more vigorously than they have for many years. These issues, played out on the terrain of legal personhood, are also simultaneously moral issues. At the same time, however, the current debates are always in necessary, if sometimes silent, dialogue with the powerful historical legacies of personhood – who or what has been declared a person in the past. 'The different understandings of person bequeathed by history thus continue to play a profound and troubling role in modern life and thought' (Hunter, 2005: 256). And as always, the stakes of these debates are very high – as we saw with Schiavo, personhood is a life and death matter.

These are the 'troubles' that are one key element of the title of this book. These troubles reveal our deep investment in the notion of the person; they make visible the fictions by which we order our social relations. Increasingly however, the notion of the person is unable to suture these fictions – we are different from (and better than) animals, we are different from things (because we are subjects), we are different from machines (because we have consciousness) – and our deep-seated social anxieties bubble up to the surface. And this brings up the second meaning of 'troubling' in the title. The Terry Schiavo case and the others that I will explore in the following chapters trouble the very notion of the person. They worry its easy claims, they poke at its complacency, they challenge its naturalization.

The Terri Schiavo case also helps us to see a second key aspect of personality – that questions of personhood are most powerfully produced by and through what I call liminal beings. The subject in a persistent vegetative state – with a heartbeat and the capacity to breathe but not reason, able to speak but not communicate, able to move but not interact – poses terrible dilemmas for us. Liminal beings inhabit the boundary zones between the comfortable categories of animal, vegetable, and mineral with which we prefer to organize the order of things. They are powerful because they make us uncomfortable – we recognize ourselves in them, and, at the same time, they are Other. Liminal beings are unnatural subjects. Sometimes they seem to straddle our categories – simultaneously object and subject, for example. Other times they reveal our categories for the constructed fictions that they are, exposing them as untenable at best, absurd at worst. They are always unruly, promiscuous, and troublesome entities. Liminal beings force an encounter with personhood, requiring us to recognize the instability of one of our most fundamental concepts of the self. As Amélie Oksenberg Rorty notes of the 'fringe case,' 'the real point of such thought-experiments is to untangle the various strands in our conceptions, to show that although they normally support one another, they are independent, and can sometimes be pulled apart' (Rorty, 1976b: 3). Not all liminal beings wear the mantle of personhood easily; not all desire it. And yet all provoke the working out of our anxieties around the elusive and central notion of the person because they cannot be easily rendered in person-terms.

Third, in the tale of Terri Schiavo, we can recognize the production of various technologies of personification, from feeding tubes and respirators, to 'do-not-resuscitate' orders, to 'living wills,' to legislation on disabilities, to public opinion polls. These operate as socially sanctioned mechanisms to ascribe, mark, and verify personhood. Technologies of personification operate as categorical imperatives; we use them to mark boundaries between person and non-person, between life and death, and to locate individual subjects within one of our requisite categories. These technologies emanate from the expert knowledge systems to which we, as a society, defer – most often, medical science and law. Science and law offer manifest, 'objective' measures by which we recognize our mutual personhood, while other knowledge systems do not. In the case of Terri Schiavo, medical science, pre- and post-mortem, confirmed non-personality through claims regarding brain size, nerve function, and so on, verified through electroencephalograms, autopsies, and diagnostic language and categories. Religion, on the other hand, can provide no objective measure of the 'soul' that could also be understood as the anchor of Schiavo's personality, and even secular ethics requires for its credibility a performance of social acceptance as to right and wrong that is somehow not captured by mere public opinion polling.

One of the most significant technologies of personification is, of course, language. Doctors in Schiavo's case were continually frustrated with the media's use of a language of 'starvation' to describe what would happen to her once the feeding tube was withdrawn. They felt that this terminology raised the spectre of starving children in Africa and implied that Schiavo would feel discomfort and pain (Schwartz, 2005: 14). More than semantic quibbling, it matters whether we call someone a human being, an individual, a higher life form, or a person. It matters when we anthropomorphize seemingly inanimate objects and objectify seemingly animate ones. It matters whether the dispute in the Schiavo case was over the disposition of a person or the disposition of a body. In language, the woman Terri Schiavo became the symbol 'Terri,' a semantic resource to be deployed by a number of interest groups.[8] Language is, in short, our most powerful technology of personification and the one upon which all others are reliant.

One could tell the story of Terri Schiavo as a sequence of legal events, applications for injunctions, trials, appeals, constitutional challenges, and so on. However, that telling would be far too spare, missing many of the noteworthy elements that made this dispute a significant public event, made Schiavo a compelling public figure. In this way, the Schiavo 'case' highlights the fourth element – that issues of personhood are always, necessarily, but only ever partially, imbricated in legal relations. Personality has long been, if not a juridical question, then at least a juridified one. Who is or is not a person is, in many ways, a fundamentally legal question; it often begins its public dialogue in law. There is no particular common law of persons, but rather, personhood disputes are found across a great variety of types of law, from patent to contract. However, as we can also see, personality is not only, nor is it perhaps most significantly, a legal question. Questions of the person, the treatment of liminal beings, always exceed law's capacity to render them sensible. The complicated embeddedness of these issues prevents any single knowledge system from determining their resolution. Instead, what we see is a playing out of different technologies of personification across myriad social and cultural locations with wide-ranging effects, structured in various social, political, economic, and cultural relations, and yet never determined by them. Tellingly, law is not always the most powerful of those social locations; its is not always the authoritative telling. Too often, we look only to law, politics, and science to resolve questions of personhood, rather than looking to our cultural narratives for other ways of looking, other epistemologies. It is necessary, I suggest, to look elsewhere as well.

And this begins to highlight what I suggest is the fifth central element of our twenty-first-century grappling with personhood that the events around one severely disabled woman allow us to discern: our preferred modality for thinking about persons is the story. In order to make the determination of whether or not Terri Schiavo is a person, we want to learn about what her life was like 'before'; we want to know how it happened; we want to see her family. This is arguably why the illicit videotape made such a difference. It put a face to the name, and we know that behind each face is a story. In this way, each otherwise possibly esoteric, technical, or legal dispute of personhood is always the story of some one's personhood. As Ross Poole claims, '[t]he concept of personhood invites us to abstract our identity from those very narrative resources – birth, growth and development, sexuality, procreation, friendship, decay, death – which we require to make sense of our lives' (1996: 50). Persons necessarily have 'life' stories. Thus, while Poole's claim that '[p]ersonhood does not provide a story at all' (ibid.) is accurate if one considers the abstracted notion of the person, liminal beings, on the other hand, are determined to tell their stories.

At the same time, the story has always been a première instrument for the working out of our troubles, for thinking about, if not resolving, issues that are morally divisive or apparently irresolvable. For example, the animated series *South Park*, after Schiavo's death, placed its character Kenny (who is regularly killed within the episodes and appears again in the following week) in a vegetative state, kept alive with a feeding tube. The doctor tells Kenny's parents, 'Kenny is the same as he ever was. It's just that he's more like a tomato.' The question of whether to remove the tube divides the other three South Park protagonists: two want him to live and one wants him to die so that he can inherit the Sony PlayStation that Kenny has willed to him. Although many would see this as in bad taste, creator Matt Stone noted in an interview in April 2005, '[t]here's kind of nothing funny about the Terri Schiavo thing, so that's why we did it. ... We, like everyone else, found the whole thing fascinating. That show, and humor in general, is how we work it out' (in Arthur, 2005: 8). While this is an extreme example, it is in and through media that these institutional and individual battles over personhood become public; it is in popular culture that we narrate these issues back to ourselves, putting faces to them; it is through these stories that we 'work out,' although not necessarily to simple resolution, what intrigues, bothers, and impassions us about who and what gets to be a person, why and with what social effects.

Stories generally have a beginning, middle, and end. They have protagonists and antagonists. They have plot lines, climaxes, and dénouements. The best stories do not always have happy endings, but we learn about our selves from reading them. Rorty suggests that the thought experiments of personhood fringe cases are 'always underdescribed' (Rorty, 1976b: 3). I am trying to remedy that shortcoming with the life stories of my liminal beings, my fringe cases. Throughout, I adopt the story as an epistemological strategy, both reproducing and analysing the stories about persons told elsewhere, but also attempting to weave these into, and construct, my own narratives in order to expose our disquiet with liminal beings, and ultimately with our selves, as persons. As well, these tales of personification remind us that cultural activity – collective sense-making, representation, and experience – takes place in a variety of social locations and arenas and through a variety of different social processes. In many ways then, what follows is a series of loosely interlinked stories about some of the liminal beings that have become important to us over the twentieth century and into the twenty-first: corporations, women, clones, computers, and celebrities. Each of these beings, in different ways, articulates anxieties that we have about persons: at this point in history, can the person be a moral agent, should they be, what might that even mean? Is the person a sex-neutral concept, or is it always already sexed and/or gendered? Whither the line between human being and object, between human being and animal? Can personality be constituted in the mind alone, in reasoned activity? In other words, what is the status of the human body? And finally, how can we represent the person? What are the effects of doing so? What is and should be the relationship between our 'selves' and the public performance of our personality?

All stories, including each of those detailed here, in addition to their main 'plotline,' offer a web of tangled subplots. In my stories, these subplots are other developments, concepts, and power formations that become visible as an effect of the personation of liminal beings. This is because the ways in which we denote persons are a potent articulation of how we order our society. Therefore, we see subplots of national sovereignty, commodities, animals, and heroes, of prudence and expertise, of social science fictions and imitation games. My stories, therefore, reveal these subplots, all indebted, but none determined by or limited to, the main storyline of impersonation.

In each of these five cases, I suggest that a dynamic is visible – that between person and persona. A persona is a socially active, culturally produced trace of the person, a copy of the person, and yet never subordinate to its original. The persona is the concrete manifestation of the necessarily individuating abstraction that is the person. To render something a person is to make it abstract, to make it generalizable, to individuate it, to place it in a larger category with other similar entities. And yet, in the case of liminal beings, the lived articulation of that person, the experience of that particular aspect of personhood, takes place in the persona. Consideration of the persona is therefore necessary in order to ground the discussions of the person, and to recognize the gaps between categorizing personhood and doing it. Liminal beings inevitably leak out of the categories of personhood, regardless of how complicated we attempt to make them. The notion of the persona helps us to understand this always incomplete process and the citizens, bystanders, and interlopers who are produced by and within it. Personae and persons are intimately linked and often difficult to separate, and yet, at the same time, if we want to understand what else is produced in our encounters with issues of personhood, we need that Other concept. For example, the corporation has always been a problematic person, if measured according to the categories of Western liberal personhood. However, I suggest that as an imitation person, as a partial person, simultaneously less than and more powerful than any embodied human person, the corporation has always been more persona than person.

Personae are constituted in their activity, in their performance of personality in public arenas, rather than in their inhabitance of a predetermined category or their essential characteristics. In fact, their personhood cannot be articulated in their essential characteristics. They are the products of our broader cultural unease with letting 'others' into the category of person that seems ultimately to best fit, and be modelled upon, the 'reasonable man.' As a result, personae are what results when liminal beings are subjected to technologies of personification and pass the test, sort of. Women, corporations, computers, clones, and celebrities all fail as full persons. They never quite make it. And so their personhood encounters allow us to recognize the fragility of our own concept of person, its limits, and also its normalizing power. At the same time, we see that if we want to take account of these liminal beings after their efforts at personification, we need another, richer notion. I offer persona. The liminal beings do not, as many legal or political commentators would assert, become persons, unproblematically; rather I argue, they become personae. As such, they are always somewhat discomfiting: performances of personhood that reveal as much about embodied, reasoning human persons as they do about the liminal being in question. Personae manifest our anxieties about personhood. Personae are lumpy, incomplete, and always simultaneously less and more than persons.

The distinction between person and persona is one that dates back to ancient Greece and Rome, and the linguistic split between Latin and Greek notions of the person. In Latin, heavily influenced by Roman law, the person, as *persona*, is a reference to agency, a 'being in context, as enabled by and embedded in the legal structure' (O'Hara, 1997: 20 and 42–3). One performed a particular persona in order to legitimately participate in certain privileged activities (Poole, 1996: 39). In Greek, on the other hand, *Prosopon*, meaning face, involved 'the understanding of the person as a substantial being, existence in the physical world, thinkable apart from his legal status' (O'Hara, 1997: 20). In other words, it implies a physical relationship, both biological and social — 'facing another's eyes' – rather than a necessarily legal or agential role (ibid.: 42–3). Marcel Mauss traces the historical shift from the notion of *persona* to person: '[f]rom a simple masquerade to the mask, from a "role" (*personage*) to a "person" (*personne*); to a name, to an individual; from the latter to a being possessing metaphysical and moral value; from a moral consciousness to a sacred being; from the latter to a fundamental form of thought and action – the course is accomplished' (Mauss, 1985: 22).[9]

While not disputing Mauss's progression, Mary O'Hara convincingly argues that the distinction between the two notions of person originating from Greek and Latin continues to shape our understandings of the person today: the contrast between persons as embodied beings and persons as legal entities (1997: 46–7; see also Howes, 1993). While I agree that both traditions are present in many current personality debates, O'Hara does not adequately conceptualize their messy imbrication. For example, I would suggest that a more Greek notion of the person is often used as a latent, legitimating element in a more Latin claim to legal status, rights, and responsibilities. In other words, while both are present in much contemporary discourse, they often operate in a dynamic manner, rather than as relatively exclusive notions. I am not suggesting that we are encountering a historical shift from person to persona, but rather that both figures operate in interesting dialectical tension, mutually constitutive and mutually influencing. To focus on the person, to the exclusion of the persona, as much scholarship does, is to miss half of the story.

It is, in part, this dynamic that I wish to capture in the stories I tell here. It is for this reason that I want to resurrect the terminology of persona to accompany person. The encounters of personality that I recount in the rest of the book are productive of more than persons, as we understand them. There is a shadowy figure that continues to haunt our discussions of the person and that cannot be captured in a more robust definition of the person, itself. Further, it is not, as most scholars would claim, merely the classical split personality of the person reappearing. I argue that while we have been focusing our disputes on the notion of the person, another entity – the persona – has always been present and merits scrutiny. She, it, and only rarely he are always the other half of the dialectic of personality that we have forgotten. And so this book, in taking up its various events of personhood, is always attentive to the personae lurking in the wings.

Philosophy and the Person

While persona has largely fallen out of our intellectual (and popular) lexicons, person has not. Two types of scholar have been primarily concerned with persons and their attributes: philosophers and legal scholars. Rorty (1976b) recognizes that the notion of person has been very important to philosophy, as do others (e.g., McCall, 1990; Teichmann, 1985; Bourgeois, 1995). Philosophy makes 'a near universal assumption that "person" is the most appropriate term to pick out what it is we most essentially are' (Poole, 1996: 38). In other words, person is a notion very intimate to us. However, Rorty (1990) also argues that much of the debate within philosophy has sought to determine an adequate notion of the person, a quest she suggests is likely impossible. However, there are a number of ongoing issues that philosophers have regularly taken up, as Poole notes:

> [i]t is in virtue of our identity as persons that philosophers ascribe to us special moral privileges and responsibilities. It is under this rubric that philosophers ponder the issue of our identity over time and the prospects of a future existence. And it is as persons that philosophers contemplate the possibility of an essential sameness between us and suitably programmed computers or alien life forms. (1996: 38)

(And, as we will see, philosophers are not the only ones). Key debates within philosophy have turned on whether or not person is an internal state or constituted in external relations (Harré, 1987; Robbins, 1996) or whether the person is completely mentalist, merely physical, or whether it is dualistic, implicating both the physical and mental (see Manning, 1984; Shoemaker, 1990; Atkins, 1987; Swineburne, 1987; Strawson, 1959).[10]

As Poole notes, philosophy has also taken up the question of what has been called individual reidentification, namely the problem of being able to reidentify the same person, however conceived, in different contexts and in different times (McCall, 1990: 21; Minkus, 1960). Finally, philosophers, I suggest, have addressed questions of what McCall calls 'class identification,' namely what kinds of attributes distinguish persons, as a class or group, from other classes or groups of entities. In other words, what are the important elements that all members of the group called persons share? It is this way of thinking about the person that allows us to identify attributes such as intelligence, emotional capacity, physicality, responsibility, and intentionality in attributing personality to other beings such as corporations, robots, computers, chimpanzees, corpses, and so on (McCall 1990: 22). Personhood, therefore, could be constituted in a conjunction of certain of those attributes, with or without others, all, some, or none of which might be essential. This approach thus holds out the hope that an essential description of personhood can be achieved, providing us with a mechanism of discernment.

Ultimately it is class identification that has had the most popular profile outside of the field of philosophy; it is in many ways the 'common-sense' approach to personhood. Arguably it is the dominant approach of law, too, as law is fundamentally a typological episteme, ill suited to determine questions such as internal continuity of the self over time. Daniel Dennett, for example, offers a list of six criteria that he argues have been proferred by philosophy as cumulative and necessary conditions for the ascription of personhood. These include: first, persons are rational beings. Second, persons are beings to whom intentions may be ascribed; they are intentional systems. Third, persons are the objects of a specific stance. In other words, in order for someone to be a person, we must treat them as such. Fourth, persons exhibit reciprocity – they can participate in, and reflect back, the specific stance. Fifth, persons have a capacity for verbal communication, signalling intentions through language that exceeds the mere transmission of information. (Presumably this characteristic would typically exclude machines from the category of person.) Sixth and finally, persons are moral agents who must be able to be held accountable for their actions. As a result of persons' capacities for self-consciousness and self-reflexivity, they have rights and responsibilities. Typically, this requirement would distinguish us from other animals (Dennett, 1976: 72–6). This list of attributes, or necessary preconditions for class identification, describes extremely well, for example, the terms of the Schiavo debate. Her capacity to reason, to act intentionally, to recognize others as persons and to be recognized as such herself, to communicate, and to exhibit self-consciousness were at the heart of the determination of Terri's personhood in the minds of doctors and the public, alike. I suggest that it is this question of class belonging that has been central to the public (including legal) determination of personhood, as will be clear throughout the following chapters.

I agree with McCall, however, who argues that the person, itself, is an inherently public notion. She offers a useful tripartite distinction, noting that we understand our selves as biological, self-conscious, and social entities; as a result, we need to distinguish conceptually between human being, self, and person (1990: 1–10; see also Wiggins, 1987; La Fontaine, 1985; Harré, 1987).[11] She argues that it is the term 'individual' that is used to refer to the 'single entity which is the subject of cognition in various modes' (ibid.: 12). Leaving aside the question of whether or not 'individual' can be deployed as unproblematically as McCall suggests, her framework is helpful in capturing key elements of the person that I adopt. She argues that the human being is the individual as a species being, as a biological entity where change, development, and adaptation take place in relation to biological laws. 'As biological entity, the human being is a physical object, and is therefore identified and re-identified using the same kind of criteria which are used to identify other physical objects' (ibid.: 15). The self, on the other hand, is the individual as self-consciousness, referenced by 'I.' 'This concept concerns the ability of individuals to reflect upon their actions, thoughts, intentions, and so on' (ibid.: 14). In this way, the self defines the individual through experience because we not only experience, but also recognize that we are so doing. It is an essentially private construct, remaining relatively constant regardless of the public identity of the individual (ibid.).

It is this public identity that McCall claims is the public individual – the person as social being. The person is constituted in what is known about that individual by others, what is attributed to or thought of them by other persons in the public domain (ibid.: 12). 'Both what constitutes a person-personhood – and the conditions for identifying and reidentifying persons – personal identity – are to be found in the public domain. Persons are social beings, created and constituted, and found only in society' (ibid.). In this way, attributes of personhood include: agency, accountability, responsibility for action, planning, and consistency in decision-making. Recognizing that personhood is ultimately a social judgment, something awarded by society, ties it inextricably to the allocation of responsibility and the granting of rights (ibid.: 12–13).

Others, too, have recognized the social aspects of personhood. Derek Parfit (1984) goes so far as to suggest that personhood is ultimately a useless notion as its meaning is entirely conventional. However, as a communications scholar, I find the working out of these conventional practices interesting. This is why certain creatures that we would accept as human beings – mentally disabled individuals, those declared insane, women, African Americans – have all, at various points and times in history, been denied the social distinction of personhood. Basically then, I suggest, we are a person if our society accepts us as, and names us, person. Personhood is fundamentally a social, but more precisely, a communicative outcome, an epistemological, rather than ontological, practice.[12]

Legal Personhood

Law is the second major discipline that has contributed to our intellectualization of the person. Typically, the notion of person-at-law is narrower than either the philosophical or the colloquial understandings. A person at law is defined in its most basic sense as the bearer of legal rights and responsibilities, often abbreviated as one who can sue and be sued (see Tur, 1987). For this reason, the person is of great interest to the law as it is how the law understands both its subject and object. The modern legal subject only arose in the shift from feudal to modern societies with the rise of legal relations, what Henry Maine (1883) calls the shift from status to contract. Arguably the law is completely dependent upon the notion of the person for its capacity to act. Yet as legal scholars have pointed out, the technical definition of person that legal doctrine offers gives false comfort – who or what is understood to be the bearer of legal rights and responsibilities is not a straightforward determination.

The editors of the *Harvard Law Review* suggest that person is better understood within law as a metaphor which helps us to define who or what does and does not 'count' for the purposes of law, a question which they argue is always, already to a significant degree, a question of who or what does and not count, as a human being (2001: 1745–7). They lament, as do others, the lack of theorization of the person in Anglo-American jurisprudence. However, they recognize what they call 'law's expressive dimension,' which 'attends to the social meaning of statements in statutes and judicial opinions, arguing that law does more than regulate behavior: it embodies and signals social values and aspirations' (ibid.: 1760). Unlike these scholars, I am neither surprised nor troubled by the lack of doctrinal and philosophical consistency, but like them, I am interested in law's expressive dimension, the ways in which our legal debates about personhood are not confined to its domains, but rather are windows into social values and anxieties at work in law and elsewhere. The person is, they recognize, a very powerful mechanism through which to examine these values and anxieties. 'Legal personhood is more than a metaphor; it becomes, in many cases, law's repository for expressions of anxiety about powerfully divisive social issues' (ibid.: 1766). What makes these encounters between law and social controversy significant is, in part, the powerful nature of law as a social discourse and set of institutions and practices. 'When the law manipulates status distinctions through the use of the metaphor "person," it necessarily expresses a conception of the relative worth of the objects included and excluded by the scope of that metaphor' (ibid.: 1760). Personhood in law is, therefore, I suggest, a normative statement about social status, and one which determines access to a range of resources used in the constitution and maintenance of both self and personhood.

Among the most powerful technologies of personification, legal personification is, given its liberal history, simultaneously a technique of individuation and abstraction (Naffine, 2003, 2004; Neocleous, 2003). Law's privileging of unity, of individuation, simultaneously problematizes multiplicity, seriality, repetition, symbiosis, and hybridity. Linked with a desire not to privilege some citizens over others because of group affiliation or membership, the concept of person in law is deliberately vague and abstract. This 'abstract individualism,' as Ngaire Naffine describes it, is premised on the underlying assumption that 'it is meaningful and useful to think of individuals at a high level of generality and that this allows us to identify a universal legal subject' (2003: 623–4). This abstract individualism becomes most visible in law's repeated encounters with liminal beings. Yet despite these challenges, the liberal person as a figure has proved itself remarkably resistant to change. This is why, I argue, we need to develop the notion of persona, to articulate the complicated ways in which these entities are never quite fully abstractable or individualizable.

At the same time that legal studies recognizes the significance of personality to the operation of law, like philosophy, it offers us a number of formulations for recognizing personhood. These have been most usefully characterized by Naffine (2003) as falling into three broad categories – personality types – labelled for ease P1, P2, and P3. Currently dominant in law, the P1 person, which Naffine nicknames 'The Cheshire Cat,' is the broadest of the categories, with a person being 'a formal capacity to bear a legal right and so to participate in legal relations' (2003: 350). It draws on no metaphysical assumptions about the person, nor does it render personality a moral claim. Those using the notion of the person in this way attempt to keep it an abstract, objective, and purely legal concept. Elsewhere Margaret Davies and Naffine (2001) label these scholars legal positivists (e.g. Kelsen, 1945). The P1 person lives outside of historical and social relations, unmarked by them, abstracted from them. As John Dewey suggests, '"person" signifies what law makes it signify' (1926: 655). As a result, P1 is typically the most encompassing of the three types of legal personality. It obviates the need for a distinction between artificial and natural persons. Legal persons in this category can include animals, clones, corpses, corporations, fetuses, the environment, and anything else that we choose to consider a legal person. It posits the person as fully contingent, variable, and mobile. Richard Tur famously suggests, in this vein, that the person is 'wholly formal ... an empty slot' (Tur, 1987: 121).

Critiques of this way of thinking about the person arise for Naffine in the easy separation of the issue of the person from the non-legal world. She wonders whether the purity of the notion can be maintained. The problem of language is a powerful one – in calling the corporation a person, for example, do we not already evoke a moral being? Is any notion of the person fully intelligible without reference back to the human being? The residue of the Greek understanding of the person is perhaps not so easily shed.[13] Further, as soon as the person is concretized in a particular instance, is not the conceptual purity lost as the resultant person is reinserted back into the social fabric? She notes, '[i]n the making of empirical legal persons, there have been powerful historical, political and social forces at work, ensuring the endowment of some beings with moral and social status and so with the ability to act in law ... and the denial of others'

(Naffine, 2003: 355). Personification, in other words, has been historically patterned, and once personified, persons act. Neither is a neutral
practice.

The second category of persons Naffine identifies as human beings,
what Davies and Naffine (2001) refer to as the natural law position. P2
therefore most resembles the ordinary usage of the notion of person.
Typically the P2 person comes into being at birth and expires once the
human being is completely brain dead. Tied as it is to birth and death,
this is a notion of personhood obviously dependent for its definitional
parameters upon biological science. In P2, '[l]egal rights map on to a
natural moral subject ... legal rights are natural to human beings; they
are a legal expression of natural attributes of a subject that has its own
inherent nature' (Naffine, 2003: 358). This is the concept of the person
most frequently found within human rights discourse, for example,
where the human subject precedes the subject at law. Rationality is not
a required basis for personhood, but being human is. As a result,
animals cannot be persons, but children and people in comatose states
can.

This concept can be troubled as one which naturalizes and solidifies
in or as science much more complicated social questions of who or
what counts as a human being. Our status as human beings, com-
mencing at birth, for example, is a complex determination when one
considers fetuses.[14] It is therefore, I suggest, a simultaneously morally
powerful and still relatively arbitrary category. However, hiding in the
claimed objectivity of biological science clearly does not allow one to
avoid the issue of who or what counts as an autonomous and integrated being (in nature). The problem of culture, as Donna Haraway
(1997) and others have suggested, is not so easily sidestepped by
recourse to science's 'culture of no culture.'

P3 is the narrowest of the three interpretations of legal person, com-
prising those who are rational and legally competent. This type of
person has been described as one who has the capacity to initiate
actions in court, as the typical subject of rights and duties, as 'normal,'
and as someone who can act in her or his own interest. It is also a position emanating out of natural law. 'In P3 we have the rational and
therefore responsible human legal agent or subject: the classical con-
tractor, the individual who is held personally accountable for his civil
and criminal actions' (Naffine, 2003: 362). P3 is an ideal type of legal
actor, both rational and moral (see Gray, 1909). Excluded from this
category then are the young, the adult incompetent, and animals.

Typically described in a language of the mind, P3 is, unlike P2, not interpreted primarily in biological terms. P2 status is, in fact, an insufficient but necessary condition for P3 status.[15] The P3 person is individuated, self-contained, and responsible. Historically it has been, and continues to be, the most narrow and politically desirable of the three categories of personality.

Naffine notes the incredibly powerful impact that the P3 person has had on legal thinking and the waves of feminist and critical legal critique to which 'he' has been subjected. He has historically been a white, propertied male and it is only slowly over the course of history, through much political struggle, that the face of P3 has been changed. I would suggest that much of our social history could be read as the struggle by different groups to move into the category of P2 and then to progress from there to P3. Certainly one could read the struggle for women's personhood as the fight to be recognized as P3, rather than merely P2, persons. And yet as Naffine and other feminists have shown, the attribution of P3 status may be somewhat ironic given the certain masculinist properties of the rational, self-possessed, self-reliant, wilful subject that are at the heart of the very notion, regardless of which embodied humans are permitted into the category at any particular historical moment (e.g., Davies, 1999).

Like Naffine, I find the greatest intellectual and social potential in the P1 category. P2 restricts the legal person to a particular physical form which increasingly carries a significant moral baggage and P3 limits the person to a particular mental and moral form. P1 'does not formally demand that its creatures assume a particular form or character. Instead it relies on an abstraction and relational interpretation of the person. The person is only their legal role or their legal relation and this is constantly subject to change' (Naffine, 2003: 366). Simultaneously, P1 disprivileges law as a site of ontological determination. 'The law of persons, and the law itself, is put in its place, as a more modest and perhaps mundane pursuit. It is only law trying to achieve certain effects. It is not a metaphysical enterprise; it does not entail a theory of being' (Naffine, 2004: 642). A notion of the person that can include already existing citizens, children, animals, the environment, corporations, computers, and others suggests person as a malleable, mobile concept, permitting subjects to morph into other identities. 'P1 recognizes the plasticity of persons' (ibid.). It is a relational concept which makes no reference back to a myth of origin or an authentic source of being. It is an articulation of public and social status, not ontology, making empirical and political, rather than metaphysical and moral, claims. It is a fundamentally communicative formulation of personality. Person can then offer a negotiable surface without a necessary anchoring authorial form. P1 persons are the most open to recognizing liminal beings, and are the closest relations to their troubled and troubling sibling: the persona.

Legal and philosophical inquiries into the person reveal a number of shared elements which I think are productive for ongoing inquiry. Both recognize the social significance of personality debates, offering cogent reasons for the primacy of the person as a nexus for the working out of varied and intense social concerns. Both law and philosophy recognize that personification is a fundamentally normative gesture, an award of status based on often invisible criteria. The person is, for both, an ideological construct. For both disciplines the person is a boundary metaphor, to borrow from Jennifer Nedelsky, in that 'it invites us to imagine that the self to be protected is in some crucial sense insular, and that what is most important to the preservation of such a self is drawing boundaries around it that will protect it from invasion' (1990: 168–9). They offer, in different ways, a basis for thinking about the person in relational terms, as a construct of social relations. They both recognize that personhood is premised upon, and works to produce, identity in unity and autonomy. Person, while studied, remains unquestioned in their analyses. Yet, at the same time, they are both driven by the 'dream' that philosophical or legal principles of personhood can be grounded in metaphysical personality (Rorty, 1976b; Naffine, 2003).

What the two fields do less well is step outside of themselves. It is striking that almost every treatise on the person in philosophy or law opens with the caveat that while not unrelated to the more colloquial or everyday use of person, the question will be taken up completely apart from its quotidian understanding. Of interest to me is that exact conjuncture between the philosophical or legal determinations of personhood and the everyday. Further, I resist the temptation to privilege law and philosophy over popular culture, and to compartmentalize them. As cultural studies of law thinkers have long asserted, law and culture are not fully separable. Each domain is influenced by, and productive of, the other (see Gaines, 1991; Sarat and Simon, 2003; Sarat and Kearns, 1994; Sarat and Kearns, 1999; Bower, Goldberg, and Musheno, 2001; Coombe, 1998; McLeod, 2001). While they are distinct arenas of knowledge whose specificity must be acknowledged, the relative power or relevance of either to effectivity in a personality debate can never be known in advance. Perhaps in part for this reason, both legal studies and philosophy are reluctant to 'get their hands dirty,' to examine the messy embeddedness of personality within lived social relations. There are too few empirical inquiries into the social working out of what it means to be a person, despite both philosophy's and law's laments of an excess of abstraction. My project, instead, *begins* with the messy embeddedness of personality.

In different and interesting ways, discussions of the person in law and philosophy both focus too exclusively on that very notion. The person operates as an always present abstraction whose necessity or relevance is rarely questioned. This abstraction is problematic, as it is only in its concrete manifestations that we can see its limits. When the abstraction of the person has been questioned, it has tended to happen in and through the formal legal processes. The law inevitably offers a binary response. While I do not discount this process, I suggest that we must not be satisfied with a legal resolution that this or that particular liminal being is or is not a person. We must go further because it is only in our robust examination of actual cultural encounters with liminal beings that we can understand *how* we personify and de-personify. Neither law nor philosophy seems concerned with what is left over when liminal beings are subjected to techniques of personification.

The very notion of liminality emerges out of, and is produced in, the encounter between experience and personhood defined categorically. The various symbolic processes through which we then negotiate, legitimate, and sanction those beings as persons or not reveal the fundamental instability of a notion in whose name much is done – the person. My project is, to a large extent, about demonstrating that what is revealed in the personality debates of these liminal subjects is not, in fact, the instability of the liminal beings themselves, but of the concept by which they are being measured. Further, this instability plays out along particular lines, with particular effects. The instability of the notion of the person, however, is not an end in itself, but rather a means to opening up the possibility of the persona as another way to take account of these personal encounters. It is with this in mind that I selected a series of personality events, events that could narrowly be understood as encounters between liminal beings and the law of persons, but which are much more than that. I have selected corporations, women, clones, computers, and celebrities as my liminal beings. This is not a complete list; one could add fetuses, the mentally incompetent, children, zombies, slaves, data doubles, labourers, dolphins, and others.[16] However, I chose my particular subjects to reveal different levels of abstraction, to span a century, and to channel different cultural anxieties. In particular, these specific case studies were selected because they leave their traces as much in popular culture as in legal relations. Each is a public event. Further, these cases permit me to explore some of the specificity of the English Canadian instance, which, while of interest to Canadian scholars, is of broader significance because many of these issues are less resolved, less final in Canada (both legally and socially) than they are elsewhere. As a result, the Canadian experience of these particular personality debates allows us to keep open questions that have been already closed, perhaps too quickly, elsewhere. Finally, of course, corporations, women, clones, computers, and celebrities were selected because they allowed me to tell a good story.

Chapter Descriptions

In chapter 2, '*Persona Ficta*: The Corporation as Moral Person,' I take up the longstanding legal (and capitalist) truth that the corporation is a person at law. Examining the historical roots of this illogical, and yet powerful, legal fiction as well as its belated philosophical justifications, I go on to suggest that we have never been completely at ease with the corporation as person. While the rights of the corporate person have been relatively easy to determine, its corresponding personal responsibilities have not. At law, this manifests in the various attempts to pierce the corporate veil, to hold individual directors responsible for the criminal or tortious actions of the corporate form. This technology of de-personification runs directly counter to the significant personifying role that the law simultaneously plays. In business, itself, the troubled nature of the corporate person manifests in the corporate social responsibility (CSR) movement. Corporate capitalists have realized that the person is not an adequate shield behind which to engage in socially risky or dangerous activities – courts, consumers, and citizens alike will look behind the person of the corporation. As a result, over the past thirty years, a movement has emerged to make corporations accountable for the social harms they cause. Some critics dismiss CSR as, at most, an effective pre-emptive strike designed to maintain self-governance and avoid regulation, while others see it as a somewhat more sincere grappling with the place of the corporation in the social structure. Like corporate veil-piercing by the courts, I see CSR discourse, as produced by both critics and advocates, as a means through which we are attempting to responsibilize the corporate person, or more accurately, render it as moral agent.

A third social site where the moral status of the corporate person is central is the recent spate of documentary films exploring the powers and limits of the corporate form. I select two of these, *The Corporation* (2004) and *Enron: The Smartest Guys in the Room* (2005), to analyse. Both films pose the question: how can we make the corporation accountable for its criminal actions? However, each offers a very different response, which reveals – as do the equally problematic attempts to responsibilize through corporate veil-piercing and CSR – that the corporate person is not easily cast as a moral agent. The person, it would seem, is not, *a priori*, a moral entity. And yet, we are clearly uncomfortable with that determination.

After taking up the moral status of the person through the liminal being of the corporation, chapter 3 troubles the gendered nature of the person. The person is currently understood as a gender-neutral concept in everything from legislative interpretation to human rights codes. However, in '"Not a Sex Victory": Gendering the Person' I posit that the person has historically been, and continues to be, fundamentally gendered, while its abstract individualism simultaneously works to efface its sexed nature. There was a time, of course, in relatively recent history, when women in the Anglo-American world were not considered to be full legal persons or full political subjects. I examine the moment of symbolic historical rupture wherein women in Canada became persons – the 'Persons Case.' Catalysed by Emily Murphy and four Prairie activist colleagues, the Persons Case was a legal challenge to the provisions of the *British North America Act, 1867* which limited appointment to the Senate of Canada to qualified persons, which the government continually interpreted as male persons. Ultimately the Judicial Committee of the Privy Council in England agreed with the 'Famous Five,' as they came to be known, and women were held to be persons for the purposes of appointment to the Senate. Of limited legal significance, the Persons Case and the Famous Five have taken on immense national symbolic importance in relation to women's political subjectivity in Canada.

More so than in the case itself, we see, in the subsequent popular cultural production around the Famous Five and the Persons Case, tensions in the notion of the person when its gendered nature is specifically drawn out. Following the controversy around the selection of the Famous Five for representation as nation builders on the re-minted 2004 fifty-dollar bills, I examine the ways in which the female person is an always unstable project. We see the limits of the law as a technology of personification; we see the complicated ways in which national iconography, as another technique for legitimating personhood, founders on the tensions embedded in its apparent gender-neutrality; and finally, we see that the Persons Case makes visible the fundamentally masculine nature of the Western liberal category of the person. An abstract, individuating, and seemingly gender-neutral notion, when it encounters the liminal being of the woman, it is deeply troubled. While men can seemingly inhabit this gender-neutral category without causing it to deconstruct, women, it would seem, cannot, suggesting that the very notion of the person, as gender-neutral, is another fiction by which we live.

While both corporations and women are liminal beings that have had their personhood confirmed and endorsed in law and by society more broadly, clones are liminal beings whose personhood status remains legally and socially unclear. In chapter 4, 'Invented Humans: Kinship and Property in Persons,' I suggest that clones trouble two fundamental distinctions upon which traditional interpretations of the person have rested: between human beings and property and between human beings and animals. While a human clone (likely) remains a creature of science fiction at the present time, it is always present in our discussions of the encounter between law, science, and persons. With the advent of recombinant DNA technology, genetic science now claims to be able not just to alter, but to invent or reinvent, life itself. And yet, a language of invention is already inflected by law in general, and by patent law in particular. As the form of intellectual property that legitimates the property held in inventions by inventors, patents are increasingly being granted on, and in relation to, the genetic elements of biological beings, and on those beings themselves. Biopatents thus endorse the biological entity as simultaneously being and property.

Therefore, when we speak of the 'invented human,' as we do in policy, legal doctrine, and popular culture, we are figuring the person as simultaneously subject and object. The liminal being of the invented human forces the realization that personhood and property statuses are not mutually exclusive. And while we have not had any legal case specifically posing the issue of the property status of the invented human being as a whole, we have considered the property status of other complete beings. I take up the journey of the Harvard Mouse through the Canadian legal and administrative systems in order to examine the tensions between person and property and person and animal that manifest in the invented mouse. I read this case alongside some tales of actual invented humans, located necessarily within science fiction narratives. The films *The 6th Day* (2000) and *The Island* (2003) map out, respectively, the kinship with animals that inevitably results once we are defined primarily as manipulable genetic information, and the inevitable property claims that will pursue any invented human. The liminality of the cancerous mouse and the popular culture tales of its cloned human cousins serve as a ground for reminding us that the person is fundamentally about distinguishing our selves from both objects and 'lesser' animals. However, in the face of biotechnological developments and the corresponding conceptual and linguistic shifts that have already taken place to render those sensible to us, these distinctions seem antiquated. The clone as persona is therefore a copy of the person that, from every angle, reveals the instability, and even the untenability, of the original.

In many ways, the clone is a posthuman form of the person, but it is still intimately related to the human being through the medium of our bodies understood as genetic information. Chapter 4, entitled 'Machine Intelligence: Computers as Posthuman Persons,' explores the implications of the non-organic posthuman person through the trope of the thinking machine. Our longstanding fascination with machines that think is most often read as a fascination with the externalization of the mind and as a narrative of disembodiment. It can be reread, I argue, as a story of personhood, most easily recognized in the liminal being of the games-playing machine. I tell the stories of a number of games-playing machines throughout history from the seventeenth century automaton named 'The Turk,' to IBM's 'Deep Blue,' to the more recent attempts to build machines capable of playing a convincing game of Texas Hold 'Em Poker. We see in these individual stories an overarching narrative of reason, of contest, and of deception. In every instance, the machine strains to succeed in the 'Imitation Game' – computer scientist and mathematician Alan Turing's test to determine whether a machine could 'pass' as a person, whether it could successfully impersonate.

I suggest in chapter 4, however, that the most convincing articulation of the posthuman person is found in bots, or intelligent software agents, who can form legally binding contracts in the online environment. A bot is a software program that is configured to manage information and 'act' upon it, independently of the direct instructions of its owner, principal, or programmer. Increasingly and heavily reliant on bots, e-commerce works in concert with contract law as a technology of personification to proffer personhood status on the most abstract form of machine intelligence to ever play at Turing's Game. In accepting the bot as capable of contracting, the law attributes to it intention, interactivity, and intellect, attributes, it will be recalled, that were denied the embodied Terri Schiavo. In this way, the liminal being of the contracting bot, in particular, makes visible the person as primarily and problematically a category of the mind. The body is, it would seem, not only expendable, but in fact a problem for the person. The problematic nature of the body was previously hinted at by the impersonation of corporations and of women, in particular, but is made express in the case of intelligent software agents. Yet I suggest these, too, are more accurately understood as personae, revealing how deeply embedded within the notion of person is the relationship between reason, performance, and deception. Our cultural anxiety that our creations will be able to pass as 'us,' present also within stories of clones, becomes more pointed in the seemingly even less likely context of computer software. We should be able to tell the difference, and yet, increasingly, we cannot. This is disturbing to us because it implies that the notion of the person is perhaps less than what we thought it was, or that we have already achieved the longstanding horizon point of nonorganic reproduction.

Finally, chapter 6, 'Celebrity Personae: Authenticating the Person,' takes us back to embodied persons, but also forward to the most concrete manifestation of the persona. More than 'other' to the person, more than a concept hovering in the shadows to articulate the tensions within personhood, the celebrity persona, in and through publicity law, becomes a valuable commodity form. Simultaneously a creature of the rise of late modern practices of celebrity production, circulation, and consumption, and the development of intellectual property in the representation of the abstract identity of the person, the celebrity persona as property challenges any necessary and/or determinative relationship between person and persona. While issues of property in the self emerge in patent law as well, in publicity law they are taken to the next level of abstraction. Patent law ultimately relies upon a Lockean labour theory of value to validate the person-property relation. The inventor, through his creative labour, produces value out of nature's raw materials and is transformed into its owner for his efforts; correspondingly nature's raw material becomes property. A comforting fiction in patent law, the labour theory of value becomes even less tenable in the constitution of the celebrity image as property. This is because the value is not constituted in the object itself, however ephemeral it might be, but rather in its recognition value. Thus, the person grounding the persona can only ever be partly responsible for its production.

Despite the untenability of the labour theory of value for legitimating property in the persona, this is the dominant explanatory narrative in the United States. In Canada, however, where celebrity itself is a much more unstable activity, namely where celebrities are liminal beings, we see a different rationale for constituting the persona as property. Relying more upon Hegel than Locke, the sanctity of the persona is constituted in its necessarily intimate relationship with the person, not as mere labourer, but as essence. The persona thus operates, within both Canadian celebrity discourse and Canadian publicity law, as a legitimating technology for the person. It authenticates the person, confirming her as unique, as outside of, and prior to, economic relations. And yet, the simultaneous recognition within both celebrity discourse and publicity law of celebrity as commodity form, necessarily imbricated within market relations, puts the lie to this easy separation, and to the necessary intimacy of person and persona. The celebrity persona then does the dialectical work, I argue, of simultaneously authenticating the person and severing the umbilical cord between them. Like corporations, women, bots, and clones, the celebrity persona reveals the tensions in personhood and our fears. Yet, as the story in which we can most easily see the distinction between person and persona, where that very distinction has been endorsed by audiences, cultural industries, and the law alike, we can begin to see the promiscuous power of the persona.

Finally, in the concluding chapter, 'Impersonations,' I offer a further reflection on the persona, and its relationship with the late modern person, as the cumulative effect of my different stories of personhood. The sketch of the persona that I offer there is neither final nor whole, not least because my five preceding stories are neither programmatic nor total. Yet, they do help us to begin a process of understanding why the person is still a figure through which we are working out some of the most important moral issues of our time. They help us to see not just what our fears are, but how we have attempted to assuage them through the notion of the person. And these activities of personification, taking place in the realms of the cultural, social, political, and economic, are always productive activities. Rather than merely controlling our stress, disciplining the unruly, or marking our moral or economic progress, these narratives of personification produce other, perhaps less desired, and certainly unintended, results. The most interesting of these are not, therefore, the legal resolutions, the technical outcomes of the personhood disputes, but rather the figures – the personae – that get produced along the way.

The personae who appear in this book are intended to offer openings, less fraught ways in which to contemplate the implications of our practices of politics, law, and science. Personae, rather than being the illegimate offspring of the person, can be an alternative lens through which to see our own personhood. Perhaps – like corporations, women, clones, bots, and celebrities – we are all more interesting personae than we are persons.

2 *Persona Ficta*:
The Corporation as Moral Person

Our assumption that an entity is a person is shaken precisely in those cases where it matters: when wrong has been done and the question of responsibility arises.

(Dennett, 1976: 194)

The law does not write fiction.

(Neocleous, 2003: 91)

Early on 3 December 1984, a holding tank filled with methyl isocyanate overheated in a factory owned by Eveready Industries India Limited and toxic gases were released throughout the heart of the Indian city of Bhopal. Thousands of people were killed outright, some were trampled in their efforts to escape, and gases injured an estimated 150,000 to 600,000, at least 15,000 of whom later died. Eveready Industries, then known as Union Carbide India, was using untested technology, had no action plan for accidents of this scale, and had not informed local authorities of the nature of the chemicals they were using and manufacturing. Analysts within the company had suggested that such an accident could happen and their reports were ignored. Staff had been recently laid off and safety checks became less and less frequent. The external alarm was activated to warn residents, but then silenced quickly to avoid causing panic. Doctors and hospitals were not informed of the proper treatment methods; they issued eye drops and cough medicine.

The litany of negligent acts seems unlimited. And yet, Union Carbide has never taken responsibility for the disaster, maintaining throughout that the worst industrial accident in history was caused by individual human sabotage. A lawsuit was brought for US$3 billion and a settlement reached for US$470 million. Families of the dead received an average of US$2,200 and very little has been paid to survivors. Warren Anderson, CEO at the time, remains a fugitive from Indian justice on culpable homicide charges. Yet the Indian government never produced extradition papers for him, worried that such an act might frighten off other investors. To this day, the area remains highly contaminated, with dramatic numbers of spontaneous abortions, stillbirths, babies born with genetic defects, and people contracting cancer and other serious diseases. There are vats of chemicals under the ground and the water contains pollution at more than five hundred times the maximum legal limit in India. Dow Chemical, which now owns the company, claims it has no ongoing responsibility to clean up the area and no one else can afford to do so.

When a tragedy of this nature occurs, we try to ascertain how it happened. We ask: who is responsible? Employees who did not push a button to cool the tank down? The Union Carbide managers who ignored the warning reports? Warren Anderson because he was the CEO and was paid to take responsibility for the operations of the company? Government officials who turned a blind eye towards the company's actions or who now won't pay to clean up the area? Notwithstanding the seemingly multiple contenders, the question of responsibility is a complicated one. Few, if any, of the people who worked in the Union Carbide plant in Bhopal are legally responsible for the actions of the corporation. This is because Union Carbide, itself, is a legal person. Dow Chemical Company is a different legal person. Typically, if a person commits a criminal or negligent act, the state pursues them under the criminal law or individuals can sue them in tort law, respectively. But how does one make a corporate person take responsibility – economic or moral – for its criminal or negligent actions? This begs the question, however: is the corporation a responsible person? Should it be?

In 1651, Thomas Hobbes contemplated the nature of political personhood and, in so doing, offered a distinction that shapes our thinking about personality to this day.

A Person, is he, *whose words or actions are considered, either as his own, or as representing the words or actions of an other man, or of any other things to whom they are attributed, whether Truly or by Fiction.* When they are considered as his owne, then he is called a *Naturall Person*: And when they are considered as representing the words and actions of an other, then is he a *Feigned* or *Artificiall person.* (Hobbes, 1968: 111; italics in original)

Artificial persons did not have to be sentient or animate. Hobbes elaborates: '[e]ven an inanimate thing can be a person, that is, it can have possessions and other goods, and can act in law' (in Neocleous, 2003: 75). For Hobbes, then, corporations, churches, hospitals, bridges, 'children, Fooles and Mad-men' were artificial persons, but persons nonetheless, and from the late 1800s in England and the United States, courts agreed with Hobbes, endorsing the modern business corporation as a person at law. For much of the nineteenth and twentieth centuries, this intriguing characterization continued unscathed and unremarked. Originally developed primarily to offer limited legal liability to shareholders, the unassailability of corporate personhood began to fray around the edges, I suggest, after the Second World War with the rise of a broader social climate of reflexivity, a climate in which we began to question the power of science and technology and the unassailability of expertise (see Beck, 1992; Giddens, 1991). During and after the 1980s with the rise of economic globalization, the trend to governmental deregulation of many social sectors, and the seemingly rapid and unchecked development of science and technology, the power of corporations increased dramatically. At the same time, however, their capacity to cause serious social harms also became more visible – witness the Bhopal tragedy, the Exxon Valdez disaster, or Shell's involvement in the apartheid regime in South Africa. Clearly corporations did more than merely make money for their shareholders. Corporations were not benign.

Yet, as late as 1991, Bruce Welling, in his law textbook *Corporate Law in Canada: The Governing Principles*, makes the following startling claim: '[w]ithin the realm of legal analysis, corporate legal personality is unquestionable; outside the realm of legal analysis it is doubtful whether corporate legal personality is of any interest at all' (80). While this claim was likely shaky in 1991, by the twenty-first century, both elements of Welling's claim no longer hold true. Arguably more than at any other time in North American history, the corporation's status as a person is under scrutiny, and even attack.

Since well before the landmark British decision of *Salomon* v. *Salomon* (1897) until the present, legal analysts have questioned both the theory and practice of corporate personality. Ngaire Naffine has gone so far as to suggest that the broader literature on the notion of the legal person is 'to a large extent preoccupied with the meaning of corporate personality' (2003: 347). But this preoccupation extended over the latter part of the twentieth century into other social domains as well. No longer a self-evident truth, the personality of the corporation is being rethought in legal, corporate, and popular cultures. In all three contexts, these efforts to rethink are, fundamentally I suggest, 'practices of responsibility,' as Nicola Lacey identifies them. Practices of responsibility 'are *normative and constructive* in that they organize both our practices and our interpretation of the world in distinctive and contingent ways' (Lacey, 2001b: 253; emphasis in original).

As a society, we are struggling with the issue of how to make corporate persons, be they artificial or natural, responsible for their actions. Debate centres on the capacity for the corporate person to be a moral agent. Within the legal realm, this has resulted in various attempts to 'pierce the corporate veil' – to deny the personhood of the corporation in order to get to its directing (human) minds, as well as less successful attempts to hold the corporation itself accountable. Within corporate culture, the rethinking of corporate personality has resulted in the 'corporate social responsibility' movement – an arguably pre-emptive attempt from within the corporate world to acknowledge that with the benefits of personhood come certain social responsibilities. Here we see the attempt to morph the corporate person into a respectable citizen. Finally, within popular culture, the rethinking of corporate personality has taken the form of, first, a problematization of the taken-for-granted nature of corporate personhood; second, a condemnation of the nature of corporate personality; and then third and finally, a probing and somewhat confused inquiry into corporate culture and how to make corporate persons accountable. In all of these contexts, responsibility acts as a 'normative device – a matter of construction and ascription' (Lacey, 2001b: 275).

In each of these three social contexts, we see the tensions inherent in the relationship between responsibility and the corporate person. This is because, in many ways, the corporation has never been a person, in the classical sense. While having agency and rights, it has not been required to perform the duties of other embodied persons or citizens. It is a collective unity – a whole produced from a number of parts. It has no body to punish; therefore retributive justice seems, somehow, unsatisfying when visited upon the corporation. These tensions result in large part, I suggest, because the corporation has always been more persona than person. This is most evident when we examine the ambivalent, confused, and ultimately failed attempts to responsibilize it, to make it a moral being, to make it a person *like us*. As a persona passing for a person, the corporation has been pressing the boundaries of personality for more than a century. To truly make the corporation a responsible person requires radical changes to corporate capitalism. Most are unwilling to make those changes, and so the corporation, acting as persona, yet recognized as legal person, continues to destabilize our comfortable frames of personhood and moral agency. It is not merely the fact that the corporation is not a human being that places pressure on our notion of person; as Amélie Oksenberg Rorty notes, '[n]ew conceptions of actions and agency sometimes relocate the conditions for responsibility and liability' (1976b: 6). However, the corporation has proved to be an entity notoriously difficult to responsibilize.

Corporate Person as Agent in Legal Theory

Hotly contested at the turn of the last century, there are four broad ways in which the personality of the corporation has been generally theorized: concession theory, legal fiction theory, group theory, and real entity theory. Legal fiction theories suggest the impersonation of the corporation is a convenient legal fiction designed to recognize certain rights and responsibilities of the group entity that exceed the individuals it comprises. Concession theories also view the corporation as a fictional person, but with the authority of that personification stemming directly from the state. (Sometimes both of these theories are grouped together as 'creature theory.') Group theory recognizes the legal utility of understanding the corporation as a separate unit, but posits that the rights of the corporation are nothing more than the rights held by the component members. Finally, real entity theory holds that the corporation is a real person, a real social organism that pre-exists its capture within jurisprudence or legislation. Each approach implies a different understanding of the person and each has different social, political, and ethical implications.[1]

Often improperly conflated with legal fiction theory, concession theory is a product of the rise of the nation state, and holds that all corporations exist only as separate entities by explicit authorization of the state. The right to incorporate is viewed as a special privilege granted by the sovereign and the corporation's rights and duties are limited to those in its establishing charter. Any action taken in excess of those terms is *ultra vires*, or beyond its legitimate authority. For example, prior to 1832 in England, a Royal Charter or special statute was required for an entity to receive corporate status. The granting of corporate status by the state was tied to the assumption that the corporate enterprise served some broader public good. In terms of its relationship with natural persons then, the corporation could be formed of persons, but not by them. Corporations were seen as inherently collective in nature. As John Dewey (1926), Marc Neocleous (2003), and others note, it is clear in concession theory that the legitimate power of the corporation is derived from the state and the state alone.[2] It was, therefore, a means by which the state might control, or at least contain, the potential unruliness of groups of citizens who had the capacity to undermine the rights of individuals or the authority of the state itself. Generally, as corporate law in the West moved away from the charter system, the concession theory lost its relevance to the explanation of corporate personality.

The second, and currently still significant, approach to corporate personhood is that of fiction theory. Legal fiction theory holds that the corporation is a person solely as a result of its legal construction as such. Emerging out of Canon law,[3] the person of the corporation is an entity recognized as distinct from the smaller entities which it comprises. In other words, the corporation is more than the sum of its parts. Here corporate personification also requires an act of creation authored by a human subject, be that shareholders or a court. This enthusiastically endorsed legal fiction served, and serves, a number of important legal and economic purposes, including permitting the corporation the freedom to own and act upon its property independently of its shareholders; providing limited liability for shareholders; facilitating a separation of expertise between the owners of the corporation and its directing minds (Board of Directors); and providing for the continuation across time of the legal entity, an immortality unburdened by the life cycles of its human participants. Thus while not tied so directly to the sovereign as concession theories require, the possibility of incorporation is comprised within statute or the courts.

Fiction theory rests on a differentiation between real or natural persons (i.e., human beings) and artificial persons (such as the corporation or other social groupings), positing this is a self-evident legal and social distinction. Commentators often demonstrate the differences between a 'real' person and an 'artificial person,' such as the corporation, by pointing out that corporations can buy and sell property, can sue and be sued, but can neither vote nor marry.[4] The artificial, intangible, invisible person of the corporation was classically understood as disembodied and without mind or consciousness. Yet corporations take actions that have consequences in our lives. 'Within the realm of *legal* analysis then, there is nothing artificial or fictional about the legal personality of a corporation' (Welling, 1991: 80). *Persona ficta* is, therefore, the legal mechanism whereby a unified rights-bearing unit is created; it is a singular technique of individuation accomplished through make-believe. It is the classic P1 person within Naffine's characterization. Yet, for all its imaginary nature, the impersonation of the corporation has been one of the most powerful legal fictions of the last century because, as Dewey astutely remarked in 1926, 'imaginary creatures are notoriously nimble' (668).

The third approach to corporate personality recognizes human beings as the original and only bearers of rights. One of those rights is, of course, to join together to conduct business. The resulting entity, however, does not morph into something else through fiction or otherwise. Rather, while it is convenient to use a business name, for example, to apparently denote a particular distinct entity, rights are held only by the individuals whom the organization comprises. Those individuals have the same protection under the law that they would have as single individuals, no more, no less. Sanford Schane draws a parallel to a family name, which serves as a 'cover term' for members of a family, but which serves only as a convenient identifying mark (Schane, 1987: 566). In law, group theory resulted in the corporation being treated very similarly to partnerships. However, while partnerships are premised upon stability in membership, corporations exist despite often complete changes in their human participants. Partnerships do not reflect the limited liability that was sought in the corporate form and partners often share in decision-making. Corporate structures, particularly for larger entities, resulted in decision-making being delegated to management by shareholders. Shareholders no longer participated in the decisions of day-to-day business. In other words, this approach, in foregrounding the individual's right to contract, does not provide the benefits of other theories in recognizing a distinct corporate personality (whether fictional or real). Group theory, as a result, very quickly failed to meet the needs of burgeoning corporate growth in the nineteenth century and was abandoned.

The fourth approach to corporate personality, also of contemporary relevance, holds, in direct contrast to group theory, that the corporation is a real, not fictitious, person. Indebted to the English Pluralists and their attempts to disassociate groups from the state, it has been variously called organism, real entity, and person theory.[5] Real entity theory suggests that the treatment of the corporation as a person by the state or a court is not the creation of a legal entity, but rather the recognition of one that already exists. In this way, real entity theory recognizes the social life and identity of groups. Here, the corporation is more than the sum of its parts, and for some theorists, possesses a non-reducible group will. It pursues its own goals and its life continues regardless of changes in its human membership. German scholar O.F. Gierke went furthest of the real entity theorists when he suggested in 1902 that a 'corporate body ... is a living organism and a real person, with body and members and a will of its own. Itself can will, itself can act. ... It is a group-person, and its will is a group-will' (Gierke, 1902: xxvi). Some critics have suggested that this is too romantic a view, which 'confuses verbal imagery (i.e., the collective will) with observable phenomena' (Welling, 1991: 81).

Thus, in real entity theory, the social reality of group association is translated into legal reality, without the need for a state or much imagination. What is a simile in fiction theory – the corporation is *like* a person and so we can treat it as a person – becomes more than metaphor in real entity theory. The corporation *is* a person. This can either radically decentre the human being from our notion of the person or humanize the corporation, requiring a more thorough contemplation of its body and mind, or both.[6] If a corporation is an organic entity, then presumably a notion of sovereignty attaches to this person. It can both act and be responsible for its actions without any additional requirements. Real entity theory seemingly gives us a basis to reunite the legal and moral persons in one being. It posits the corporate person as a P3 personality, or a responsible subject, within Naffine's schema. The corporation's independence from the generative capacities, and the resulting control, of the state seems assured.

Finally, thinking of the corporation as an actual person enables us to talk about the personality of that person.

Mutually Exclusive? Denying the Person to Moralize the Action

Interestingly, while legal theorists have debated the merits and implications of these four approaches to thinking the corporate person, legislation and case law developed largely independently of such characterizations. In Canada, the personhood of the corporation is currently established by statute. The *Canada Business Corporations Act*, for example, provides in section 15(1): '[a] corporation has the capacity and, subject to this Act, the rights, powers and privileges of a natural person.'[7] Indeed, any Canadian corporate law textbook will likely open its chapter on the status or nature of the corporation with the bald statement that the corporation is a legal person.[8] Courts in Canada have even found that corporations have certain rights under the *Charter of Rights and Freedoms*, such as freedom of expression, the right to be tried within a reasonable time, the freedom to associate, and the right to be secure against unreasonable search and seizure.[9] The state of Canadian law certainly empowers vanDuzer to confidently say, '[i]ncorporation brings into existence a new legal person whose rights and obligations may be thought of as analogous to those of a human person' (2003: 98), and yet, it is not quite as simple as that.

In Canada, over the first half of the nineteenth century, a distinct legal personality had not yet developed for the corporation; however, limited liability had been a practice since at least 1830, becoming established in legislation in 1850.[10] After a variety of changes which weakened the statutory claim to corporate personality in many jurisdictions, it was not until the 1970s that Canada and Ontario moved to the present system in which corporate personality is assured, with most other provinces following suit over the 1980s and 1990s. Interestingly, with all of the statutory variation, however, the British case of *Salomon* v. *Salomon & Co.*, decided by the House of Lords in 1897, has long been interpreted as the Canadian authority for the proposition that the corporation is a distinct legal entity from its shareholders. In that case, a successful leather boot merchant, Aron Salomon, converted his business from a sole proprietorship into a limited corporation, with himself, his wife, and their five children as directors. As part of the consideration paid for the transfer of the business, the corporation issued him debentures secured against the assets of the corporation. Salomon himself held an overwhelming majority of the shares and was in effective control of the corporation.

When the company went through serious financial difficulties, the issue arose of whether or not Salomon as an individual was liable for the corporation's debts. The liquidator was required to pay the secured creditors first (Salomon in this instance) before paying the unsecured creditors, such as suppliers, etc., and to do so would have left nothing for the unsecured creditors. The liquidator argued that the corporation was a sham, that it was basically Salomon carrying on business in another name only. Making history, the House of Lords held that at law a company is a person capable of perpetual succession, quite distinct from the natural persons who may comprise it (*Salomon*, 1897). They went on: '[e]ither the limited company was a legal entity or it was not. If it was, the business belonged to it and not to Mr. Salomon. If it was not, there was no person and no thing to be an agent at all; and it is impossible to say at the same time that there is a company and there is not' (ibid.: 31). All of the justices agreed that the individual motives in the creation of the corporation were irrelevant. Once the corporation was legally created, it was a free-standing and fully independent legal entity.

This finding of a separate corporate persona was upheld in subsequent cases, coming to be known as the separate entity principle. Yet, if the corporation is a separate entity from its human shareholders, then we need to determine if it is an intentional and responsible actor. '[T]he fundamental question is whether an organization can be blameworthy in itself, or is it always a function of the blameworthiness of the individuals involved?' (Quaid, 1998: 72). Many scholars have lamented, however, that what has resulted from the personification of the corporation in Anglo-American law is that corporations receive the rights and benefits of legal personhood without any responsibilities above those of acting in its own best interest (Wells, 1993; Neocleous, 2003). As Jennifer Quaid notes, '[a]scriptions of responsibility do not flow from the current notion of the legal person' (1998: 73).

When considering questions of liability, courts in Canada have adopted an approach called identification theory, 'provid[ing] us with a method of analyzing whether the corporate person has done something of legal significance' (Welling, 1991: 115). Identification theory rests on the behaviourist principle that the acts of a company's organs – its directors, managers, employees, and so on – as long as they are within the scope of their proper authority, are not their own actions, but the acts of the company. One Canadian judge stated, 'the essence of the doctrine of identification is that the individual is treated as the company's self. They are one and the same' (*Canadian Dredge*, 1985: para. 82).[11] Therefore, if one wishes to know the 'mind' of the corporation, one must merely investigate the minds of certain managers who are empowered to take key decisions. The company should then only be held responsible for the actions of those charged with its primary management in its corporate constitution. At the same time, the individuals in question cannot be held liable for actions taken within the scope of their authority, because they are corporate acts. If one cannot find that directing mind, however, then the prosecution fails; the corporation has acted without an ascertainable legal intention.

The general test for identification can be framed: '[i]s the human actor who committed the crime a vital organ or a directing mind and will of the corporation?' (vanDuzer, 2003: 172). For example, a used car sales manager was found to be a directing mind when odometers were fraudulently being turned back on cars in the sales lot (*Waterloo Mercury Sales*, 1974). On the other hand, a truck driver was found not to be a directing mind in relation to transporting hazardous waste without authorization (*Safety-Kleen*, 1997). R. v. *Canadian Dredge and Dock Ltd.* (1985) is the leading Canadian case on corporate criminal liability. There, several companies conspired in advance to inflate the lowest bid for a contract. The lowest bidder, after receiving the contract, was to make pay-offs to the other corporations. In that case, the court held that if the individuals involved were doing something fraudulent and benefiting personally to the complete exclusion of the interests of the corporation, then identity theory could not apply. However, as the benefits were shared between the corporations and the fraudulent managers, identity doctrine did apply and the corporations were found liable.[12]

Despite the well-established nature of the identity doctrine, the separate entity principle, and statutory provisions across the country providing for the corporate person, critics have lamented that Canadian courts have taken upon themselves the right to regularly disregard the separateness of corporate legal personality (vanDuzer, 2003; Welling, 1991; Neyers, 2000). This judicial creativity has come to be known by the 'somewhat antiquated and ultimately obscuring' (and I would add gendered and racialized) expression of 'piercing the corporate veil' (vanDuzer, 2003). What is really being lifted in these instances is the personhood of the corporation. Concern is also expressed that it is by no means clear when courts will be prepared to pierce the veil and when they will not. VanDuzer suggests, '[u]nfortunately, the many cases in which this approach has been taken "illustrate no consistent principle."'[13]

He suggests three primary instances where courts have tended to discount corporate personality: first, when it is 'just not fair' not to do so; second, when the corporation in question was incorporated for an objectionable purpose; and third, when the corporation in question is acting as a mere agent for another person at law. Courts will ignore the separate personality of the corporation when not doing so would lead to a result 'flagrantly opposed to justice' (*Kosmopoulos*, 1987: 10). This is, of course, quite a subjective determination but does have a certain appeal. For example, then Chief Justice Lamer of the Supreme Court of Canada noted in *R. v. Wholesale Travel Group*,

> [t]he corporate form of business organization is chosen by individuals because of its numerous advantages (legal and otherwise). Those who cloak themselves in the corporate veil, and who rely on the legal distinction between themselves and the corporate entity when it is to their benefit to do so, should not be allowed to deny this distinction in these circumstances (where the distinction is not to their benefit). (1991: 171)

Courts have noted, however, that this subjectivity is not and should not be interpreted as a *carte blanche* to ignore the corporate person (*Transamerica Life*, 1997). The courts are arguably more likely to lift the corporate veil to protect innocent third parties such as creditors or tort victims, rather than shareholders trying to benefit from both the enforcement and denial of corporate personality.

Second, courts will often ignore corporate legal personality where the corporation has been incorporated for the very purpose of doing something illegal or improper. Fraud and avoidance of taxes have been typical purposes under this head for which courts have been likely to look behind the veil (e.g., *De Salaberry*, 1974; *Big Bend Hotel*, 1980). The third basis upon which Canadian courts have avoided the corporate person is by finding that the corporation is merely an agent of another legal person (typically a controlling shareholder that is, itself, a corporation). These corporations are often described as 'shams,' 'cloaks,' 'conduits,' or 'alter egos.'[14] It is important to recognize that this third approach does not really pierce the corporate veil so much as suggest that the actions of a particular corporation have a different legal status than if undertaken outside of an agency relationship.

While piercing the corporate veil, and thus ignoring corporate personhood, may enable the punishment of individuals at fault in a particular situation, the rationale does not take into account the realities of the complexity of current corporate action. 'Such an approach cannot accommodate the situation where corporate harm is caused by system failure or a cumulation [*sic*] of various faults by many agents of the corporation neither of which are sufficient to sustain an individual attribution of blame' (Quaid, 1998: 91). In such instances, there may be some utility in 'blaming' the corporate person. This was the approach advocated by Canada's Law Reform Commission in its Working Paper on *Criminal Responsibility for Group Action* (1976), which took more of a real entity perspective on the corporate person. The Commission noted, '[o]ur interest in corporations, then, reflects a more general concern about the impact groups have on society, and how group processes provide a vehicle through which power can be exercised anonymously, often without feeling or responsibility' (1976: 3). The Commission argued that corporate responsibility must be seen as a form of 'collective fault' for which the corporation provides the 'symbolic focus' (1976: 21). Yet, it also acknowledged that the primary means to sanction corporations has been through fines, an ultimately unsuccessful and socially unsatisfying mechanism, and the Commission called for more creative measures.

The recent passage of Bill C-45, *An Act to Amend the Criminal Code,* is arguably part of a long-awaited reply to the calls by the Commission. The introduction to the bill states:

> Critics of [the identification] approach have pointed out that it does not reflect the reality of the internal dynamics of corporations, particularly in the case of larger corporations. Rarely do high-level corporate officials personally engage in the specific conduct or make the specific decisions that result in occupational health and safety violations or in serious workplace injury or death. However, they can often, through actual policy decisions or otherwise, create or contribute to a corporate environment where subordinate managers, supervisors and employees feel encouraged or even compelled to cut corners on health and safety matters, even in the face of legal prohibitions or official corporate policy.

The legislation was passed as a result of the Westray mining disaster in which twenty-six miners perished as a result of corporate negligence, and yet no one was held responsible. As one commentator notes, the legislation potentially expands the assignment of liability as it 'eliminates the prosecution's duty to prove that a person is a directing mind of the corporation. Instead, a "senior officer" must be implicated in the criminal activity' (Macpherson, 2004: 11). Therefore, the legislation replaces the identification doctrine with a broader regime of criminal liability, expands the principles underlying the attribution of criminal responsibility for fault-based crimes, loosens the availability of potential defences, and includes both increased fines and sentencing guidelines particular to organizations.[15] It remains to be seen, however, how this will change the face of corporate criminal responsibility in Canada, as, to date, only one set of charges has been laid under the new legislation, and those charges were later withdrawn.

Responsibilization of the corporate person in the Canadian legal system, therefore, has tended to occur through the device of piercing the corporate veil, namely looking behind the corporation to the directing minds (and bodies) of the human beings that comprise its leadership and holding them personally accountable for the actions taken within the corporate context and by the corporation. This denies the legal personality of the corporation, rendering it, at best, a legal fiction. Corporate personhood then becomes a convenient technical device to be invoked for economic and legal purposes in the regular course of business, and one to be removed when there is a compelling moral reason to do so. It in no way describes a state of affairs where a unity exists in collective action that can serve as the basis for social responsibility. It suggests that the personality of the corporation is an impediment to, rather than an enhancement of, moral action. Recent legislation reaffirms the notion of the corporate person and attempts to make it easier to pursue it as a responsible agent, but perhaps the most powerful attempt to responsibilize the corporation, while at the same time recognizing its personality, has been from within the corporate world itself, in the corporate social responsibility movement.

Fusing the Moral and Metaphysical?

It will no longer do for a company to go quietly about its business, telling no lies and breaking no laws, selling things that people want, and making money. That is so passé. Today, all companies, but especially big ones, are enjoined from every side to worry less about profits and to be socially responsible instead.

(*Economist*, 2005d: 11)

A quick perusal of any major business's website is very likely to reveal the presence of a corporate social responsibility (CSR) policy, a number of initiatives designed to achieve philanthropic, social, or environmental goals, and a reporting mechanism of some kind such as environmental annual reports. Sometimes described as a 'triple bottom line' of business – social, environmental, and economic – CSR policy is emerging in a context where it has become increasingly difficult for corporations to insist that their responsibilities to society are continuous with, and limited to, those owed to their shareholders, namely the legal pursuit of profit. While the notion that corporations have some broader social duties than profit-making dates back to at least the nineteenth century, it was after the Second World War that these ideas began to coalesce into something that one could describe as a social movement towards corporate social responsibility. Early discussions featured two fundamentally different conceptualizations of the corporation.

The first approach assumed that corporations have an inherent moral character, that business has an obligation to pursue social goals which cohere with the values of the broader society, and that businesses cannot be extracted from their social context (Bowen, 1953 and Eells, 1956). This contrasted dramatically with a more classical economic view advocated by Milton Friedman (1962), Theodore Levitt (1958), and others (e.g., Livingston, 1958 and Kelso and Adler, 1958), which claimed that the only moral obligation a business has is to be profitable. The assumption made by classical economists was that if a society's corporations were making profits, then that society inevitably benefited. In personhood terms, the latter is, at best, passively responsible, whereas the former implies a more engaged citizenship model.

Unfortunately for the classical economists, a whole host of converging social factors rendered their view of the corporate person as solely a profit-making entity publicly untenable (De George, 1996: 18). Some of these social factors included the social unrest of the 1960s; the environmentalism of the 1970s; the rise of neoliberal globalization in the 1980s (and the corresponding rise of anti-globalization politics nationally and globally); the public dissemination of corporate wrongdoings (from promoting baby formula in the Third World, to supporting the Apartheid regime in South Africa, to clear-cutting old-growth forest, to human rights violations of labourers in off-shore work sites); the rise of international NGOs focused on corporate mis-behaviour such as Greenpeace, Pollution Probe, or Amnesty International; the ongoing work of international labour unions; the rise of consumer advocacy groups; and most recently, the rise of the Internet as a tool for groups publicizing corporate misdeeds and organizing consumer boycotts and culture-jamming (see Coombe and Herman, 2001). The groups at the centre of these various initiatives were able to force the notion of corporate citizenship further up the corporate and political agenda. Thus, while no one can agree on exactly what CSR means, and its effectiveness is regularly disputed, it is clear that from the 1960s onward, we have seen a radical reconfiguration of the public roles and responsibilities of the corporate person under the guise of something called CSR.[16] This reconfiguration is one which the *Economist* dubbed a 'significant victory in the battle of ideas' (2005a: 3). 'Over the past ten years or so, corporate social responsibility (CSR) has blossomed as an idea, if not a coherent practical programme. ... Today corporate social responsibility, if it is nothing else, is the tribute that capitalism everywhere pays to virtue' (*Economist*, 2005a: 3).

Still a highly contested concept, CSR has no one accepted meaning and no agreed-upon set of measures for its achievement. In 1979, Archie B. Caroll proposed the base model which suggested that after a foundation of sound economic performance, one considers the ethical, legal, and discretionary duties of the corporation, the latter of which involves being a 'good corporate citizen' through philanthropic acts. Others built upon that model over the next decade (e.g., Wartick and Cochran, 1985, Wood, 1991a, 1991b). I suggest one can locate the various models into three broader categories which I call economic, social obligation, and corporate citizenship, each of which implies a different conception of the person.

The economic approach to CSR suggests that the corporation is socially responsible by virtue of pursuing profit within the constraints of the law. (Of course, any illegal behaviour is not responsible.) Indebted to the classical economists' view of the corporation, this perspective has four primary arguments raised in its support. First, corporations are accountable to their shareholders/owners, therefore managers are responsible for managing the corporation in ways which maximize the owners' interests. Second, programs to improve society should be determined by the law and left to the contributions of private citizens. Businesses then participate in such government-driven social initiatives through the payment of taxes. Third, allocating company profits to social improvement programs is a violation of the management contract, and fourth, such activities can drive the prices of good and services up, thereby, in fact, harming society. This is the minimalist approach to CSR which suggests that corporations do contribute to the overall social good, but do so primarily and ideally solely through their primary activities of profit-making. In other words, as *homo economicus* the corporation fulfils its part of the social contract. The moral and metaphysical persons can be separated.

The second approach is social obligation and assumes that a corporation reacts to broader social norms, values, and performance expectations. In other words, in the current context, society expects corporations to go beyond the mere provision of goods and services. As a result, corporations should be accountable for the environmental and social costs incurred by their actions, and be required to participate in the solution of problems they contribute to generating. A typical definition within this rubric would be that CSR 'means that a corporation should be held accountable for any of its actions that affect people, their communities, and their environment. It implies that negative business impacts on people and society should be acknowledged and corrected if at all possible' (Frederick, Post, and Davis, 1992: 30).

'Stakeholder theory' or the stakeholder approach, which emerged in the mid-1980s, is a key development in this category. Stakeholder theory holds that corporations are accountable to their stakeholders, but that their stakeholders include not only shareholders and potential investors, but managers, employees, customers, business partners, the natural environment, and the communities in which the corporations operate (Freeman, 1984). Corporations are seen as implanted social actors with an *a priori* relationship with the public that exceeds their economic activity. Therefore, in this conception, the corporation remains *homo economicus*, but is simultaneously recognized to be an effects-causing agent. This capacity to cause effects produces a social, if not moral, obligation to be accountable.

Third and finally, I suggest there is the corporate citizen approach. It begins with the operating assumption that there is an inevitable tension between private profit and public interest. The terminology of 'responsiveness,' for example, is advocated by some American scholars (Ackerman and Bauer, 1976) because 'responsibility' connotes a process of assuming an obligation and therefore places its emphasis on motivation, rather than performance. Motivation is simply not adequate for advocates of this approach, whereas responsiveness or putting into action what a corporation has decided to do is a more accurate description, suggest some, of what CSR should stand for (Hopkins, 2003). This school of thought goes the furthest, demanding action from the corporate person, rather than merely intention, and it is the approach most frequently adopted by anti-corporate activists. As CSR has turned, for many corporations, into a public relations exercise smacking of tokenism, corporate citizenship advocates would seek out corporate social responsibility standards defined universally (often in relationship to human rights objectives), and enforced through institutions and governments, rather than the more typical voluntary mechanisms. Thus, the metaphysical and moral persons merge in the corporate citizenship model. *Homo economicus* is understood as amoral, if not potentially immoral, and demands are made to place moral, not merely social, obligations upon the corporate person.

Overwhelmingly, the bulk of current CSR initiatives fall within the social obligation approach. One well-known example of a CSR initiative is the United Nations Global Compact. Announced in 1999 and launched in 2000 by United Nations Secretary General Kofi Annan, the Global Compact includes ten principles pertaining to human rights, labour, and the environment. Companies participate by sending a letter from their CEO to the secretary general in which they commit to integrating the ten principles into their mission statement and activities, as well as informing their employees, shareholders, customers, and suppliers about them. Companies must then report their progress on these objectives in their annual reports. The UN does not audit the reports, as the Compact is non-binding; it functions primarily as an educational forum. This poses significant limitations, argue advocates of the corporate citizenship approach.

Other international and national agencies are participating in the CSR buzz. At the World Economic Forum in Davos, Switzerland in January 2000, President James D. Wolfensohn of the World Bank launched 'Corporate Social Responsibility' and 'Corporate Governance' programs (World Bank Group, 2004). Those themes have been present regularly in conferences and discussions of the World Bank since 1998. Britain has appointed a government minister responsible for CSR. In Canada, the Canadian Business for Social Responsibility organization was established in 1995 and is a 'non-profit, business-led membership organization of Canadian companies that have made a commitment to operate in a socially, environmentally and financially responsible manner' (see CBSR, 2004). In 1998, the Canadian Centre for Corporate Ethics and Social Responsibility posed an amendment to the *Canada Business Corporations Act* permitting, but not requiring, management to take account of non-shareholder interests when determining the best interests of the corporation. In this way, there would be non-mandatory but still legislative recognition of CSR. The change was not included in the 2001 amendments to the legislation, however. Similar amendments have been included in more than half of American states.

Yet even without legislation, analyses such as *Building Confidence: Corporate Sustainability Reporting in Canada* (2003) and the *National Corporate Social Responsibility Report* by the Conference Board of Canada demonstrate the rapid rise of awareness of CSR issues and a corresponding rise in reporting practices in Canadian companies (Greenall, 2004). The Organization for Economic Co-Operation and Development (OECD) recently analysed the contributions that voluntary CSR initiatives have made (OECD, 2001). Some of their findings show that voluntary initiatives are indeed a global phenomenon, but that they differ significantly across regions. There are a variety of informal pressures (legal, regulatory, employee, brand, public) which influence implementation of even voluntary strategies, as well as wide divergences in the commitment to CSR values. Management expertise has advanced to the point where compliance with CSR policies can be made fiscally possible, but other measures and reporting standards remain weak. The costs of these initiatives remain unclear. The potential benefits of CSR initiatives are numerous, including corporations' improved legal compliance with existing legislation, management of litigation risks, brand and reputation enhancement, improved relations with shareholders and society, and improvement of employee morale. The various guidelines produced, such as the *OECD Guidelines for Multinational Enterprises*, the United Nations *Global Compact*, and Amnesty International's *Human Rights Principles for Companies*, play an important role in strengthening an emerging consensus of values, as well as distributing expertise.

In practice, therefore, while seemingly prolific, there are no overarching shared definitions, standards, or set of institutions. As a result, CSR practices are voluntary and largely unregulated. They tend to be dominated by corporate philanthropy, namely the donation of funds or time to charity, rather than to more substantial engagements with labour relations, environmental sustainability, and so on. Critics have suggested that while the single bottom line can be measured and accounted for, the triple bottom line is considerably more difficult to measure. As a result, much CSR does not radically alter how a company does business; it does not fuse the moral to the metaphysical person. 'The human face that CSR applies to capitalism goes on each morning, gets increasingly smeared by day and washes off at night' (*Economist*, 2005a: 4).

Critiques of CSR emerge across the political spectrum and include that it reinforces the idea that business and social responsibility are unique and independent thought processes and activities and that social responsibility of business involves doing good deeds to make up for the fact that the underlying structure of business is either bad or neutral (Velamuri and Freeman, 2006). Another concern voiced by critics of CSR is that it is primarily conceived of as an 'after-profitability' concern, and that to be meaningful, socially responsible principles have to be embedded in the corporation from the beginning (Kang and Wood, 1995). Some critics have suggested that CSR is nothing more than a public relations smokescreen (Bakan, 2004), while others continue to argue the classical economic position that CSR distracts businesses from their primary profit-making activities, wastes resources, and that this profit-making, in itself, provides significant social benefits to society (see *Economist,* 2005a, 2005b, 2005c, 2005d, 2005e).

But whether it is a public relations sham or a sincere rethinking of the role of corporations in our social fabric, something called CSR has taken the corporate world by storm. The metaphysics of the corporate person are in high relief, yet, at the same time, corporations are mobilizing a strategy that 'employs powerful ideological and practical devices designed to stabilize the field around voluntary and legally nonbinding practices of social responsibility' (Shamir, 2004: 659). Therefore, rather than the triple bottom line or a corporate smokescreen, we can more productively think about CSR as 'a site of struggle over meaning, where public pressures and corporate response to such pressures assume a more or less definitive structure, with "authorized" agents who occupy certain "recognized" positions from which they assert "what is at stake" and from which they try to control the definition and scope of the very notion of responsibility' (ibid.: 644). In this way, we can rewrite CSR as a technique of personification which necessarily makes visible the tensions in the person as moral agent, in the P3 person.

Responsibility and Blame:
The Corporate Person in Popular Culture

> Corporate social responsibility is their [companies'] new creed, a self-conscious corrective to earlier greed-inspired visions of the corporation. Despite this shift, the corporation itself has not changed. It remains as it was at the time of its origins as a modern business institution in the middle of the nineteenth century, a legally designated 'person' designed to valorize self-interest and invalidate moral concern.
>
> (Bakan, 2004: 28)

Joel Bakan, lawyer, author, and filmmaker, is clearly sceptical of the apparent responsibilization of the corporation through the corporate embrace of CSR. This scepticism permeates the 2004 documentary film *The Corporation*, based on his book of the same year, *The Corporation: The Pathological Pursuit of Profit and Power*, and is linked, for Bakan, to the corporation's identity as a person. In the very well-received film, Bakan, director Mark Achbar (of *Manufacturing Consent* fame), and director and editor Jennifer Abbot explore the personality of the modern business corporation, ultimately with a view to making it accountable to society for the huge perceived social harms it produces. Another recent documentary film also seeks to lay blame and enforce accountability for egregious corporate behaviour. *Enron: The Smartest Guys in the Room* (2005), based on a book by *Fortune* magazine writers Bethany McLean and Peter Elkind, is directed by Alex Gibney, and tells the sordid tale of the rapid rise and even faster fall of one of America's largest, most successful, and most notorious corporations. Yet while *The Corporation* seeks to blame the corporate person, *Enron* immediately and unquestioningly pierces, or even ignores, the corporate veil. Thus, in these two popular culture engagements with corporate personality and socially harmful corporate activity, we have two very different perspectives on the relationship between corporate persons, law, and social responsibility.[17]

The Corporation played in theatres across Canada, the United States, the United Kingdom, and Europe. It won audience awards at the Sundance Film Festival and at numerous other international film festivals, drawing both critical raves and vitriol, depending on the politics of the reviewers and/or their media outlets. Overwhelmingly, however, it was widely acclaimed by the press, with many reviewers comparing it favourably to Michael Moore's *Fahrenheit 9/11* (2004), released at about the same time. Powerful adjectives abounded: 'compelling,' 'powerful,' 'scathing,' 'a sensation,' 'meaty,' 'rigorous and challenging,' and 'hard-hitting.' It obviously struck a nerve with the viewing public, screening very widely for a documentary film and actually making a profit.

In addition to its critical acclaim, the film made its mark on the corporate world. At a 2004 business meeting event, the organization Canadian Business for Social Responsibility posed to its members the question 'Is CSR Just PR?' It was framed as a response to *The Corporation* and panel participants included Mark Achbar and Ray Anderson, the CEO of Interface who features prominently (and heroically) in the film. Joel Bakan has become well known in business circles and was referred to in a special issue of the *Economist* on CSR as 'an angry law professor' and the 'scourge of the modern corporation' (2005e: 20). In short, *The Corporation* was a film that made its mark on both corporate and public imaginations.

The Corporation opens with a litany of images of corporate misconduct and its rationalization, immediately posing the corporation as capable of acting immorally, as a candidate for blame.[18] The corporation is, we are told by the narrator, 'an institution that creates great wealth but causes enormous and often hidden harms.' Deploying close to forty talking heads, representing current and former CEOs of some of the world's largest corporations, investigative journalists, anti-globalization activists, authors, academics from a number of disciplines, medical doctors, corporate spies, and a born-again eco-businessman, the film explores those harms in detail. The usual suspects are presented: Michael Moore, Naomi Klein, Noam Chomsky, Maude Barlow, Vandana Shiva, as well as a few other suspects, less likely and more suspicious: Sir Mark Moody-Stuart, former chairman of Royal Dutch Shell; Milton Friedman, Nobel prize winning economist and favourite of Margaret Thatcher; Sam Gibara, chairman and former CEO of Good Year Tire; and Tom Kline, affable senior vice-president, Pfizer Incorporated.

This excess of irresponsible corporate activity is directly linked in the film to the corporation's identity as a person. This legal turn of events is represented as a misuse of power; historian Howard Zinn states:

> [t]he fourteenth amendment was passed at the end of the civil war to give equal rights to black people and therefore it said, no state can deprive any person of life, liberty or property without due process of the law. And that was intended to prevent the states from taking the life, liberty or property from black people as they had done for so much of our history. And what happened is the corporations come into court, and corporation lawyers are very clever, and they say no, you can't deprive a person of life, liberty or property. We are a person. The corporation is a person. And the Supreme Court goes along with that.

Another commentator volunteers the troubling statistic that between 1890 and 1910, of the 307 cases brought before the courts under the Fourteenth Amendment, 288 were brought by corporations and 19 by African Americans.[19]

This treatment of the corporation as a legal person is thus framed as a tricky manoeuvre by corporate lawyers, and as a fundamentally counter-intuitive, if not immoral, development. And it is the very fact of the legal personality of the corporation that is focused upon in almost all popular press about the film. For example, a journalist in the *Washington Post* notes, '[p]erhaps the most disturbing of all the material set forth in the informative yet entertaining film is the notion, which arose in the nineteenth century, of the corporation as a legally defined "person," with the same rights, but only some of the same responsibilities, as flesh-and-blood people' (O'Sullivan, 2004: WE39).

The press's treatment of the fact of corporate personhood mirrors the film's own incredulity. The Supreme Court's decision to recognize Fourteenth Amendment rights for the corporation is 'truly bizarre' (Wilmington, 2004; Lehmann, 2004; LaSalle, 2004), an 'elaborately absurd piece of legal fiction' (Robinson, 2004), and a cooptation of civil rights law (Lehmann, 2004). Thus the corporation's personhood is understood as an unlikely and inappropriate legal fiction. In this way, blame is easily laid at the feet of crafty lawyers and short-sighted judges, forestalling a more sustained critique of the social conditions of capitalism producing such an outcome as possible, effective, and even desirable.

The film then veers sharply away from the viewer's lesson in legal fiction theory towards the real entity approach in order to frame its operating conceit: 'having acquired the legal rights and protections of a person ... what kind of person is the corporation?' The film takes the stance that the legal person is a moral person. As a reviewer from the *Boston Globe* notes, 'the film portrays the corporation as a living, breathing, individual (male) entity that's wholly responsible for its actions, inactions, and moral, social, legal, and ecological transgressions. It also has a face, a voice, and for most of this epic's runtime, a psychology' (Morris, 2004). Its psychology is, the film claims, psychopathic.

The filmmakers deploy the Personality Diagnostic Checklist of the World Health Organization's Manual of Mental Disorders to make this claim. The diagnostic checklist for psychopathology contains the following elements, each in turn 'proved' within the film. First, the callous unconcern for the feelings of others is illustrated through the example of sweatshop labour and the Kathie Lee Gifford scandal, where the former television hostess had lent her name to a line of clothes for Wal-Mart which were being produced in conditions far below acceptable. Second, the incapacity to maintain enduring relationships is captured in the global mobility of international labour – once a country or region hosting a sweatshop becomes politicized, wages rise and the multinational corporation packs up and moves somewhere else less problematic for its interests. Third, the reckless disregard for the safety of others is illustrated through the example of corporations trivializing the risks associated with the development and use of synthetic chemicals. Particularly haunting is the archival footage of Native American children being dusted with DDT by technicians in hazmat suits. The fourth item on the checklist is deceitfulness, or the repeated lying and conning of others for profit. Here Monsanto Corporation's coverup of the risks and negative test results of bovine somatrophin serves as the exemplar case. Fifth, an incapacity to experience guilt, where again, Monsanto's actions are *apropos*. This time it is their exposure of Vietnamese citizens and American soldiers to Agent Orange during the Vietnam War that is featured. While veterans ultimately sued for the health damages caused to them, and Monsanto settled out of court for millions, it never admitted its culpability (and Vietnamese citizens received no compensation). The failure to conform to social norms with respect to lawful behaviour is the final attribute. A long list of corporate criminal fines is offered as proof. After ticking off each of the above personality flaws, Dr Robert Hare, MD (an FBI consultant on psychopaths), confirms:

> ... if we look at a corporation as a legal person then it may not be that difficult to actually draw the transition between psychopathy in the individual to psychopathy in a corporation. We can go through the characteristics that define this particular disorder one by one and see how they might apply to corporations. They would have all the characteristics. And in fact, in many respects, corporations of that sort are the prototypical psychopath.

Viewers then nearly drown in the subsequent sea of corporate misconduct and resulting social harms. Yet it is not merely the wrongdoings that we are invited to remark; what the film offers as particularly galling is the corporation's lack of remorse. Throughout the film, neither the corporations themselves, nor the executives who represent them, take any responsibility for what happens. Geoff Pevere wrote in the *Toronto Star*,

> [w]atching the film ... one may be dumbstruck by the fact that so many spokespeople for what the film's makers clearly regard as the primary evil of our era would even sit for the camera, let alone smile so openly in its gaze. But that merely serves the movie's dramatically ingenious diagnosis of the corporation as legally recognized 'person.'
>
> If this self-interested, profit-driven, globally omnivorous capitalist structure is like a person, the film argues, then this person is a psychopath. And the psychopath smiles easily for it believes it is doing absolutely nothing wrong. ... It's easy to be happy if you're rich, powerful and utterly incapable of guilt and remorse. (2004: B01)

And yet, who should feel the remorse?

The film's creators do query whether all the people behind the corporate person are as malignant as it is. They clearly reject the metaphor that corporate misconduct is due solely to a 'few bad apples.' There are even attempts to humanize some of the executives. The former chairman of Shell and his wife are seen serving tea on the front lawn of their country home to anti-corporate protestors who have hung a banner crying 'murderer' across the roof. They apologize to the vegans in the group for having no soy milk. The film's hero is an executive who has redeemed himself, holding out hope for others. Ray Anderson, CEO of Interface (the world's largest carpet manufacturer), had a seemingly sincere environmental epiphany and now preaches the gospel of sustainable capitalism to all who will listen. Describing himself as a plunderer, he notes: '[s]omeday people like me will be in jail.'

And in his comment, we see the dilemma the film faces. The attempt to retain the real entity of the corporate person when it comes to not merely the laying of blame, but the taking of responsibility or forcing of accountability, falters. If the corporation itself, not merely the executives, is to blame, as the film repeatedly tells us, then should it be sent to jail? As one Harvard scholar suggests in the film, we need to 'look at the very roots of the legal form that created this beast and ask, who can make them accountable.'

The issue of moral accountability is put squarely on the table in one of the final sections of the film, entitled 'Psychotherapies.' Yet ultimately the film leaves us with a sense of dissatisfaction about how to approach individual or collective corporate psychopathology. Individual instances of resistance and forced accountability are the proferred therapies. The towns of Point Arena and Arcata California, poised to pass an ordinance challenging corporate personhood and framing the corporation as a threat to democracy, voted ultimately to merely limit the addition of chain restaurants in their community. Two jurisdictions in Pennsylvania took the bold step of revoking the personhood status of corporations, yet the film gives this move – seemingly the act it has been calling for – surprisingly short shrift. Finally, the residents of a city in Bolivia resist, to the point of civil unrest, injury, and death, the attempts by the World Bank to privatize their water system, including the rain. So, the power of the state or the people is pitted against the power of capital. And yet in this 'psychotherapy,' the corporation as person continues, unchanged, unscathed, and still irresponsible.

Ultimately *The Corporation* blames, but is unable to demonstrate how one might reform, corporate nature. However, in *Enron: The Smartest Guys in the Room*, the filmmakers, also desirous of blaming, focus instead on corporate culture, specifically, the corporate culture of Enron and the men who made it in their image. Enron was, at its height, the seventh largest corporation on the American stockmarket and valued at $70 billion. It is also notorious as one of the largest, and the first, of a long string of corporate bankruptcies resulting from misdeeds, including WorldCom, Tyco, Adelphia, and Global Crossing. Yet with all the recent instances of flagrant corporate misbehaviour, it is Enron which has become symbolic of the failure of corporate responsibility and public trust, shaking American culture to its roots. Enron single-handedly 'proved' that *homo economicus* is immoral. Who in North America can forget the televised images of pale, shocked employees flooding past the silver, tilted E with a mere thirty minutes to vacate the head office; the images of tons of shredded paper at accounting firm Arthur Anderson; indignant congressmen of all political stripes grilling the principal actors in the inquiries that followed; Chief Financial Officer Andrew Fastow 'taking the Fifth'; Kenneth Lay and Jeffrey Skilling incredibly maintaining their lack of knowledge and innocence throughout? Everyone was asking: how did this happen?

Kenneth Lay, oil tycoon and close friend of the Bush family, founded Enron in 1985 by merging a number of pipeline companies. From its early beginnings selling natural gas, it grew to become more of a stock-market for natural gas, and then expanded into markets in electricity, broadband, and even, near the end, the furthest point on the spectrum of virtuality, the weather. The company benefited from the deregulation of the energy markets in the United States and was permitted to adopt a system of 'mark to market' accounting. This allowed it to reflect future profits in its current books, regardless of whether those profits ever actually materialized. This drove up Enron's (apparent) quarterly profits, which correspondingly drove up the stock price. However, it also put incredible pressure on the company to continue to show ongoing significant profits, opening up the books to interpretive abuse.

With its go-getter team of young, ambitious, macho officers, Enron was the poster-child of the new American entrepreneurialism. Jeffrey Skilling, the president and chief operating officer from 1997 to February 2001, infused the company with his naked ambition and cut-throat style of management. Bonuses were huge for good performance, but there was also a policy of firing 10 per cent of the workforce annually after peer review, a practice dubbed 'rank-and-yank.' Loyalty was rewarded; questions were not. One infamous incident involved Skilling calling former Enron investor relations head Mark Koenig an 'asshole' during a telephone conference call, after he dared to suggest that it was difficult to make sense of Enron's books. But this neoliberal dream-come-true appeared to be working, according to the stock market. The charisma of the principals became the charisma of the corporation. Stock analysts, company executives, the financial media, lawyers, accountants, and the major banks all got on board with the success that was Enron. For six years, *Fortune* magazine voted Enron the most innovative company in America.

However, the business was not going well: projects were failing, competition was expanding, and it became increasingly difficult to show huge profits. Creative accounting became fraud as Andrew Fastow, chief financial officer, was charged with hiding huge amounts of debt. He created a variety of shell companies with the knowledge and consent of the major banks and the approval of Enron's independent auditor, Arthur Andersen. The fall of Enron was as rapid and surreal as its rise to supremacy had been. The Securities and Exchange Commission began an investigation in late 2000. In February 2001, Skilling took over as chief executive officer from Kenneth Lay, and then in August he suddenly quit. On 2 December 2001, in New York, Enron filed for Chapter 11 bankruptcy, at that time America's biggest corporate bankruptcy.[20] Around the world, close to 20,000 people lost their jobs; more than $2 billion in retirement funds disappeared; 25,000 more people lost their jobs when Arthur Andersen also collapsed; investors are estimated to have lost US$30 billion; and shareholders are suing Enron and the banks for $20 billion. Insiders were later revealed to have sold off several billion dollars of their stocks in the months before the company went bankrupt, much of which has not been recovered.

Enron's collapse sent shock waves throughout North America. Analysts scrambled to make sense of how this could have happened. Ironically, Enron's company slogan was 'Ask Why' and many factors were identified in the immediate fallout to explain why: Wall Street's 'loss of objectivity' (Lashinsky, 2001: A27); the brutality of the marketplace (*San Francisco Chronicle*, 2001: A28); an ineffective board of directors (*Toronto Star* 2001: D01); irresponsible accounting (Turner, 2001: BU5; Hilzenrath, 2001a: A01; 2001b: E01); deregulation (Geewax, 2001: 3E); combinations of all of those (Ivanovich, 2001); and trusting public utilities to the 'equivalent of Mississippi riverboat gamblers' (Milner, 2001: B2).

While many commentators acknowledged the roles of Skilling, Lay, and other principals, many looked elsewhere to blame as well. As a *Globe and Mail* reporter noted,

... let's not heap all the blame for what is likely to turn into the most spectacular and costly business failure in modern annals solely on the heads of Mr. Skilling, Mr. Lay or other arrogant executives who built the staid Texas pipeline operator into a global energy trading colossus, and then presided over its remarkably rapid fall from grace. There's plenty of blame to spread around among directors, auditors, regulators, rating agencies and the bankers and investors who provided all the money to put Enron into flight in the first place. (Milner, 2001: B2)

In fact, often the company itself and its key human actors were framed in the financial press, in the early days after the collapse, as a relatively small part of a larger problem. The *Philadelphia Inquirer* noted, 'the real issue at Enron isn't how the company violated the regulations. It is what the regulations allowed the company to get away with' (Brown, 2001: E01). 'The most unsettling corruption is not in the souls of the people in charge of Enron but in the heart of the financial markets,' claimed a reporter with the *Toronto Star* (Lewis, 2001: E06). Don Bauder at the *San Diego Union-Tribune* did not mince words: '[i]t is fortunate that the Enron scandal involves two cancers that threaten to cripple capitalism: phony accounting and excessive top management pay' (2001). Thus, it is the context and not the corporate person that produced the immoral behaviour. Enron is not responsible.

Greg Hassel of the *Houston Chronicle* is one of few to single out Enron's corporate culture as more than a mere detail of its downfall:

If the incredible collapse of Houston's most powerful company were written like a whodunit, there would be no shortage of clues to sift through in search of the culprit behind it all: questionable bookkeeping practices that hid high-risk deals – some of which defied standard definitions of acceptable business practice – from the prying eyes of the investing public. Headlong forays into uncharted waters like selling space on broadband data lines. But a prime suspect is the culture of Enron itself – a potent brew of aggressiveness and powerful intellect, fearlessness toward risk and a disregard for anyone who dared question the inner workings of the corporate juggernaut.

For those who accept that corporate culture was to blame for the company's demise, the initial reaction has been to heap most of the criticism on the brash and abrasive Skilling. ... That line of thinking tends to place little or no responsibility at the feet of Ken Lay, the polished and professorial chairman of Enron. (2001: A1)

Whether more blame should lie at the feet of Lay or Skilling is a moot and unanswerable question, but it is interesting that individual persons are figured as the authors of the destructive corporate culture at Enron. It would seem that for the financial press, the corporation as moral person is a *non sequitur*. This is also the angle emphasized by director Alex Gibney in the 2005 film that chronicles the Enron saga.

Opening with the reenactment of the suicide of Enron executive John C. (Cliff) Baxter, framed as an act of admission and remorse, *Enron: The Smartest Guys in the Room* is a film that seeks to explain how the event that is Enron happened. However, it is also, and I would argue primarily, a film about laying responsibility and seeking accountability for immoral actions. The macho, entrepreneurial, innovative, and success-mad culture at Enron is clearly part of the problem. Some of the most chilling footage takes place during the 2001 California energy crisis with the rolling brown-outs and devastating forest fires. The film argues that Enron's direct interference in the power grid at the time was largely responsible for the crisis, and then implies that the subsequent election of Republican Arnold Schwarzenegger as California governor followed suit. Traders at Enron are featured on tape laughing at the plight of Californians and saying 'burn, baby, burn' because they know that, the higher the price of electricity goes, the bigger their bonuses will be.

At the same time, *Enron* is very much a film seeking to lay responsibility at someone's feet. To this end, it operates as a series of mini-biographies on the assumption that the corporate culture is reflective of the identity of its principal actors. We learn about Kenneth Lay, a self-made man from humble roots, with golden political connections, who became the ambassador of deregulation. Lay was a close personal friend of the Bush family and Enron was the single largest contributor to George W. Bush's presidential campaign. We learn about Lu Pai, the CEO of one of the related companies, Energy Services, who divorced his wife and left the company with $250 million to marry a stripper pregnant with his child. He was famous for the parties and 'girls' in his office and is claimed to be the single largest individual landowner in Colorado. Andrew Fastow is represented as clearly the most overtly fraudulent, setting up a huge network of sham companies in which he was often directly interested, in order to hide Enron debts.

The film focuses its punitive gaze on Skilling, however.[21] Represented as a self-remade man, a huge risk taker, charismatic, and a legend within the macho culture of the company, he is credited with the innovative ideas that virtualized the business of the company. Skilling is framed as someone who knows exactly what is going on in the company at all times and as a controlling and dominant force in its corporate culture. Undoubtedly this is why the viewer feels so sick watching Skilling on the stand denying both knowledge of, and responsibility for, any of the illegal activities that took place at Enron. The screen shows him as utterly without remorse. The viewer 'knows' that Skilling is lying and is invited to be angry at his contemptuous lack of repentance. We do not know if justice was achieved because the film's narrative ends before the trials of Lay and Skilling which followed its release.

The off-screen convictions did eventually happen. Fastow pled guilty to conspiracy and received an agreement for a reduced sentence of ten years in order to secure his testimony against Skilling and Lay. The other charges against him were dropped. In September 2006 he was sentenced to six years in prison. Lay was convicted in May 2006 of six counts of fraud and conspiracy and four counts of bank fraud. He died on 5 July 2006 at the age of sixty-four before he could be sentenced; he likely would have spent the rest of his life in jail.[22] Jeffrey Skilling was convicted in January 2006 of eighteen counts of fraud and conspiracy and one count of insider trading and was acquitted on nine other counts of insider trading. On 23 October 2006, he was sentenced to twenty-four years and four months in prison for his role in the securities fraud. It was one of the harshest sentences for corporate crime in American history.[23] The judge sentenced Skilling after hearing statements from seven victims. While Skilling was out on $5-million bail awaiting his sentence, the court required him to wear an electronic monitor, and he will be in prison as he appeals his sentence. He was also ordered to pay $45 million in restitution, which will require the sale of almost all of his personal assets, including his home. He, like Lay, maintains his innocence of the charges to this day.

Enron: The Smartest Guys in the Room was released to critical acclaim. More so than with *The Corporation*, which drew a conservative backlash for its unabashed corporate bashing, everyone could agree that what happened at Enron was appalling. It was repeatedly compared favourably to Michael Moore's documentaries, and in particular *Fahrenheit 9/11* (2004), as less polemical and, as a result, more credible. Reviewers were clearly drawn to the human drama at the heart of the film – a 'gobsmacking tale of corruption and greed' (Braun, 2005), a 'horrifyingly potent vision of ruthless avarice' (Schager, 2005), and 'a classical tragedy of greed and hubris, proceeding apace from rapacious entrepreneurship to frenzied, evil avarice to epic delusion' (Winter, 2006). Skilling, Lay, Fastow, and others are held accountable in the press: '[g]amblers all, the men who ran Enron into the ground seem to share a general amorality that really has to be seen to be believed' (Braun, 2005).

At the same time, however, David Ansen at *Newsweek* recognizes that the documentary 'calls into question not just a handful of rogue corporate outlaws but an entire business ethos' (Ansen, 2005). While the narration in the film itself poses the question, '[w]ho was responsible for the downfall of Enron ... the work of a few bad men or the dark shadow of the American dream,' it lays the blame at the feet of corporate culture and the men who made it, rather than on corporate nature, as *The Corporation* seeks to do. While it seems to embrace a classic formulation of the doctrine of identification, it does not do so, as the law does, to responsibilize the corporate person, to attempt to unify the metaphysical and moral personalities of the corporation. However, the conclusion of *The Corporation* is very unsatisfying: after being convinced that the corporate form is incredibly destructive in practice, if not in principle, and that 'a few bad apples' are not the real problem, we are left with very little by way of solution. We get the satisfaction we seek in *Enron: The Smartest Guys in the Room* because we know that the smartest guys have been caught and are likely to go to jail. While both films operate on a model of moral blame and both seek retribution, only *Enron* is successful in producing a sense of satisfied retribution, because it pierces the corporate veil to blame the human persons at the heart of the corporate person.

As one of the authors of the book upon which the film was based, Bethany McLean, notes in an interview:

[e]veryone has a line of argument about why this wasn't their fault. And each is actually kind of believable. You can embrace that logic. We even made the title of the chapter where we wrote about that, 'Isn't anybody

sorry?' But if we take all of those arguments, and we agree that everyone did everything right, then we are saying that Enron was an accident. That America's seventh largest company can have a stock price of $180 one month and be bankrupt the next and can have financial filings that totally don't represent the company, and that's nobody's fault. I can't subscribe to that thought. Someone has to take responsibility. You can't be a CEO who takes $300 million in compensation out of a company and then say to the rest of us, 'I didn't know.' You have got to have greater moral responsibility than that. (in Sinha, 2005)

This focusing in on the embodied individuals as the receptacles of blame, responsibility, and accountability according to a model of retribution has a number of effects. First, it permits retributive justice to be visited upon the perpetrators as identified. Fastow is in jail, Skilling will be a very old man before he leaves federal prison, and Lay, were he still alive, would have likely spent the rest of his life in jail. These men are embodied individuals who can be punished viscerally in a way that provides us with moral satisfaction. It is a model of punishment that we recognize as a society and reserve for our most significant immoral behaviour.

In addition to this arguably socially salutary effect, however, it is important to recognize that there are two other less desirable and more complex effects of the focus on the humans involved. First, this approach does not get to what some argue is the root of the problem. As many commentators remarked at the time that it declared bankruptcy, Enron was likely caused by a variety of factors ranging from deregulation to corruption, to bad governance, to the decline of objective standards, to a larger entrepreneurial spirit within American business and culture. As one reviewer noted of the film,

> Enron was far from a fluke or a rogue operation; it was late-'90s American business at its finest, embraced by almost every leading financial analyst and commentator. If it looks in the rear-view mirror like a wacko cult run by thieves, liars and maniacs, what does that tell us about the functioning of the so-called free market? (O'Hehir, 2005)

Thus any broader critique of corporate capitalism or the nature, rather than the culture, of the corporation is dulled by the focus on the individual, human perpetrators.[24]

The second related and less desirable effect of blaming the 'bad apples' is that the tale of travesty and tragedy ultimately turns into one of redemption. Eventually Enron did fail, the individual perpetrators were caught and jailed, and the mechanism designed to catch such problems is retroactively assumed to have worked. Enron becomes an opportunity to legitimize the market. The *San Francisco Chronicle* suggested, after noting Kenneth Lay's mocking of California officials' naïveté about market dynamics, 'Lay has been proved right about one thing: the marketplace can be brutal and unforgiving, even to its biggest champions' (*San Francisco Chronicle*, 2001: A28). An editorial in the *Boston Herald* also noted how the market clearly punished the abuse of trust that Enron executives had wreaked upon it (*Boston Herald*, 2001: O38). This is echoed in the *Economist*: 'The resultant backlash comes as a bitter reminder that the market forces that Mr. Lay once worshipped can prove a double-edged sword' (*Economist*, 2001). The anthropomorphized market is not held accountable for producing Enron, but is found responsible for its demise. '[O]ne lesson also seems to be that the market does sort out winners from losers. Eventually, in its own fashion, the system works' (Cassel, 2001: C01). If we think that more than 40,000 people out of work in a week, the loss of more than $2 billion in pension funds, the loss of $30 billion by investors, and the huge personal gain of executives such as Lu Pai who were smart enough to take their millions and run before the house of cards came down is 'the system working,' then we may want to examine the standards by which we measure the system. That argument insulates the market, here figured as a personification of corporate capitalism, from critique. The events that could presumably ground such a critique – Enron's fraud on investors, its employees, and the public – instead are used to affirm, legitimate, and, without a wisp of irony, to redeem. The corporation as moral agent is rendered moot, because the real moral person is the market.

Thus, both popular inquiries into the possibilities of the corporate person as a responsible agent fail. *The Corporation* is ultimately seeking a retributive form of justice that must be enacted upon the body of an offender. Fines and boycotts will never balance the moral scales for the scope of hardship and suffering that corporate capitalism has caused, in the eyes of the filmmakers. We are overwhelmed by the size of the problem, left with a feeling of futility: the corporate person is unassailable, although morally culpable. The film abstracts the corporate person, leaving us with no strategies to address the particular corporate persons with which we might deal. It affirms the untenability of the corporation as moral person, while ostensibly seeking its recognition. *Enron: The Smartest Guys in the Room*, by ignoring the corporation and seeking retribution on the minds and bodies of the greedy men at the top, offers a seemingly more satisfying outcome. Somebody got what they deserved; some body paid. However, at the same time, this denies the widespread nature of corporate misdeeds, ignores the specific agency of the corporation, and reproduces a model that only persons can be morally responsible social actors. It does little to ensure the next corporate person will not do the same thing. Finally, it obscures the existence of the corporate person, diverting our attention. Both films ultimately deny the potential to rethink corporate responsibility or accountability outside of a model of retribution and corporeal punishment. Both deny, in different ways, that the corporation is, can be, or should be a moral person.

Conclusion: Responsible Persons

The diverse domains of corporate law, the boardroom, and popular culture all operate as sites for the production and negotiation of practices of responsibility. This is because, as Davies and Naffine correctly suggest, '[c]losely allied with the legal concept of the person is the moral concept of the person. For, to be a legal person is also to have moral standing' (2001: 51). In the documentaries' search for retribution, in the CSR codes and discourse of community implication, and in the doctrines of separate identity and identification, practices of veil-piercing, and new criminal legislation, we see the attempts to recognize this doubled articulation, to write or rewrite the moral status of the corporation. In these processes, the norms by which we understand corporations become visible. Naffine suggests,

> [i]n the corporation ... we have a legal creation which is called a person, but which appears to lack any obvious moral status, precisely because it is a legal abstraction and not a flesh-and-blood human being. At first blush, the personification of the corporation might seem to lend weight to the proposition that legal personality can be divorced from moral personality. (2003: 348)

And it would seem that the corporation is notoriously difficult to figure in moral terms. The corporate person does not wear the mantle of the responsible subject easily. If we read each of these three cultural locations as organized sites for practices of responsibility as Lacey exhorts us (2001b: 253), and as I suggested in the introduction to this chapter, then we can see that they construct our practices and interpretation of the world in normative terms in a number of different ways. In addition to the specific problems of responsibilizing the corporate person, of trying to suture its moral and metaphysical personhood together, I suggest there are two other effects of these techniques of personification that here also operate as practices of responsibility.

What the varied attempts to responsibilize the corporation discussed in this chapter have demonstrated most effectively is, I suggest, not whether the corporation should be conceived as a person or not, but rather what else is at stake in our struggle to reunite legal and moral personality. We have never been completely comfortable with their separation; the corporation has always been a problematic person. Problematic because it does not have a body; problematic because it has no conscience, feels no remorse; problematic because it puts its own (self) interest before that of the community; in fact, it exists to do, and is exalted for doing, that very thing. The failed responsibilization of the corporation can be understood, therefore, as an attempt to rewrite the corporate person from the personality type of P1, the empty vessel, to P3, the responsible subject. We see that this project is neither simple nor seamless. The difficulty we encounter may suggest that the P1 person is fundamentally amoral; it may suggest that the P3 person is necessarily an embodied human being. However, even for P3, rational action is apparently not enough to ground the requirement for moral response.

A normative ideal of the responsible subject emerges from these stories of corporate (ir)responsibility – a subject who is individuated, a subject who has rights, a subject who can act, a subject who can assess self-interest, but also a subject who is always already implicated as a member of a broader community, a subject who has responsibilities, a subject who is implicated in the social first through its embodiment, a subject who does not always act in its own self-interest. We have assumed, I suggest, that these attributes flow from personality at law, that they can be both achieved and recognized through legal personhood. Ninian Smart (1972) has suggested that the idea of the person, as a universal and cosmopolitan notion, has always brought with it the implication of a moral stance (26). But the corporation forces us to regard that stance as complacent. We see that responsibility, or moral subjectivity, does not necessarily flow from personification, and this troubles us. So many of our political struggles are organized through the lens of the quest for personhood – as we shall see, in particular, in the next chapter – and yet, this quest carries no necessarily moral outcome. We are forced to ask, if the corporation as legal subject is not necessarily a moral subject, are we?

In addition to requiring an examination of our unquestioned assumption that personhood is a necessarily moral endeavour, the corporate person also reveals the ways in which real entities leak out of our personal categories. The corporate person is an attempt to individuate out of collectivity, yet we see in the piercing of the corporate veil, in both jurisprudence and legislation, how fragile that effort can be. The corporate person is an attempt to separate embodiment, material existence, from rational action and social embeddedness. We see in the popular culture struggles with the criminal effects of corporate action and in the inherent paradox that is the 'good corporate citizen' that this, too, is a conflicted venture. We see in law, popular culture, and business that the person as a notion is intimately tied to the formation of the social contract, and yet the corporation appears to stand outside of this bargain. The corporate person does not trade away anything of value. The corporate person really is therefore *persona ficta*, not because it is imaginary, but because it is not a person at all. I suggest that the corporation is best understood as persona.

The persona looks both like and unlike other persons. Law is invested in the likeness of the corporation to the responsible human subject; metaphysics recognizes that the corporation is very unlike that P3 entity. Personae are often produced in the quest for legal personhood, particularly in the struggle to shift from either the categories of P1 or P2 into the exalted heights of P3. Yet that quest is always only partially achieved and leads us to question the value of P3. Personae are, however, both produced in, and as easily recognizable in, other cultural locations outside of law. It is in the non-legal struggles around personhood that we can recognize the broader social implications of personification as an organized set of social practices. It becomes evident that the reason why the controversies around corporate responsibility are occurring is because the entity that I am calling the persona does not fit easily within, and certainly cannot be contained by, the boundaries of the person. Those boundaries, despite law's best efforts, are leaky. Thus personae offer valuable critical insights into the limits of, and our anxieties around, personhood. However, personae also demand that we take account of them. We are not yet through with *persona ficta*. He/she/it is a powerful entity, all the more powerful because, in some lights, it looks like a person. But ultimately even more because our techniques of personification do not, and cannot, render it a necessarily moral agent.

3 'Not a Sex Victory':
Gendering the Person

In the legal world, we are obliged to assume different *personae*. To have a presence in this world at all as legal beings, we must qualify as legal persons: that is persons as law defines them. If one is a live-born human being, one is automatically a person, but then one is further required to be a person of a certain sex, a man *or* a woman, one kind of person, not both or neither.

(Naffine, 2004: 621)

It should be made clear that we and the women of Canada whom we have the high honour to represent are not considering the pronounce-ment of the Privy Council as standing for a sex victory, but rather as one which will permit us to say 'we' instead of 'you' in affairs of state.

(Murphy in Cormack, 1969: 116)

The 'very antithesis of the short-haired woman reformer,' Cairine Reay Wilson, was appointed Canada's first woman senator in 1930.[1] Upon taking up her history-making seat, she stated, 'I owe my appointment to the bravery of the five pioneer women from the Province of Alberta who took the plea for the admission of women to the Senate to the highest court, His Majesty's Privy Council: they are, Judge Emily F. Murphy, Mesdames Nellie F. McClung, Louise C. McKinney, Henrietta Muir Edwards and Irene Parlby' (*Canadian Annual Review*, 1928–9: 66). These five women are collectively known as the 'Famous Five' and the 'plea for the admission of women to the Senate' is more frequently referred to as the 'Persons Case.' Led by Murphy, this high-profile group of suffragists and social activists –

indeed the very epitome of short-haired women reformers – brought a reference to the Supreme Court of Canada in 1928 requesting an interpretation of the provision of the *British North America Act, 1867* (*BNA Act*) which empowered the prime minister to appoint 'qualified persons' to the Senate. In particular, Murphy and her colleagues wanted to know if a female could be appointed to the Senate of Canada, if a female qualified as a person.

As one commentator wryly notes, the Supreme Court 'did not distinguish itself on this occasion' in holding, unanimously, that women were not 'qualified persons' eligible for appointment to the Senate (Normey, 1993: 12). Undaunted, and with some support from the Government of Canada, the Famous Five appealed to what was then the final court of appeal for Canada, the Judicial Committee of the Privy Council in London. The British Lords took a more expansive view of their task of constitutional interpretation, noting that '[t]he exclusion of women from all public offices is a relic of days more barbarous than ours' (*Edwards*, 1929: para. 10). They ultimately held that 'the word "persons" in sec. 24 includes members both of the male and female sex and that, therefore, the question propounded by the Governor-General must be answered in the affirmative and that women are eligible to be summoned to and become members of the Senate of Canada' (*Edwards*, 1929: para. 98).

Legally, the case enabled the subsequent appointment of Wilson and other women to sit in the Red Chamber and offered up the 'living tree' metaphor of constitutional interpretation, namely that a constitution is intended to grow and develop with the times and circumstances of a nation. At the same time, as Supreme Court Justice Claire l'Heureux-Dubé noted in an address in 2000, 'I think it is safe to say that while this case had a positive impact on the lives of a relatively select group of women, it did not take us very far along the road to equality' (l'Heureux-Dubé, 2000: 389). Even contemporary participants wondered about the significance of the case: '[n]ow that we are persons, I wonder if we will notice any difference' (McClung in McCallum and McLellan, 1980: 77). Most current commentators agree, noting that while women's eligibility for Senate appointment and their legal personhood status was decided in 1929, we still have some distance to go to achieve gender equality in public life (e.g., *Maclean's*, 1999: 29; Alberta Women's Secretariat, 1991). And yet, while the Persons Case may be of limited legal significance, I suggest that it has been, and remains, of significant symbolic importance to Canadian history and identity, and most importantly for my purposes, to the gendering of the person. This is because the intertwined myths of the Persons Case and the Famous Five work to suture three tensions in the Canadian public imaginary, namely prudence to politics, historical specificity to abstract cultural values, and sex to personality.

In many ways, dominant Canadian narratives frame the Persons Case, *qua* myth of origin, as a site which makes visible, on a national scale, the performance of women's equality, where Canadian women 'come of age' as political subjects. Yet, like all origin myths, it depends on a 'myth of original unity, fullness, bliss and terror' (Haraway, 1991: 151). Ultimately the case, itself, does not bear the weight of an origin story, and instead demonstrates the limited political value of both the law in general, and the claim to personhood in particular. I draw upon the work of Michael Dorland and Maurice Charland (2002) in exploring prudence in relation to Canadian women's suffrage, to suggest that the Persons Case is a prudential tactic which, by its very nature, deradicalizes political possibilities. As a result, it makes for a somewhat lacklustre myth of origin, remaining strictly within the legal system and the traditional configuration of state authority.

Second, at the heart of any mythic narrative is the heroic figure overcoming hardship and triumphing in glory. While a number of historians and analysts suggest, unproblematically, that the Famous Five are heroes (e.g., Famous Five Foundation; Wright, 2004a, 2004b; L'Heureux-Dubé, 2000; Normey, 1993),[2] I would suggest it is not quite that easy. Heroine is a contested status. What we have witnessed is a sustained effort to produce the Famous Five as heroic, and it is in these various public culture efforts that the tensions of history, memory, and national identity emerge and are played out. Inextricably mired in their historical specificity, the Famous Five, as women, resist abstraction and thus fail as national heroes, which by definition must embody values which are timeless, universal, and non-gendered.

Third and finally, my goal in re-examining the stories we tell of the Persons Case and the Famous Five is not to debunk them, or to offer a more accurate telling, but rather to refocus our scrutiny on the fundamental question that grounded the whole affair in the first place: the person. Too often analysts have overlooked the significance of the fact that this tale of conflict – between the Prairies and Central Canada, between women and men, between militant social reformers and a comfortable political elite, between Conservatives and Liberals, between rural and urban politics – is also a story of personhood. As such, when we examine the Persons Case as an issue of personality, we see the fundamental tension between sexed identity and personhood. We see the impossibility of the feminine person when it collides with the seemingly gender-neutral, but in actuality masculine, person. The challenge by the Famous Five results, not in a rethinking of liberal, individual personhood, but rather in the insistence upon gender-neutrality. Indeed, as Murphy claimed at the time, it was not a 'sex victory.' The technologies of personification, thus, operate to erase the sex difference of subjects. The Persons Case, I will suggest in this chapter, performs a prudent feminist politics, reaffirms the national hero as an abstracted rather than historically located figure, and most significantly, reasserts the universality of the person – all fundamentally unstable, gendered, and gendering projects.

Reform, Women's Suffrage, and Prudential Politics

The early 1900s was a heady time for radical politics in Canada, particularly in the newly minted Western provinces. From 1900 to the 1930s (and beyond) there was an explosion of political parties organized around labour, progressivism, socialism, social democracy, and farm issues.[3] Women were active participants in this public reshaping through various movements, including social reform, farmers' unions, temperance, and suffrage. This gendered combination of simultaneously politically radical and socially conservative politics (often referred to as 'maternal feminism') served as the complicated ground upon which Canadian first wave feminism played out.[4] Yet it was during this period, between the years of the late 1800s and 1920s, that Canadian women emerged as political subjects, largely due to the efforts of rural and prairie women.

Women's formal political subjectivity became a national issue as early as 1885 when Prime Minister Sir John A. Macdonald proposed legislation in the House of Commons to extend the federal franchise to unmarried and widowed women who otherwise met the necessary property qualifications. While Macdonald's Conservative party held a strong majority of seats, he permitted a free vote and the motion was soundly defeated, as he had predicted it would be.[5] Interestingly, however, this relatively early masculine gesture towards women's enfranchisement was not framed as a necessary step to right a wrong committed against women; it was not figured in a language of rights.

Rather, it was understood as a necessary step on a telos of progressive national development. That same telos confirmed women's political enfranchisement as an eventual inevitability, perhaps contributing to the subsequent civility of the debate in Canada.

The framing of the female franchise in a language of progressive politics and national identity was in part produced by, and contributed to, the coupling of that issue with a broader Progressive movement in the Western provinces. Not surprisingly, it was Saskatchewan, Manitoba, and Alberta that first granted women the franchise in 1916. British Columbia and Ontario followed suit in 1917. At the federal level, Prime Minister Sir Robert Borden, in support of his policy on conscription, changed the voting laws in 1917 for the duration of the war, granting the right to vote to anyone who had served in the armed forces, including women, and then to the adult wives, sisters, mothers, and daughters of those who had served in the Great War. Having taken this step, at the end of the war in 1918, the government extended the federal franchise to all women meeting the necessary provincial criteria. Nova Scotia granted the franchise to women in 1918, New Brunswick in 1919, and Prince Edward Island in 1922. Quebec, on the other hand, held out until 1940![6] The right to hold public office was granted federally in 1919 and Agnes MacPhail was the first woman elected to the House of Commons in 1921. She was the only female federal parliamentarian until 1935 when Martha Black of the Yukon Territories was elected.[7]

The battle for enfranchisement in Canada is generally understood by historians as less militant than its counterparts in Britain and the United States (Dorland and Charland 2002; Bacchi, 1983; Cleverdon, 1974). Whereas those nations' suffrage movements were marked by a politics of unrest and demonstration, Canada's involved civil public intellectualism, mock parliaments, legal challenges, and considerable support from key male political actors. Dorland and Charland suggest that '[s]uffrage advanced and a new woman subject was constituted through a rhetoric that mobilized elite complicity, an ethos of moral obligation, and a conception of Canada as an ethical project, dedicated to progress' (2002: 196). Borrowing from Eugene Garver (1987), they go on to argue that Canadian women were participating in a national tradition of prudential politics:

> ... prudential politics are rhetorical, structured by contingency, and they subordinate purity of principle to practical possibility. In contrast, ideo-

logical politics, including 'rights talk,' are driven by principle and not directed toward the contingent good. They are categorical. They are, as such, anti-rhetorical (in the persuasive sense) because they are unwilling to proceed from their opponents' premises ... (197)

Women's suffrage, as a quintessentially prudential politics, succeeded for three central reasons, the authors suggest. First, the exclusion of women was more rhetorical than structural, namely that the legitimacy of the state did not turn on the exclusion of women. Second, women's political subjectivity could be figured coterminously with broader Canadian constitutional objectives and rhetoric, as part of the 'narrative of progress,' and finally, suffrage was ultimately a reform movement, not a form of identity politics (ibid.). While Dorland and Charland do address the Persons Case, their project focuses on its treatment of the place of Canada in British common law.[8] While it is certainly true that significant aspects of Canada's constitutional identity play out within this case, at the same time, it is, I suggest, likely the most compelling instance of the tensions within feminist prudential politics in Canada, a feminist politics without a gendered subject, and it is in this sense that I first revisit the case.

The Persons Case

Emily Murphy was fond of saying of the Persons Case that it was 'a woman's fight started by a man' (in Sanders, 1945: 214). It was also a battle that both ended and began in a courtroom. On 1 January 1916, Emily Murphy was appointed the first female judge in the British Commonwealth. She sat as magistrate in the newly created 'Woman's Court' in Edmonton, Alberta.[9] On her very first day in court, while hearing the case of a bootlegger, enterprising defence counsel Eardley Jackson suggested to Murphy that any decision she rendered would be void because, as a woman, she was not fit to hear the case. Women were not, he alleged, persons as defined in the constitution. Murphy mused in one instalment of a 1919 series in *Maclean's* magazine outlining her experience as magistrate, '[n]ow I had always known I was not *persona grata* but I had an idea that I was still a person, in spite of the ancient disabilities of the statute books' (Murphy, 1919: 35).

Persona non grata

While Murphy continued, undaunted, to hear cases, the issue of the fitness of female persons to sit as provincial magistrates did not go away. It was resolved, in Alberta, in the appeal of the case of Lizzie Cyr, a woman accused of prostitution. The case was decided by Murphy's colleague Alice Jamieson, appointed to the bench shortly after Murphy in 1916.[10] In 1917, Lizzie Cyr was convicted by Magistrate Jamieson and, on appeal, one of the grounds offered was the legitimacy of Jamieson's presence, as a woman, in the post of judge. On the second appeal, the Supreme Court of Alberta, Appellate Division, ultimately upheld the conviction of Ms Cyr, confirming that women were persons for the purpose of holding public office in Alberta. Mr Justice Stuart, for the court, held that:

> I therefore think that applying the general principle upon which the common law rests, namely that of reason and good sense as applied to the new conditions [in Western Canada], this court ought to declare that in this province and at this time in our presently existing conditions there is at common law no legal disqualificiation for holding public office in the government of the country arising from any distinction of sex. And in doing this I am strongly of the opinion that we are returning to the more liberal and enlightened view of the middle ages of England and passing over the narrower and more hardened view, which possibly by the middle of the nineteenth century, had gained ascendancy in England. (*Cyr*, 1917: 850)

Significantly, the court here rejects a long line of British cases denying political personhood to women, instead preferring the American precedent of *Missouri* v. *Hostetter* (1898).[11] So, by 1921, at least in Alberta, Alice Jamieson and Emily Murphy were persons at law. This in no way resolved the issue at the federal level, however, and the issue of her personhood was to continue to haunt Murphy.

Emily Murphy was born in Cookstown, Ontario on 14 March 1868. She married the Reverend Arthur Murphy in 1887 and had two daughters, in addition to two other children who died at birth. In 1889, the family moved to England, where Murphy began her writing career as Janey Canuck.[12] In 1901, however, the Murphys returned to Canada, first to Swan River, Manitoba, and then to Edmonton, in 1907. Concerned with the conditions of women and children, in 1910, Murphy was the first woman appointed to the Edmonton Hospital Board. A prolific writer, she served as the national president of the Canadian Women's Press Club from 1913 to 1920, as vice-president of the National Council of Women and the first president of the Federated Women's Institutes of Canada. She was the first female magistrate in the Empire, and honing her legal skills and her experiences in the Woman's Court led her to write two prominent books, *The Black Candle* (1922) concerning the drug trade in Canada and *Pruning the Family Tree* (n/d) on birth control.[13] She also worked for the establishment of public playgrounds and the election of women as school trustees. An ardent supporter of women's role in the public sphere, she was known across the country, more generally as an author, and in the more specific emerging network of formalized women's groups linking the nation, as an activist.

With these credentials and with women having had the vote for more than a decade, when a seat in the Senate opened up, many felt the appointment should be a woman, and further, thousands of people across the country felt it should be Emily Murphy. Members of the Federated Women's Institutes, the National Council of Women, and the Montreal Women's club were among the more than 10,000 citizens who signed petitions and wrote letters in her support. In 1921, the National Council of Women, representing 450,000 women, unanimously supported a resolution at their annual meeting that Emily Murphy be immediately appointed to the Senate (Price, 1921). In 1922, when a senator from Alberta died, the calls for Murphy gained renewed vigour. Editorials in newspapers across the country got behind the cause.[14] Murphy herself, originally surprised at the suggestion that she serve as a senator, soon set her sights on that goal.[15]

The *BNA Act* governed appointments to the Senate. To be eligible, the candidate had to be at least thirty years old, be a natural or naturalized citizen of the Commonwealth or Canada, hold real property of a value of at least $4,000, and reside in the province for which they were appointed. Murphy met those criteria, but no appointment was forthcoming. In response to the demand for a woman senator, the Liberal government of the day responded, '[t]he gentlemen would like nothing better than to have women in the Senate but the *British North America Act* made no provision for women and the members feared that women could not be appointed to the Senate until this great foundation of our liberties was amended and that would take time and careful thought' (McClung, 1945: 186). The government was clinging to Section 24 of the *BNA Act*, which provided: '[t]he Governor General shall from time to time, in the Queen's name, by instrument under the Great Seal of Canada, summon qualified persons to the Senate; and subject to the provisions of this Act, every person so summoned shall become and be a Member of the Senate and a Senator.' Based on the advice of its lawyers, the government's view was that women were not 'qualified persons' within the meaning of Section 24, and, as a result, its hands were tied. Mackenzie King's government took the further position that an amendment to the *BNA Act* would be required to appoint a woman to the Senate and that this would be no small thing. An amendment to the *BNA Act* required, not only the agreement of all the provinces (with Quebec vociferously opposed to women's suffrage and Ontario very reluctant to 'tinker' with the *Act*), but also the concordance of the sitting Senate, which did not relish the prospect of women members in its midst, and the approval of the Dominion Government, which had recently denied the right of a woman to sit in the House of Lords.[16] Mackenzie King did go so far as to ask Senator McCoig from Chatham to propose an amendment to the *BNA Act* in 1923. The motion was recorded on the agenda of 25 June 1923, but was neither proposed that day nor revisited at a later point. It became apparent to Emily Murphy and various advocates of a woman senator that the *BNA Act* was being used as a 'convenient screen behind which the senators and the federal government could hide their refusal to take action' (Benoit, n/d: 5).

Between 1917 and 1927, five consecutive governments indicated that they wanted to appoint a woman to the Senate, but could not do so because of Section 24.[17] After years of being frustrated by the government's lack of commitment, Murphy's brother William Nassau Ferguson, himself a judge, brought to her attention a little-known, and even lesser-used, section of the *Supreme Court Act*. Section 60 permitted any five concerned citizens acting together to bring forward a reference, through the Cabinet, to request a clarification from the Supreme Court of Canada of any section of the *BNA Act*. It further held that the costs of such an undertaking could be borne by the government.[18] Having found civil persuasion to be ineffective, as it enabled seemingly perpetual stonewalling by the government, Murphy decided to pursue her action through the legal system. She could force an answer to the question of whether or not women were prohibited from Senate appointment by the requirement in Section 24 that they be 'qualified persons.' Thus this newfound awareness of an obscure section of the *Supreme Court Act* precipitated what is likely Canada's most famous 'tea party.'[19]

Always politically savvy, Murphy wanted the petition to be signed by five prominent women who would bring credibility to it. She first contacted her good friend Nellie McClung. McClung was a novelist, reformer, teacher, journalist, and suffragist. Born in Chatworth, Ontario on 20 October 1873, she had moved to Manitoba in 1880. In 1896, she married Wes McClung, with whom she had five children. In 1908, she wrote *Sowing Seeds in Danny*, her first and most popular novel, going on to write fourteen other books. In 1911, she began to champion the rights of women to vote and run for office, becoming an avid supporter of the Women's Christian Temperance Union (WCTU). In 1914, she wrote and starred in a mock Parliament which asked, 'Why Should Men Have the Vote,' which has been celebrated in a *Heritage Minute* (Historica Foundation, 1990). During the First World War, she was the only woman to serve on the Dominion War Council. As the MLA for Edmonton (1921–6), she actively campaigned for mothers' allowances, birth control, free medical and dental treatment for school children, public health regulations, temperance, and the rights of women. She subsequently served as the first woman appointed to the Board of Governors of the CBC and, in 1939, represented Canada at the League of Nations in Geneva (the only woman in the delegation).[20] McClung responded enthusiastically to Murphy's request and consulted with her on the selection of the other three petitioners.

After McClung, Murphy contacted Louise McKinney, Henrietta Muir Edwards, and Irene Parlby. McKinney was the first woman elected to serve as member of any legislative assembly in the Commonwealth in the first election where women could vote or run for office in 1917.[21] She was born in 1868 in Frankville, Ontario to a farming family. In her early career, she taught school and in 1893 moved to North Dakota and began organizing for the WCTU, a cause that was to dominate the rest of her life. In 1896, she married James McKinney and they had one child. She applied her American-gained organizational skills when she moved to Claresholme, Alberta in 1903, travelling for the next few years throughout Western Canada organizing twenty WCTU chapters. After serving in the legislature for four years, during which time she was central in having the *Dower Act* passed, she was defeated in the 1921 election because of her staunch opposition to drinking and smoking.[22] During her time in office and afterwards, she helped introduce laws for immigrants and more effective liquor laws, as well as raising public opinion regarding the unjust status of widows and separated wives.[23]

Henrietta Muir Edwards was the eldest of the women Murphy approached – eighty years old at the time the reference was launched. She, too, had a very distinguished career as an advocate for women's rights and a social reformer. Born into a privileged family in Montreal on 18 December 1849, she published Canada's first women's magazine in 1875, entitled *Women's Work in Canada*. While still in Montreal, she helped to establish the Working Girls' Assocation in Montreal, which became the prototype for the Canadian YWCA. In 1876, she married Dr Oliver Cromwell Edwards, with whom she had three children, and in 1883, the family moved to Fort Qu'Appelle, Saskatchewan. With Lady Aberdeen, in 1893 and 1897, she established the National Council of Women and founded the Victorian Order of Nurses, respectively. In 1903, the family resettled to Fort McLeod, Alberta and with her colleagues McClung and McKinney, she lobbied for Alberta's *Dower Act*. A member of the Alberta Government Advisory Committee on Health, she was concerned with issues such as prison reform, helped organize public libraries, urged the establishment of mothers' allowances and equal parental rights, and pressed for divorce to be granted on equal grounds. Valued by Murphy and her colleagues for her legal knowledge, she was well known for two law handbooks entitled *Legal Status of Women in Canada* (1917) and *Legal Status of Women in Alberta* (1921).[24]

Irene Parlby rounded out the 'Famous Five.' An advocate for rural farm women in Alberta, she was appointed the first female cabinet minister in 1921 (the second in the British Commonwealth). Born in 1868 to an aristocratic family in England, she travelled to Lacombe, Alberta to visit friends in 1897, and never left. In 1898 she married Walter Parlby and had one son. In 1916, she organized, and became the first president of, the United Farm Women's Association of Alberta. In 1920, she was appointed to the University of Alberta's Board of Governors and, in 1921, was first elected to the Alberta legislature as a United Farmers of Alberta candidate from Lacombe. That same year, she was appointed a cabinet minister without portfolio, a position which she held until her retirement in 1935. In that position, she successfully sponsored the *Minimum Wage Act for Women* and seventeen other laws affecting the lives of women and children, including bills to improve the quality of rural education, to provide municipal hospitals and public health nurses to rural districts, as well as to establish child welfare clinics, and to place obstetrical nurses in outlying districts of the province without doctors. After the reference, she went on to represent Canada at the League of Nations in 1930, and has the distinction of being the first woman to receive an Honorary Doctorate of Laws from the University of Alberta.[25]

These five eminent public figures in national and prairie politics met on Murphy's porch on a sunny afternoon in August 1927 to discuss her proposal. There, during what was reputedly many pots of tea and slices of date and nut loaf, they traded stories of the challenges they had encountered in their various travels, and strategized how best to bring the case forward. All agreed to sign the petition, which they ultimately did. All the women were careful to note that despite the presence of their names in alphabetical order on the petition (at Murphy's insistence), it was Murphy who was the driving force behind the petition, and the one who did all the research, letter writing, and so on, necessary for its ultimate success.

Murphy wrote to the Ministry of Justice in order to secure the agreement of the government, both to posing the reference and to defraying the petitioners' legal costs. On 27 August 1927, Emily Murphy and her four companions petitioned the Canadian government to ask the Supreme Court of Canada to answer two questions:

1 Is power vested in the Governor General in Council of Canada, or the Parliament of Canada, or either of them, to appoint a female to the Senate of Canada?
2 Is it constitutionally possible for the Parliament of Canada under the provisions of the *British North America Act*, or otherwise, to make provision for the appointment of a female to the Senate of Canada?

Prime Minister Mackenzie King sent the petition to his minister of justice, Ernest Lapointe, who recommended to the government that the petition be accepted. The Privy Council memorandum stated that:

[i]n the opinion of the Minister the question whether the word 'Persons' in said section 24 includes female persons is one of great public importance. The Minister states that the law officers of the Crown who have

considered this question on more than one occasion have expressed the view that male persons only may be summoned to the Senate under the provisions of the British North America Act in that behalf. The Minister, however, while not disposed to question that view, considers that it would be an act of justice to the women of Canada to obtain the opinion of the Supreme Court of Canada upon the point. (Privy Council, 19 October 1927, IH/5, P.C. 2034)

However, rather than the two questions of the petition, the government referred the following question to the Supreme Court: 'Does the word "Person" in section 24 of the *British North America Act, 1867* include female persons?'

When Murphy learned the wording of the question submitted to the Court, she wrote on 9 November 1927 to the deputy minister of justice, W. Stuart Edwards, stating that the question was not that of the petitioners 'either in word or meaning' and that it was 'in consequence, a matter of amazement and perturbation' to the five petitioners (in Benoit, n/d: 7). The petitioners had deliberately avoided using the word 'persons,' as that had been the basis upon which the Crown had repeatedly declared publicly that women were not eligible for appointment. She emphasized the omission of the second question, which provided constitutional guidance should the petition fail, and finally, to clarify the situation further and avoid potential delays, she asked a third question: '[i]f any statute be necessary to qualify a female to sit in the Senate of Canada, must this statute be enacted by the Imperial Parliament, or does power lie within the Parliament of Canada, or the Senate of Canada?' (Benoit, n/d: 7).[26] Edwards declined to alter the wording of the question posed to the Supreme Court and so the reference proceeded on the government's terms.

The reference itself is an interesting technique of prudential politics, infrequently but significantly employed by the Government of Canada, in order to diffuse politically volatile conflicts. These have included a number of early disputes between the provinces and the federal government as to their respective areas of legislative authority, the Quebec secession issue, and most recently, the same-sex marriage debate. Unlike other legal actions, it does not require a specific conflict between litigants; thus the problem is simultaneously intellectualized, distanced, and potentially depoliticized. The government shifts public scrutiny from itself to the courts, thereby attempting to separate law and politics.[27] Indeed, the archival records show the complexity of this issue for the government as officials within the Department of Justice debated the merits of putting forward the question on behalf of the women, paying their legal expenses, and whether or not to formally oppose the position of the petitioners at the Supreme Court of Canada hearing. The government did not want to appear hostile to women's political participation, but at the same time were clearly not prepared to make such a change without a push.

No Vast or Dangerous Changes: The Supreme Court of Canada

In order to instigate that push, the petitioners hired well-known Toronto lawyer Newton Wesley Rowell, recognized as sympathetic to women's suffrage. The Supreme Court heard the petition on 14 March 1928. Rowell argued that 'the word [person] in its natural meaning is equally applicable to female persons' and that if Section 24 of the *BNA Act* was read in conjunction with the other provisions in that legislation, then it was clear that 'persons' could not refer only to male persons.[28] On the other side, Lucien Cannon, solicitor-general for Canada, suggested it was a question only of law and legal interpretation and that if women were to be included in the Senate, then the *BNA Act* had to be amended. 'Under the present act no "legal mind" could construe the word "person" as including women' ('Five Judges,' 1928: 2). Quebec was the only province that exercised its right to be represented at the reference, opposing the petition. Lucien Lafleur, Quebec's lawyer, suggested that including women in the Senate would be 'revolutionary' (ibid.).

The Supreme Court rendered its decision six weeks later on 24 April 1928, holding that '[t]he question being understood to be "Are women eligible for appointment to the Senate of Canada" the question is answered in the negative' (*Edwards*, 1928: para. 76). The court separated law and politics, carefully defining its mandate in an unambitious manner:

> [i]n considering this matter we are, of course, in no wise concerned with the desirability or the undesirability of the presence of women in the Senate, nor with any political aspect of the question submitted. Our whole duty is to construe, to the best of our ability, the relevant provisions of the B.N.A. Act, 1867, and upon that construction to base our answer. (Ibid.: para. 8)

Chief Justice Anglin's judgment relied upon the long history of women's disenfranchisement in British common law.[29] He took the perspective that legislation must be interpreted in accordance with the intention of the legislature at the time of its drafting, and that in 1867, women were under a 'legal incapacity to hold public office' (ibid.: para. 13). By implication, women were excluded because in other instances, such as the enfranchisement legislation, they had had to be expressly included. 'Such an extraordinary privilege is not conferred furtively' (ibid.: para. 20).

While the chief justice conceded that '[t]here can be no doubt that the word 'persons' when standing alone *prima facie* includes women ... It connotes human beings – the criminal and the insane equally with the good and the wise citizen, the minor as well as the adult' (ibid.: para. 21), each of the criminal, the lunatic, the imbecile, and the minor were all necessarily excluded from the phrase 'qualified persons.' Women were thus categorized with criminals, lunatics, imbeciles, and children. Further, while the court acknowledged that there had been changes in the status of women in the sixty years since the drafting of the Canadian constitution, 'surely it is a significant fact, that never from 1867 to the present time has any woman ever sat in the Senate of Canada, nor has any suggestion of women's eligibility to that House until quite recently been publicly made' (ibid.: para. 19). Finally, the chief justice claimed it would be 'dangerous' to assume that, through the use of the 'ambiguous' language of person, the Imperial Parliament meant to 'bring about so vast a constitutional change affecting Canadian women' (ibid.: para. 25).

Mr Justice Duff, while concurring with the result proposed by the chief justice, took a different line of reasoning. He suggested that it was inappropriate in the Canadian context to draw upon British authority to determine the issue; he challenged the historical interpretation that presented women as generally ineligible for public office; and he argued that the language of the *Act* did not support a restricted interpretation of 'qualified persons.' Having made the case effectively for the petitioners, he then – in an about-face – held that the Senate was intended to be a chamber modelled on the Legislative Councils of 1791 and 1840 from which women were clearly excluded. Finally, Justice Mignault, also concurring in the result, felt the term 'person' was far too ambiguous to be assessed in the abstract and to be considered apart from the notion of 'qualified.' 'The word "persons" is obviously a word of uncertain import. Sometimes it includes corporations as well as natural persons; sometimes it is restricted to the latter; and sometimes again it comprises merely certain natural persons determined by sex or otherwise' (ibid.: para. 71). Further, the notion of 'person' could not ground 'the grave constitutional change which is involved in the contention submitted on behalf of the petitioners' (ibid.: para. 71).

The telegram from Wesley Rowell to Emily Murphy read, tersely: '[r]egret Supreme Court have answered question submitted to them in the negative' (in Cormack, 1969: 114). The Five were very disappointed, Murphy most of all. She was very careful, however, not to be publicly critical of the Supreme Court justices and indicated her pleasure that the government was restating its intention to act. Headlines around the world pronounced 'Ban on Women,' 'Woman Not a Person,' 'No Women Senators in Canada' (National Archives, RG 13, vol 2525, p. 71, Box Misc.). Women's groups across the country were shocked by the result. The Ontario Liberal Women's Association called the ruling a 'manifest injustice to a large proportion of the electorate' (*Toronto Daily Star*, 1928a: 1). Mrs Mary Ellen Smith, a member of the British Columbia provincial legislature, suggested that women across the country had not been united enough or aggressive enough in their tactics. 'The iron dropped into the souls of women in Canada when we heard that it took a man to decree that his mother was not a person' (*Toronto Daily Star*, 1928b: 8). The *Toronto Daily Star* reported an overheard conversation between two women at the court house. 'A woman may marry a person, may bring a person into the world, care for and educate persons all her life ... and yet she is not a person,' said one woman, to which her colleague replied, 'this opinion is given by persons for persons, evidently, yet a woman may marry a chump, bring a chump into the world, raise and educate chumps but it does not follow that she herself is a chump. The whole thing is ridiculous' (1928c: 1).

On the very day that the Supreme Court of Canada decision came down, Ernest Lapoint, minister of justice, declared in the House of Commons that women did have a legal right to sit in the Senate and that measures would be taken by Mackenzie King's government to amend the *BNA Act*.[30] Murphy was understandably sceptical, not only of the government's commitment to this process, given its past dillydallying, but also of the real possibility of its being able to take place. She formally wrote to the Ministry of Justice requesting that the government appeal the decision to what was then the final court of appeal for Canada, the Judicial Committee of the Privy Council (JCPC). In a highly prudent move, by appealing to the British Privy Council, she wished 'to remove the issue from the political arena and have it addressed from a purely legal aspect' (Murphy in Benoit, n/d: 9). The appeal was filed with the Supreme Court of Canada on 12 October 1928 and on 16 November 1928, Murphy and her co-appellants obtained permission to appeal to the JCPC, complete with a commitment from Prime Minister Borden to finance the process.[31]

'Pleased in Edmonton': The Judicial Committee of the Privy Council

Again with the cooperation of the government and its financial support for the appeal costs, Wesley Rowell journeyed to England to present his case to the Law Lords at 1 Downing Street. The arguments were largely the same; however, significantly, Quebec was not represented. Murphy was very gratified when Premier Taschereau agreed not to oppose the appeal. Alberta expressly endorsed the appeal, sending their attorney general, the Hon. H.F. Lymburn, to assist Rowell with the case. Murphy initially wanted to go to London to participate in the proceedings, but ultimately decided for strategic reasons not to do so. Suffragist groups in England were very eager to have her speak and to honour her for her work, but she worried that this might politically taint the case she was working so hard to depoliticize.

The hearing took place on 18 July and continued on the 23rd and 25th, with the JCPC reserving its decision for six months, finally releasing it on 18 October 1929. In an unusual break with tradition – testifying to the significance of the case – the fourteen-page judgment was read aloud in full by Lord Sankey to the audience in the court.[32] The British Law Lords unanimously overturned the Supreme Court of Canada decision and held that Canadian women were eligible for appointment to the Senate in a judgment one early commentator described as a 'scholarly and human analysis' (Sanders, 1945: 244).

Lord Sankey reviewed the word 'person' in relation to the British legal incapacity to hold public office, as well as in the context of the development of public roles for women in Canada. He recognized that in instances where women had been excluded from public office and from voting, such limitations had been made expressly. Acknowledging that the word 'person' is 'ambiguous and in its original meaning would undoubtedly embrace members of either sex' (*Edwards*, 1929:

para. 44), he suggested that the fact that women have not in practice served in such public offices does not hold much weight as such exclusion was likely customary. 'Customs are apt to develop into traditions which are stronger than law and remain unchallenged long after the reason for them has disappeared. The appeal to history therefore in this particular matter is not conclusive' (ibid.: para. 46). Thus the basis for Chief Justice Anglin's reasons at the Supreme Court of Canada was dismissed.

In interpreting the section on women being summoned to the Privy Council, i.e., Cabinet, Lord Sankey stated that there should be a presumption that persons includes females unless someone could successfully demonstrate the contrary (ibid.: paras. 65–6). The qualification of the word 'persons' by 'qualified,' which troubled the Supreme Court, refers back, the JCPC held, to the qualification of property and citizenship stated expressly within the legislation, nothing more. Within the *BNA Act* there are provisions where males are specifically mentioned and the Court argued that this means that in the absence of such a qualifier, the term 'person' must be given a broad interpretation.

Significantly, Lord Sankey offered a new metaphor for constitutional interpretation, rejecting the Supreme Court's position that one must interpret a constitutional text in relation to the values of the time period of its drafting, and instead suggesting that courts should interpret constitutions as 'living trees' whose tenets must be flexible enough to accommodate shifting societal values. Giving Canada licence to develop its own political culture, 'their Lordships do not think it right to apply rigidly to Canada of to-day the decisions and the reasonings therefore which commended themselves, probably rightly to those who had to apply the law in different circumstances, in different centuries to countries in different stages of development' (ibid.: para. 48). While the *BNA Act* is legislation of the Imperial Parliament, it creates a constitution for a new country. Thus different considerations apply:

> The British North America Act planted in Canada a living tree capable of growth and expansion within its natural limits. ... The object of the Act was to Grant a constitution to Canada ...
>
> Their Lordships do not conceive it to be the duty of this Board – it is certainly not their desire – to cut down the provisions of the Act by a narrow

and technical construction, but rather to give it a large and liberal interpretation so that the Dominion to a great extent, but within certain fixed limits, may be mistress in her own house, as the Provinces to a great extent, but within certain fixed limits, are mistresses in theirs. (Ibid.: paras. 54–5)

The decision speaks powerfully to Canadian sovereignty and the young nation's relationship with Britain. Yet, again, while a watershed case in terms of constitutional interpretation and much welcomed by the Famous Five and their supporters, the decision is ultimately also prudent. Sankey was careful to note that the court is not deciding 'any question as to the rights of women but only a question as to their eligibility for a particular position' (ibid.: para. 59).

This time the national headlines were jubilant. The decision was figured as a victory for Canadian Women (*Toronto Daily Star*, 1929: 1). While officials in Ottawa were not expansive in their response, the Famous Five were happy: Murphy was reported as being 'pleased in Edmonton' (*Globe* 1929: 6). Women's groups across the country were ecstatic. *Le Soleil* suggested, '[d]écision accuellie avec joie partout' (1929: 1). Mrs J.A. Wilson, the president of the National Council of Women, stated, '[s]ince women were enfranchised it has really been an anachronism that they were not allowed to take their position in the Senate, and it was also painful to women to feel that they were not even a "person"' (*Globe*, 1929: 6). Women in Ontario recognized that they owed much to the Prairies, and the other members of the Famous Five were effusive in handing the victory to Murphy. The *Ottawa Evening Citizen* reported that, '[i]n every instance, those interviewed regarded it as a great moral victory, and recognition of the fact that woman suffrage was more and more being recognized as an extension of the principle that women are eligible to occupy seats in the highest governing bodies' (1929: 1).

In retrospect, a number of commentators wondered why the issue had had to come to this (*Toronto Daily Star*, 1929: 1). An eyewitness to the JCPC hearing, Canadian Press journalist Lukin Johnston, wrote a piece that circulated widely. He concluded: '[a]t the end of all these endless speeches, lessons on Canadian history, and questions by five great judges of England, it will be decided, if one may hazard a guess, that women undoubtedly are Persons. Which one may say, without exaggeration, most of us know already!' (in Sanders, 1945: 244). The front page of the *Regina Morning Leader* followed up the title, 'So a Woman's a Person' with:

The average man may not be able to digest mentally the fine points of the law involved in the argument that went on as to whether a woman is a person in relation to the Senate of Canada but it [*sic*] will freely concede that common sense is altogether on the side of the decision of the Privy Council that a women [*sic*] is a person ... The strange thing about it all is that it was necessary for the women of Canada to go to the courts to establish that point. (1929: 1)

Thus, while the victory was recognized as one for women, at the same time it comes as a bit of an anti-climax politically, being framed retrospectively as common-sensical, and not particularly radical.

Ironically, none of the Famous Five was ever appointed to the Senate. As noted previously, Cairine Reay Wilson was the first woman appointed in 1930, 'bilingual, a liberal, and a lady' to quote Mackenzie King. A wealthy woman devoted to good works and the Liberal party, she was a member of a family which was friendly with the prime minister. At a banquet honouring her, one Senate colleague jested, '[w]e of the humble and gentle sex were apprehensive that one of those strong-minded and determined women with a mission in life and a pair of horned rimmed spectacles would be appointed and that if so she would immediately commence to reform a number of matters that we did not wish reformed' (Hill, H.P. MG 27 III, C. 6, vol. 8). In contrast, Wilson's femininity was continually emphasized, with frequent reference to her slim figure and youthful appearance (Benoit, n/d: 11). She was known as the 'Betty Crocker of the Senate' (*Maclean*'s, 1999).

When a Senate vacancy occurred in Edmonton several years after Wilson had been appointed, hopes were high again that Conservative R.B. Bennett would appoint Murphy (who was also Conservative); however, Senator Patrick Burns, a Liberal, was ultimately appointed. The reason was given by the government at the time that it was because a Roman Catholic had to be appointed to that seat.[33] Perhaps the reasons lie elsewhere. One senator from Edmonton remarked a few years after the Persons Case when the question of Murphy's non-appointment was put to him, '[o]h, we never could have had Mrs. Murphy in the Senate. She would have caused too much trouble' (in Sanders, 1945: 259). Emily Murphy died of complications arising from diabetes in 1933.

Thus, we see the limits of prudential politics. In order to bring the constitutional reference, Murphy and her four colleagues were already accepting the legitimacy of the Canadian (and British) states to determine the legal and political status of women. Rather than seeing the law, too, as a fundamentally political institution, the Famous Five accepted the separation of politics and law deployed by the Canadian government, the Supreme Court of Canada, and the JCPC alike. For this reason, their challenge had the effect of legitimating, rather than challenging, Canadian state power. Arguably, the Canadian nation state, rather than women, was the winner of the case. Women having won the right to be appointed to the Senate, the legal decision offered no resources to change the social mores of the day, as we see in the exclusion of the more radical women from official political realms. As one colleague said shortly after Murphy's death, '[d]espite the noble efforts of Janey Canuck – peace to her ashes – politics is still a stag party' (R.M. Harrison in Mander, 1985: 126). The support of the reference and the embrace of its outcome by Mackenzie King's government (and those subsequent) constituted the government as forward-thinking and progressive. The Famous Five, as 'manly,' 'flamboyant' agitators, were more radical than their court challenge had been and, therefore, had to be contained, first within law, the very tool they were wielding, then through political marginalization. Women as political subjects were recognized, provided they did not gender politics. In this way, it was clear to all Canadians that gender, like politics, should be performed prudently.

Persons but Not Heroes:
The Famous Five in Popular Culture

While the Persons Case is an exemplar of prudential politics and its limitations as a politics of gender, it has been understood historically as a significant legal and political landmark that opened the door to women being appointed to the Canadian Senate. In recent years, we have seen the attempt by liberal feminist historians to recover the role of the Famous Five from the obscurity of mainstream Canadian history. However, alongside that more intellectual exercise, we have also seen attempts to remake the Famous Five as national heroes. Primarily mobilized through the work of the Famous Five Foundation, an organization founded in 1996 to raise awareness about the Five as the seventieth anniversary of the case approached, this attempted heroicization also operates within a broader cultural nationalist project of popularizing Canadian history.[34] In recent years we have seen a virtual explosion of popular culture recovering the Persons Case and the Famous Five from historical obscurity.

In addition to plaques of recognition at the entrance to the Senate chamber in the Parliament Buildings and in the Alberta legislature, and urban parks in their names in Edmonton and Calgary, one of the oldest traces of the national commemoration of the Famous Five includes an annual award from the governor general, inaugurated in 1979, on the fiftieth anniversary of the JCPC decision. The awards are presented annually on 18 October, 'Persons Day,' to individuals who have made outstanding contributions to the quality of life for women in Canada. The function is marked by a brunch attended by the award recipients, the governor general, the minister of Canadian heritage or status of women, and various other feminist activists. Like the Persons Case itself, as an act of commemoration and recognition, it is a safe, feminist gesture. As one journalist noted tellingly, regarding the 2006 ceremony, '[t]he event is a *gentle reminder* that the ongoing struggle for women's rights is far from over' (emphasis added, *Chilliwack Progress*, 2006: A12).

More recently, Emily Murphy was featured in a Canadian *Heritage Minute* (now called Historica Minutes) reflecting on the case (Historica Foundation, 1992). The actress playing Murphy is considerably slimmer and more stereotypically attractive than the photographs of Murphy suggest is accurate, and the case is cast in more conflictual terms than those in which it actually transpired, making for better drama. A vignette in the television mini-series *Canada: A People's History* situates the dispute, appropriately, within its rural politics and suffragist context (2001). Necessarily then, the women's individual roles are downplayed. But not so everywhere. Elsewhere the Famous Five are being touted as heroes.

The attempt to heroicize exploded in the late 1990s. The National Library and Archives produced a special exhibit for the seventieth anniversary of the case and maintains a website on the Persons Case, featuring primary materials from the case within a user-friendly narrative. The site notes: '[w]hile commemorating this major step in women's entrance into political life in Canada, this exhibition is aimed at promoting awareness of those five famous Alberta women and highlighting their role in the admission of women to the Senate' (National Library and Archives, www.lac-bac.gc.ca/index.html). On 18 October 1996, the Famous Five Foundation was founded with Frances Wright as its president. The mandate of the Foundation is to 'honour the Famous 5 and other Canadian women, commemorate the "Persons Case 1929," and inspire, recognize and celebrate their achievement' (Famous Five Foundation). It takes as its founding assumption that the Famous Five are national heroes. As Wright stated at the time: 'it is now time for these heroes to be known and appreciated by Canadians and others because their work affects us today and tomorrow' (in Bright, 1998: 100).

In anticipation of the seventieth anniversary of the case in 1999, the Foundation lobbied heavily for a number of initiatives designed to cement the Famous Five as nation-building heroes. These included duplicate monuments at Olympic Plaza in Calgary and on Parliament Hill, featuring a larger-than-life Famous Five receiving the news of the JCPC victory.[35] The Famous Five appeared on the millennium series of Canadian postage stamps promoting 'nation builders,' and were featured, with Quebec human rights advocate Thérèse Casgrain, on the fifty-dollar bill in 2004.[36] It is interesting that in each of these highly symbolic, national sites, the attempt to render the Famous Five as national heroes drew a very strong counter-discourse and their heroicization ultimately foundered on the complexities of history, sovereignty, memory, and gender.

A hero 'transcend[s] ordinary human qualities embodying the divine, the ideal, the quest, the courageous, the virtuous, the superior,' suggest Susan Drucker and Robert Cathcart (1997: 1). However, scholars of contemporary heroes note that in our postmodern, heterogeneous, reflexive, and somewhat cynical era, the hero is increasingly denigrated (see discussion in Drucker and Cathcart, 1997: 4–5). Lance Strate (1997), for example, suggests that mass media trivialize heroes and that as a result, they are no longer known for any intrinsic qualities. A number of scholars are essentially arguing that mass-mediated celebrity has replaced the hero, and that our cultural environment is, as a result, filled with pseudo-heroes.

This scholarship rightly troubles the constitution of current heroes in the media age as problematic and explores the important relationship between celebrity and heroes. At the same time, however, the national hero is arguably of a different type, particularly when recovered from history. If heroes reflect an agreed-upon set of norms, in the national context, I suggest, they embody a set of norms and values in and through which a national culture imagines, and symbolically reproduces, itself. National heroes are essentially communicative phenomena, constituted in the traces of commemoration, in the practices of performing an agreed-upon public history.[37] Typically, history has served to insulate the national hero from the saturation and cynicism of current celebrity heroes.

However, Gary Gumpert (1997) identifies an interesting phenomenon about the process of heroicization. He argues that we are presently more fascinated with those that fall from grace than with those who remain within it. Some of the reasons for this instability and ultimate unsustainability of the hero as a cultural figure include:

> ... the combination of photographic acuity, media's ready access ... to event and persona ... and the extraordinary amount of programming that is required by media organizations and devoured by the American public that dissolved the distance that protects heroes from an invasion of privacy. The aura of necessary invincibility cannot withstand constant and penetrating visibility. The role of heroes has changed. It is not catharsis that the audience seeks, but rather revelation. Most persons, even heroes, would like to protect their wrinkles from public exposure, but it is the collective medium that has created a national pastime – the revelation of the wrinkle. An audience nurtured by penetrating media comes to expect the elimination of the public face and demands insight into the private. Heroes cannot withstand such scrutiny. (59)

While Gumpert is referring to the current constitution of contemporary celebrities as heroic figures, his claims do point out a seemingly inevitable cultural process that I call moral scrutiny. Heroic status is only awarded from public opinion once moral scrutiny is complete. I suggest that this process operates in the contemporary context according to certain axes, the specifics of which in the Canadian national context become visible in the ultimately futile attempts to reconstitute the Famous Five as heroes.

Finally, the very notion of the hero is 'biologically male and culturally masculine,' suggests Joan Fayer (1994: 24). Edwards (1984) asserts that, 'insofar as she resembles the male hero, she questions the conventional associations of gender and behavior' (48). These scholars suggest that the very fact of the female hero is threatening to masculine authority, highlighting its instability, necessarily marking the woman as transgressive and hence problematic. Certainly, as we saw in Murphy's own time, efforts were made to contain her potential to transgress at the federal political level. However, in the intervening years, we see that the category of hero continues to be shaped by gender norms. This results in the curious outcome that while Murphy and her colleagues could be recognized as persons in 1929, they could not hope to be heroes in the 2000s.

In 1997, Parliament voted to create a memorial in honour of the Famous Five on Parliament Hill, its location thus marking it as a *national* monument. The Famous Five Foundation commissioned a statue from Edmonton artist Barbara Paterson. Unveiled in October 2000, it is a large bronze of the Famous Five in a circle, receiving the news and holding up a newspaper proclaiming 'Women are Persons.' The monument is in a circle, at ground level, featuring Louise McKinney and Henrietta Muir Edwards sitting at a table and toasting the victory with teacups; Nellie McClung and Irene Parlby standing with a newspaper, which declares, 'Women are Persons;' and Emily Murphy standing before an empty chair inviting the viewer to join the women in the circle. As Tracy Kulba observes in her interesting interpretation of the monument and the controversy it generated in Alberta, the statue 'attempt[s]s to reconcile a narrative of equality with a narrative of difference' (2002: 77). She continues, '[a]gainst the narrative of equality marked by the very "personhood" that the statue commemorates, the monument attempts to register a sense of gender difference' (ibid.). Arguably, I suggest, this tension between equality and difference is a tension present in the very notion of the person, and not merely in Paterson's monument.

Kulba reads the statue against the backdrop of the controversy that arose in Alberta, in particular, about the heroic status of the Famous Five.[38] At issue was the support for policies of eugenics by a number of the Famous Five, but by Emily Murphy in particular. Incendiary quotes were pulled from her book *The Black Candle* (1922) as proof of her racism and these circulated widely in the Western Canadian press. The Famous Five Foundation then responded with a section on their website entitled, 'Were these heroes perfect?' and offering a justification of historical locatedness. Kulba correctly points out that:

> [i]n one sense, this controversy emerged from internal feminist critiques that sought to make current feminist practices attentive to differences between women; in another sense, however, this controversy marked the appropriation of those critiques by conservative interests, who mobilized race to dismiss feminism and its insistence on women's right to control their own bodies. (2002: 82)

She also recognizes that the debate became about whether the statue was an appropriate monument for contemporary Canada. Either it was appropriate because of the ongoing value of these women's contribution to a story of national and/or feminist progress or it was inappropriate because some of the politics of these women are not progressive and are outdated. Both approaches, however, do not really aid in 'negotiat[ing] the legacies of first-wave feminism as a historical subject' (Kulba, 2002: 83).[39] Kulba's project is one of attempting to complexify the politics of feminist memory. In addition to this, however, I suggest that we can see what happened with the statues as a broader strategy of moral scrutiny that reveals certain tensions within, not just the politics of feminist memory, but within Canadian national memory and gendered personhood. Because, this was not to be the last controversy.

In 2000, the Famous Five were poised as the first Canadian women to grace our national bank notes (along with Casgrain) – the first time in Canadian history in which 'identifiable women other than the Queen, [had] appeared on Canada's currency' (*Vancouver Province*, 2004). This was part of a redesign of Canadian currency, aimed, in practical terms, at countering increasingly sophisticated counterfeiting techniques, and in symbolic terms, at replacing the various birds on the back of the bills with images that would reflect Canadian national identity back to Canadians. The Famous Five Foundation and the National Liberal Women's Caucus had lobbied, unsuccessfully, for the five-dollar bill, in much more common circulation, but the fifty-dollar bill was the tender ultimately selected.[40] What resulted was yet another national brouhaha which played out in the press, as it had with respect to the national monuments in Calgary and Ottawa, largely along partisan lines. Once again, at issue was the appropriateness of, first, the location of the Famous Five on national tender, an arguably even more symbolic location than a commemorative monument. But more broadly, in this incident, the Five's candidacy for national heroic status was again at stake.

Deborah Yedlin in the *Globe and Mail* noted,

> [t]hese five women were clearly pioneers of the feminist movement and should be recognized for their accomplishments. ... But to put them on the back of a banknote that passes through our multicultural society is one step too far. It legitimizes racism and xenophobia, and ultimately taints the bill. (2004)

Michael Platt stated the problem somewhat more baldly in his *Calgary Sun* editorial: '[t]he redesigned fifty, due out in October, will mark a gutter-level low in the history of Canada's currency. And in honour-ing the squad of racist, elitist bigots known as the Famous Five, it will serve as a legal-tender insult to millions of Canadians' (Platt, 2004). He goes on to suggest that the Famous Five would be more aptly labelled 'the Fascist Five' (ibid.). What Yedlin, Platt, and the other journalists who weighed in on the Famous Five are referring to was the fact that, not entirely surprisingly, as women of a particular class and historical moment, a number of the Famous Five held views which would be unpopular today. Murphy, while writing about the debilitating effects of drugs, also cautioned readers about the 'black and yellow' races in *The Black Candle* (1922). As part of her overall concern about poor single mothers and their position within the law, as well as her belief that mental illness was a disease, not a crime, she also advocated eugenics, as did Nellie McClung and Louise McKin-ney. They lobbied extensively for Alberta's 1928 *Sexual Sterilization Act* where wards of the court, usually mentally disabled individuals, could be forcibly sterilized.[41]

The media, and in particular the conservative press, were eager to weigh in on the moral flaws of the Famous Five. Having had the advantage of 'doing the research' and developing the ammunition through the previous statue controversy, they had already selected the favoured quotations from *The Black Candle*; among them the passage where Murphy labels the Chinese 'traitors' and 'men of fishy blood who might easily be guilty of any enormity, no matter how villainous' (in Liu, 2000; Aubry, 2000). This and other 'unfortunate' quotations cir-culated widely in the press. Platt succinctly captures the function of the moral scrutiny when he notes that the Persons Case 'shouldn't make heroes of people who deserve as much criticism as they do applause' (2004). Another journalist asks, '[i]f we are going to install new national icons for Canada, would not a celebration of the present multicultural Canada be a preferable choice than reminiscences of the past?' (Liu, 2000). Again, as with the statue controversy, race and mul-ticulturalism are deployed to trump gender.

The advocates of the Famous Five, some of the more liberal press, and the Bank of Canada itself suggest, predictably, that the women were of their historical period, that their views were not atypical, and that their accomplishments remain considerable. The chair of the National Liberal Women's Caucus recognized the Five's historical specificity in a strong letter to then finance minister Paul Martin: '[m]embers of the Women's Caucus are also very aware that the Famous Five held some views that would be unacceptable today. Nevertheless, members believe that people must be viewed in the context of their times and that this should not detract from the enormous impact of their accomplishments' (in Aubry, 2000). Frances Wright, on behalf of the Famous Five Foundation, becomes a regular figure in the media, defending the potential heroes, locating them in their time, and countering with data and quotations of her own to suggest that the Famous Five also held progressive views.

A journalist for the *Calgary Herald* notes that history is apparently adaptable: '[t]he fact remains these women were remarkable, and among the first to fight for ideas which today seem obvious, but then required brass nerve to advocate. Must we condemn them because in walking a mile, they failed to walk two?' However, this argument in favour of historical specificity is then countered quickly by comparing the Famous Five to 'real' heroes such as Susan B. Anthony, Elizabeth Cady Stanton, and other nineteenth-century feminists who were abolitionists (Lakritz, 2004).[42] Here we see the notion of the authentic hero who passes moral scrutiny, and transcends her or his location outside of history, pitted against the historically specific failed hero mired in the complexity of the values of their day. 'The Famous Five ... deserve credit for the Persons Case, but in the rush to canonize them as Canada's feminist icons, their sickening views have been overlooked as nothing more than some quaint blight of the period, like corsets' (Lakritz, 2004).

As in the debate around the monuments, the Famous Five become a site in which other debates play out. 'And so it is that today's mavens of political correctness try to adapt history to promote their faction, by taking cheap shots at people who were once admired, because the attitudes they once held are now unfashionable. Destroy your heroes and I destroy you,' claims one journalist (Hannaford, 2004). Another counters: '[m]oney talks, and when Canada honours a group of racists and eugenicists by featuring the Famous Five on the $50 bill, it says we're sadly short of heroines these days' (Lakritz, 2004).

Interestingly, the legitimacy of the decision to feature the Five is justified by advocates as democratic. Geoffrey King, spokesman for the Bank of Canada, defends the controversial choice by noting that it was the outcome of focus groups participated in by four thousand everyday Canadians across the country. Wright states, in one of her defences, that prime ministers, governors general, chief justices, and parliamentarians have all honoured the Famous Five on Persons Day for the past twenty-five years. She labels the Five 'preeminent democratic champions' and suggests that they are revered, respected, and adored by 'the people' (Wright, 2004b).[43]

So, what does the 'minor foofaraw over the suitability of five Alberta women to adorn a bank note,' as one commentator put it (Hannaford, 2004), tell us about scrutiny and heroism? First, we can see that the terms of the debate are normative. The attacks on the potential heroes are figured in very dramatically moral terms. This simultaneously figures the scrutineer as already a moral actor, as a defender of a certain set of values under assault by the very prospect of their nomination as heroes. In this narrative of the Famous Five, the conservative press takes the somewhat ironic position of defender of immigration and the mentally disabled, ardently championing the values of multiculturalism. Further, casting the debate in moral terms quickly claims the high ground for the scrutineers, leaving the heroic defenders in the inevitable and unenviable position of historical apologists.

Second, we see the polarization of the debate. Hero is an absolute status – one is or is not a hero. The press structures its coverage in a yea or nay fashion, frequently inviting readers to write in in support of one position or the other. Third, we see how the debate around the Famous Five becomes a location for the playing out of larger political debates. There is, at times, an almost palpable sense of glee on the part of some critics that the 'feminists' were foolish enough to back such a controversial group of women. In this way, feminism more broadly is discredited. The fourth element of scrutiny we see at work is the use of democracy as a trope of heroic legitimation. Claims of democratic approval are relied upon as a legitimating tactic by the Famous Five advocates. Interestingly, democracy is also used as a weapon by the critics. 'The Famous Five are a rotten choice, because the country's money is public domain – and many members of the public are people the Five wouldn't have wanted as Canadians' (Platt, 2004). National heroes clearly have a troubled relationship with democracy.

In the playing out of the fifty-dollar-bill contestation, we see the final element in the process of scrutiny. As noted previously, a Canadian national hero must reflect the values at the heart of Canada's self-image – tolerance, equity, multiculturalism, and so on. Almost as soon as the racist epithets were hurled in the statue controversy, it was clear that the Famous Five would not, indeed could not, be effectively constituted as national heroes. Jennifer Henderson makes a point about Murphy's quest to be recognized as a legal person that applies very well to the attempted heroicization on her behalf. 'The crusade for recognition by an *outsider* to personhood required a demonstration of qualifications in the form of an exemplary embodiment of normativity' (2005: 83). While exemplary in many ways, the Five did not embody Canada's imagined national norms. Failure was a *fait accompli* even before the fifty-dollar bill is mentioned. Instead, the process of scrutiny itself becomes a means in and through which to rearticulate those national values as universal and eternal. In this way, scrutiny serves as an authenticating process for Canadian self-image (in the same way that the Persons Case itself did). Because we denied these women their heroic status, because the process of scrutiny worked and their unsavoury history was revealed, the scrutineers and their activities of scrutiny are legitimate. It renders our existing heroes more heroic and 'us' more discerning. Canadian society itself emerges cleansed of potential false idols, regardless of whether or not the Famous Five joined Thérèse Casgrain on the re-minted fifty-dollar bill. At the same time, however, we also cleanse ourselves of history. 'They thought differently than we did. *Quelle surprise.* At worst, we become the grave robbers of reputations, kicking out the foundations of our society to the detriment of the whole house' (Hannaford, 2004).

In this process of the moral scrutiny of heroes, or more particularly in this instance, heroines, we see the difficulty of co-articulating a gendered national hero. 'In today's multicultural society and in an era ruled by political correctness, it is amazing to see how the Famous Five could have been given an honour usually reserved for the Fathers of Confederation, monarchs or dead prime ministers' notes one journalist (Liu, 2000). Our currency currently features Prime Ministers Borden, Mackenzie King, and Macdonald, individuals who had dubious racial politics themselves and checkered personal lives. One need only think of the first significant use of the new Canadian Pacific Railway to move the army out to quash the Northwest Rebellion and slaughter the Métis, or the internment of Canadian citizens of Japanese, German, Polish, and Italian descent during the Second World War. Macdonald had a well-known drinking problem and Mackenzie King held séances to talk to his deceased mother and dog. One might also surmise that the Fathers of Confederation, like the Famous Five, were also likely people of their times, and the values of 1867 were very different from those of today.[44] Yet no one challenges the right of these individuals to be featured on our national currency or to be represented on Parliament Hill. In making these observations, I am not suggesting that Prime Ministers Borden, Mackenzie King, and Macdonald should not be on our currency, but rather that, in the absence of controversy around them, we see how the Famous Five, unlike our prime ministers and other 'national heroes,' were considered as specific subjects, and their character, rather than their actions, therefore was brought under moral scrutiny. The Five were not abstracted from history and the resulting politics that arises from specific location, but rather remain always embedded within it. In this way, they can never be heroic, because the hero is a figure out of time. Like the person, the hero is a liberal individual, always an abstraction, and arguably, still masculine.

Gendering the Person

When responding publicly to the decision of the JCPC, Emily Murphy was quick to suggest that it was not a 'sex victory' but rather an act of civility, of inclusion in public affairs. Murphy's statement was likely prudent in relation to calming the worries of those opposed to women's participation in the Senate (and elsewhere in public life). As well, it is also coherent with the absence of a strong rights discourse at the time. However, her framing is accurate in a way that she did not perhaps anticipate. Not merely because of its prudence is the Persons Case limited in its political effect. It is not only because the actions of the Famous Five are inevitably anchored within their specific historical moment and values that the Persons Case does not lead to a rethinking of gender and personhood. Rather, in its focus on the question of women's personhood, the Persons Case and the Famous Five run into the fundamental tension involved in the person as a gendered identity. Recognizing the sexed subject poses an irreconcilable dilemma for the law. The abstract individualism at the heart of the legal person, therefore, makes visible the gendered person when it encounters the sexed subject. Gendering operates as an exclusionary tactic from the abstract individualism at the heart of the legal person.

In the typology of personhood that Ngaire Naffine (2003) offers, and which I discussed in chapter 1, none of the definitions mentions sex, and indeed, they all assume that legal personality can be articulated in a completely gender-neutral manner. Naffine further argues elsewhere (2004) that the reason for the absence of sex is that sexing the person is counter to all three formulations of personhood. Personification as a fundamental liberal project is an activity of individuation; it produces us as distinct and unique, after the law. On the other hand, sexing the subject places us in a pre-existing, pre-legal category, defining some of our important characteristics in common and thus distinguishing us from each other according to which group we belong to (Naffine, 2004: 629).

For the P1 person, 'the person, as abstraction, resides in shifting con-stellations of legal rights and duties that are in turn constitutive of legal relations. Persons exist in the particularity of a given legal rela-tion; their natures are not set beforehand' (ibid.). On the other hand, P2 personality explicitly evokes the embodied human being, seemingly raising issues of sex. However, P2 also operates on the basis of an abstraction – the 'human being.' 'The paradox of this P2 person is that "he" is intended to give legal life to real embodied human beings and yet at the same time, "he" is highly abstracted – a thought experiment' (ibid.). Finally, P3, constituted solely in the capacities of the mind, denies the body altogether. As a result, sex can have no place in its con-stitution (ibid.).

Legal definitions of personhood mark themselves off from the 'natural,' where sex is seemingly located. Sex 'is a natural fact, not a legal fiction, which law is bound to accept in its natural form. In other words, it is not truly a legal concept even though it is firmly within law's lexicon. It is thought to draw its meaning entirely from another discipline: the biological sciences' (ibid.: 632). The sexed body moves in and out of law as necessary, but is always subservient to the more powerful, abstracted notion of the person (ibid.: 633). We see this at work, for example, in our principles of statutory interpre-tation. Section 33(1) of the Canadian *Interpretation Act* provides: 'words importing female persons include male persons and corpora-tions and words importing male persons include female persons and corporations.'[45]

In the ideal posited by the person, we are legal persons first and sexed beings second. However, in many instances 'the law still requires a sexed individual before it is prepared to recognize them as the sort of person who can participate in certain legal relations' (Naffine, 2004: 635). Prior to the Persons Case, for example, the word 'persons' in Section 24 of the *BNA Act* was not gender-neutral, as we saw. One had to be already sexed a male person to fit within the qualification of persons. Yet at the same time, masculinity has not been a limiting condition on personhood; rather, historically, being male has served as an enabling characteristic, a precondition of personhood. 'Male sexing has been so proximate to personification that male sexing has been all but invisible' (ibid.: 638). Just as the Persons Case caused 'gender trouble' for the notion of personhood, making visible its masculinism, we see in other moments of gender trouble the ongoing tension in thinking the sexed person. More recently, Canadian law required that individuals be hetero-sexed before it was prepared to grant marriage to legal persons.[46] The law has repeatedly demonstrated its unease both with non-gendered or complexly gendered beings, sometimes brutally requiring that they be defined as sexual beings before considering their personhood rights. For example, in a recent case in British Columbia the court upheld the exclusion of a post-operative male-to-female transsexual from a training program for peer counsellors in a rape crisis centre because she had not been born and raised as a girl and woman. What is even more interesting than the outcome, however, is the court trying to deal with the seeming malleability of gender when it collides with the assumed fixity of identity (*Vancouver Rape Relief*, 2005). 'That is why,' Naffine suggests, 'sex neutrality is always a feat of the imagination' (2004: 636).

> Sexing and personification would seem therefore to be inextricably linked and yet fundamentally in tension. Both are elementary to our social and legal thinking about what and who we are and why we have moral and legal status and yet they co-exist unhappily. Personification gives dignity essentially through individualization – through rendering someone individual and distinctive. Sexing gives (and removes) dignity essentially through attribution of sameness or similarity with others of the same sex, the attribution of difference from the other sex, and through the simultaneous avoidance of the third term: 'it.' To date we lack a liberal theory of the sexed person, of the sexed individual. (Ibid.: 638)

The Persons Case was a technique whereby women were able to make visible the gendered nature of the person, and yet the legal case became about including women as sexed subjects within the abstraction, seemingly reproducing a gender-neutral notion of the person. And yet repeated, subsequent treatments of the (female) person at law and in social life demonstrate that this is not the case. The Persons Case had the effect of reaffirming the position that we are supposed to be legal persons first, and sexed beings second. This does nothing to rethink the liberal, individualist notion of the person, with its concomitant incapacity to recognize collective identification or embodiment. 'The concept of personhood invites us to abstract our identity from those very narrative resources – birth, growth and development, sexuality, procreation, friendship, decay, death – which we require to make sense of our lives' (Poole, 1996: 50).

A Technology of Gender

In the lobby entrance to the Senate of Canada, a bronze plaque hangs on the wall. Placed there by the Canadian Federation of Business and Professional Women's Clubs, the plaque commemorates the role of the five Alberta women – Emily Murphy, Irene Parlby, Henrietta Muir Edwards, Louise McKinney, and Nellie McClung – for their role in gaining admittance to the Senate for the women of Canada. At the unveiling on 11 June 1938, attended by the only two members of the Famous Five who remained alive – McClung and Parlby – Prime Minister Mackenzie King intoned of the Five:

> [t]hey did more than that [brought to the fore the issues of women's rights and responsibilities in public affairs]. They helped to throw into bold relief the special gifts which it is within the power of women to bring to the organized life of the community and the nation. Endowed with special powers of intuition and sympathy, a keen insight into human values, and, in most cases an abiding loyalty to cherished institutions and principles, woman possesses and has revealed in public as in private life, a quite exceptional capacity for sustained and unselfish service. (in Maclean, 1962: 3–4)

Thus while the Famous Five and the women of Canada symbolically became 'persons' that day in 1929, they were and are always, already figured as women first, persons second. Indeed, their prudential politics was both implicated within, and productive of, that ordering. However, as we saw in the 'controversies' surrounding the attempt to rewrite the Famous Five as national heroes, once again, their sex preceded their heroism. Unlike their male political colleagues of the same era, the Five were subjected to a personal and historically specific moral scrutiny. Their burden was to be total heroes – in all actions and in belief. They were interpreted as specific historical actors, who could be neither generalized nor abstracted. In this way, both the legal and popular cultural stories of the Famous Five are most accurately understood as narratives of an enlightened national sovereignty that reinforces the 'gender-neutrality' of both the hero and the person.

Yet, more importantly, both tales reveal that the Persons Case, while not a 'sex victory,' is very much about the tensions in the personality of the sexed subject. The Famous Five succeeded in shifting women from the category of P2 persons to that of P3 – from recognizably human to legally responsible subjects. The category of P3, previously inhabited only by males, was now opened to females. I suggest, however, that there are two other aspects of gender and personality that are revealed in this seemingly successful quest that are as signifcant as, if not more significant than, women's addition to P3 personality.

The first facet made visible is that the Persons Case in Canada (and those elsewhere) reveals, not merely that the category of the legal person has been historically gendered (in both the letter and spirit of the law), but rather, that personification itself is a technology of gender. The struggle at law to be recognized as person, in the case of the Famous Five, resulted, not in reappraisal of the gendered nature of the category of the legal, rational subject, but rather the confirmation that women's sex precedes their entry into personhood. The quest for legal personality reproduces women as necessarily sexed subjects, without altering the comfortably and invisibly gendered nature of the person. Operating within, and using, the law as the technique of personification, the actors of the Persons Case necessarily accepted the 'gender-neutral' understanding of the person, while the need for their actions belied this very neutrality.

This results in the second interesting aspect of the Persons Case, namely that it reveals that women are still not persons. While they can vote and sit in the houses of government, they continue to be women first, and persons second. They continue to be specific women first, and potential heroes second. The person functions, therefore, not only as a legal fiction, but also as a gender fiction, attempting to abstract the individual from his or her embodiment and social context. The 'female person' is, as a result, not as oxymoronic as one might hope. Yet, as we have seen, the mantle of person as a gender fiction does not sit easily on women. This is because, I suggest, women are more interestingly understood as personae than persons. Women are personae in that their personification is always partial, always problematic, in turn marking personality a necessarily contested terrain. Personae there-fore offer a partial and fractured form of subjectivity, but one which does not require necessary disembodiment. Personae are specific, and never fully abstractable. They demand an encounter with history; they demand we remember. They require us to recognize that the person was not, and can never be, gender-neutral.

4 Invented Humans:
Kinship and Property in Persons

[The] excess of biopower appears when it has become technologically and politically possible for man not only to manage life but to make it proliferate, to create living matter, to build the monster.

(Foucault, 2003: 254)

When faced with the question of whether or not one should be able to patent a higher life form in Canada, the Canadian Biotechnology Advisory Committee (CBAC) assuaged our fears: '[e]ven if the act of granting a patent on an invented human were not in itself a violation of basic human rights, exercising the patent's exclusive right to make, use or sell an invented human would almost certainly violate the *Canadian Charter of Rights and Freedoms* and the *Canadian Human Rights Act*' (CBAC, 2002: 8). What is even more interesting than the advisory body to the Canadian government on biotechnology issues recommending that all higher life forms except complete human bodies be patentable is that CBAC is contemplating an 'invented human.' Typically, one finds invented humans in science fictional, rather than policy, texts. Films such as *The Boys from Brazil* (1978), with its boy-clones of Adolf Hitler created by none other than an embittered Dr Josef Mengele, or *Multiplicity* (1996), featuring four versions of Michael Keaton cloned to make busy life in the 1990s a little bit easier, are the more familiar sites exploring the possibilities for, anxieties around, and ultimate status of, an invented human being. However, over the last twenty years, governments around the world have been forced to deal with the social science fiction of the invented human. This is because the invented human is not just a product of science and popular culture – it is, by its very nature, also a product of law.

Patents are the form of intellectual property that give exclusive rights to inventors to prevent others from making, using, or selling an invention for which they hold a registered patent. To qualify for a patent, an invention must be new, non-obvious, and useful. In the past two hundred years, patents have been granted for all manner of technoscientific developments from the electric lightbulb to Prozac. Yet since the advent of molecular science in the post–Second World War era, and, in particular, the development of recombinant DNA technology, scientists and their corporate funders have been actively seeking patent protection for a different type of patentable subject matter: biological life forms. From the Flavr Savr tomato, to a goat that produces milk with drug proteins in it, to fish that can secrete human insulin, to mice modified to develop Alzheimer's disease, patent offices have been inundated with applications for genetically re-engineered beings. As a result, courts and governments have had to struggle with the social, legal, political, and ethical implications of reconfiguring the higher life form as intellectual property. An invented life form is, by its very status as an invention, already potentially patentable, already conceived of as property. In most Western nations, with the notable exception of Canada, invented life forms are patentable – they are property. And while no one has yet applied for a patent for an 'invented human,' ever since the announcement of the cloning of Dolly the Sheep in 1997, the prospect of the invented human has been in the scientific, governmental, and popular imaginations.[1]

Immediately after Dolly, headlines around the world screamed predictions about the application of that reproductive technique to human beings. The *Globe and Mail* made the connection express: '[h]uman cloning: The race is on since Dolly the sheep appeared on the scene' (Kolata, 1998: A17). The science editor of the *Guardian* predicted human clones in two years (Radford, 1997: 1) and the *Australian* reported that 'the successful cloning of a sheep proves it is possible to clone dead humans who have been frozen' (*Australian*, 1997: 7). An editorial in the *Kansas City Star* asked, '[w]hat follows Dolly? Cloning humans should not be the next scientific step' (McClanahan, 1998: C6). Dr Ian Wilmut, the lead scientist on the team that cloned Dolly, became an overnight, authoritative reference for human cloning as well. An interview with him was titled 'Human Organs Next Says Dr. Dolly' (*Daily Mail*, 1998: 7). Wilmut was quick to stress that the procedure would take place before the embryo developed a nervous system, but the journalist notes, 'his comments may fuel fears of mutant humans being bred for transplants especially after British biologists said they had created a frog embryo without a head. The creature, essentially a bag of organs, was born after its DNA genetic blueprint had been altered. It was later destroyed' (ibid.). Wilmut, himself, noted in another interview that he is regularly requested to clone human beings for people who have recently lost close relatives (in Moysa, 1997: D16). Within the media coverage, therefore, there is an evident fear of the slippery slope from the cloning of animals to the cloning of human beings.[2]

This fear seemingly materialized in 1998 when Chicago physicist Richard Seed claimed he was going to set up a clinic to clone human babies for infertile couples (and for profit).[3] Governments around the world, Canada among them, scrambled to produce legislation outlawing human reproductive cloning.[4] Many in the scientific community argued that these laws were hastily drafted, ill conceived, and destined to place undue limits on scientific research. Interestingly, many critics blamed science fiction for producing the public and political uneasiness with biotechnology generally, and cloning technology in particular. In relation to the Canadian legislation, one journalist claimed that 'public attitudes toward cloning are based on a diet of science fiction B movies and paperbacks,' arguing that governments, before they 'rush to outlaw' cloning, 'should at least consider seriously whether the opposition to human cloning is based on real dangers, or on science-fiction horror movies' (Colvin, 2000: A18). After Dolly was cloned, a notable bioethicist stated, '[h]orror stories purveyed by science fiction movies and novels (the cloned Hitler of *The Boys from Brazil*) have prepared people to think of only "worst-case scenarios" involving cloning' (in Monmaney, 1997: 12).

This link between human cloning and science fiction is neither accidental nor incidental.[5] With the 'successful' cloning of a large, adult mammal, the possibilities of cloning technology materialized. Therefore, the scientific limitations to human cloning seemed to be gone, lending a sense of increased threat from marginal scientists from the Quebec cult of Rael, to Richard Seed, to doctors Severino Antinori and Panos Zavos. The only possible barriers to the invented human then became socio-ethical and legal. But without an actual instance of a cloned human, governments were operating in a vacuum of actual scientific knowledge and experience. They were forced to regulate a technoscientific possibility, a fictional being.

William Bogard offers the notion of the social science fiction to enable us to map the effects of regulating such a fiction. He suggests social science fiction as an epistemological technique for doing future history (1996: 7).[6] It seeks to 'describe the social or institutional "effects" of an imaginary technology' (ibid.: 8). While relying on fiction, it is not an imaginary future against which we measure our current social reality (Bogard, 2003: 178); rather, it is a future always emerging out of, and speaking back to, our current context. Social science fictions are produced in the reproduction and circulation of certain figures 'in which the fictional superimposes itself on and is effective within its own past and, by extension, within the real and present order of things' (Bogard, 1996: 8).

I suggest that the invented human is such a figure, a figure of social science fiction. The lack of scientific actuality of a cloned human being does not mean we lack an image of what it is, or that we lack the capacity to imagine what the implications of it might be. We produce this inquiry in and through the figure of the invented human who moves fluidly between fictional and governmental discourses. Like all social science fictions, the invented human is a technique for managing future risk, but at the same time, it is a means by which the present is imagined and enacted. We can thus trace out the cultural effectivity of the figure of the invented human by mapping its articulation in both popular and legal-governmental sites.

In this chapter, I explore the invented human both in texts of speculative fiction addressing cloned humans and in a series of legal and policy decisions on biopatenting, taking up the question of the invention and ownership of the higher life form. I do not pursue in any detail Canada's hastily drafted, much publicized, and controversial *Assisted Human Reproduction Act*, legislation that prohibits human cloning, but which has been largely ineffective. Many thought that the passing of that legislation would cause the spectre of the invented human to recede. Not so. The site of the discussion has merely shifted. And in fact, in many ways, the fact of the legislation obscures a much more quiet and effective means through which human beings and their higher life form kin are already being invented: the technique of biopatenting. Throughout the 1980s until the present, the Canadian patent office, CBAC, and the federal courts have been involved in discussing and determining the legal question of whether or not higher life forms are patentable in Canada. In so doing, they have been grappling with the invented human in much more concrete terms than the fleeting legislative discussions of human cloning did and could.

After an introduction to Canadian patent law, I offer a brief history of biopatenting, and then take up the administrative-legal journey of the only invented mammal to make it all the way to the Supreme Court of Canada, the Oncomouse. I read Canada's grappling with the invented higher life form alongside popular narratives of invented life, specifically, Roger Spottiswoode's 2000 film, *The 6th Day*, and Michael Bay's film of 2005, *The Island*. As Debbora Battaglia correctly recognizes, cinema has a 'place of honor in bioethical rhetoric and popular debate about genetically engineered entities' (2001: 495). Through this analysis I suggest that the invented human challenges two significant ways in which we have traditionally demarcated the person, what I call the two boundaries of personal propriety. First, we know that a person is a person because he or she is not an animal. Returning to Daniel Dennett's (1976) list of personal attributes, we are rational, we communicate, we are self-reflexive and intentional, we have emotion – all characteristics which, we feel, distinguish *us*, namely human beings, from other organisms. Second, we know that a person is a person because he or she is not a thing. Subject-object relations must be maintained in their proper order. Persons are meant to be free and autonomous beings, and those moments in our history where we have permitted them to be property are now seen as a stain on our collective conscience. We are highly invested in the mutual exclusivity of the categories of person and property (see Davies and Naffine, 2001; Frow, 1995; Hyde, 1997).

Yet, the invented human, as social science fiction, troubles both of those boundaries. The invented human has become a central figure through which our broader cultural anxieties about our phylum relationship with animals and our uneasiness about understanding ourselves as property manifest. It is a rupture point in our sense of self, revealing our anxieties about the increasing instability of the easy distinctions between human and animals and between persons and property.

Patent Law in Canada

Patent law is one of a number of different areas of intellectual property for which legal protection may be sought in Canada.[7] Governed by the *Patent Act*, the technical elements of patents have changed very little over the years, but the subject matter to which those technical elements apply has obviously changed dramatically. In 1869, when the legislation first came into force, its drafters could not have envisioned the space shuttle, heat-seeking missiles, Viagra, ultrasound machines, the iPod Shuffle, and the host of other technologies that have emerged over the ensuing century and a half. The legislation has expanded, however, to take account of all of the above technologies through the expansive interpretation of what constitutes an invention. Through the concept of invention, patents and patent systems have had a dynamic relationship with the development of new technologies and scientific techniques.

A patent is a monopoly right granted to an inventor for an invention. An invention is defined in the legislation as 'any new and useful art, process, machine, manufacture or composition of matter' or any useful improvement to any of those. An invention is often contrasted with the 'mere' discovery of something, pre-existing in nature, that is not patentable. The *Patent Act* specifically states that '[n]o patent shall be granted for any mere scientific principle or abstract theorem' (Section 27(8)).

As noted above, to receive patent protection, the invention must be new, non-obvious, useful, and fully described in the application. The requirement of newness means that the invention cannot be something already in active use, or already known. It cannot have been made public prior to the patent application.[8] The invention must be non-obvious to someone trained in the particular field in which the invention operates. The usefulness criterion requires some form of industrial or commercial application. Finally, both the process for its production, and the invention itself, must be described in the application in such a way that someone trained in the field could produce the invention from the description.

Unlike copyright, a patent does not vest with the act of creation. An application must be made to the Canadian Intellectual Property Office (CIPO), the body responsible for the administration of patents. If the inventor does not file an application, she or he has no rights. If the patent is granted, it is presumed valid unless and until it is challenged, and there are no public policy grounds for CIPO to refuse a patent. A patent may only be denied if the statutory requirements are not met. The patent gives the inventor a limited monopoly right to prevent others from the unauthorized creation, use, or sale of the patented invention for twenty years.[9] Interestingly, a patent is a negative property right – it does not give the right to the patentee to make, use, or sell the invention, only to prevent others from doing so. For instance, there may be other legislation or public policy that prohibits or restricts the practice or sale of the invention, as is sometimes the case with weapons, drugs, and environmentally volatile products. If the

Assisted Human Reproduction Act were declared in force, for example, a scientist could apply for and receive a patent for the process to clone a human being, while being prohibited by law from actually producing such a creature.

The logic behind granting a patent is that the period of monopoly permits the inventor the time to exploit her or his invention free from competition in order to recoup the research investment. In this way, patent systems (like other regimes for the protection of intellectual property) seek to provide incentives for invention. In exchange, the patentee is required to make full disclosure, thus enriching the public storehouse of knowledge. After the patent period, others are free to use, produce, and sell the invention as they wish (within the bounds of the law). As a result, patents are often framed by courts and policy makers as a bargain where the inventor receives protection and financial incentives, and the public receives useful knowledge circulating openly in the public sphere.

Patents operate on the assumptions of the Mertonian ideal of non-interested, non-commercialized research carried out by individual scientists who are part of a shared community of knowledge and values.[10] Some critics argue, however, that patenting actually serves to deter innovation. Negligible adjustments are made to inventions in order to extend patent periods. Creators spend much time developing, negotiating, and often litigating licensing agreements and royalties. Holders of patents use them strategically to prevent competitors from developing new products. This occurs, in part, because an overwhelming majority of patents are not, in fact, awarded to individual scientists, but to their employers – the large corporations that are funding the research. In addition, scientists (even in the research university setting) frequently wait to publish their research until they can obtain a patent, so as not to jeopardize their ability to do so. Consequently, patents can create a chilly climate where researchers are reluctant to pursue certain avenues of research because they are concerned about infringing someone's patent.

In a November 2000 Environics Research Group study of the Canadian biotechnology community, critics' concerns were validated. Researchers, in addition to having a very low comprehension of patent issues, suggested that concerns about patent infringements were inhibiting research activity at the early stages of research. One-third of respondents reported that they had delayed their research work; another third reported postponing work; and one-fifth said they stopped work completely. The social impacts of these kinds of patent effects are significant. In 2002, leading cancer researchers in the United States charged that DuPont's troublesome licensing practices deterred them from undertaking cancer research using oncomice. In Canada in 2001, British Columbia stopped using a low-cost breast cancer test because of the threat of a patent infringement suit from Myriad Genetics Inc. of Utah, which wanted the BC government to pay triple the price for the test.

So, while patents are one of the most technical and limited areas of intellectual property, they have recently emerged as one of the most significant, in large part because of the considerable amounts of money required for investment and the substantial return on capital investment. However, patents are a very important means of framing an object because, as Mark Hanson suggests, '[a]s a rhetoric of the market and property rights, patents are a rhetoric of ownership, control, and assertions of sovereignty' (2002: 172). Ownership, control, and sovereignty become even more powerful terms of reference when attached to what have traditionally been viewed as higher or complex life forms, when attached to life. The patenting of life and its component parts has become known as biopatenting.

Biopatenting

Within the very premises of patent law – the separation of 'mere discovery' (nature) from 'invention' (culture), and the insulation of patents from politics through the elision of public policy considerations in their granting – are the seeds of key debates around biopatenting. In many ways, the story of biopatenting is one of the slow expansion of the category of invention at the expense of the category of nature. While biopatenting began slowly and quietly in North America, with patents being issued for processes of developing microorganisms in the 1960s, it was not until a patent was sought for a life form as a whole that biopatenting garnered serious and substantial public, political, and scholarly attention.

The watershed case in North America, and the one which has served as the benchmark for all subsequent American and Canadian courts, is *Diamond* v. *Chakrabarty*. In 1971, microbiologist Anandan Mohan Chakrabarty and his employer, General Electric, applied for a patent on a genetically modified bacterium which broke down crude oil components. This oil-eating bacterium was potentially very useful (and lucrative) for cleaning up oil spills. Chakrabarty's application was initially denied by the United States Patent and Trademark Office, and he appealed to the courts. In a split decision, the United States Supreme Court held, in 1980, that the issue was not one of whether the subject of the patent application was animate or inanimate, but rather whether it was made by a person, as opposed to being found in nature. The court found that the bacterium, as a living organism, was a composition of matter, and therefore a human-made invention. Microorganisms were more akin to chemical compositions than complex organisms, the justices felt. The best-known dictum from the decision, and the one which has had a revolutionary rhetorical and legal impact upon the patenting of life forms, was a statement the Court quoted with approval from the legislative history of the enactment that 'Congress intended statutory subject matter to include anything under the sun that is made by man' (*Diamond*, 1980: 308).

The distinction between nature and culture is left unproblematized by the American high court; yet nature clearly emerges as Heidegger's standing reserve for man as inventor. Nature is rendered invention through human creative agency. The focus of the court on the actions of the inventor, figured as an originary creator who remakes the raw material of nature, simultaneously transforms the inventor into author and – through a Lockean sleight-of-hand – owner.[11] However, in addition to refiguring the inventor as subject, and nature as object, *Chakrabarty* is understood by legal, social, and cultural scholars as a significant symbolic event, a marker of a broader set of shifts that were beginning to crystallize in the late twentieth century. Paul Rabinow remarks, for example, '[t]he Chakrabarty decision was less a legal milestone than an event which symbolized broader economic, political and cultural changes taking place' (1996: 132). These changes include, I suggest, the rapid rise of a global biotechnology economy dominated by gargantuan transnational firms, the subjection of life itself to regimes of commodification and biovalue,[12] shifts in subjectivity requiring prudential and risk management strategies on the part of citizens,[13] changes in how we conceive of our bodies,[14] and the increasing inability of states to manage or control biotechnology research activities.[15] While we can see these changes in a variety of related realms, their playing out in the domain of patent law renders biopatents a technique of tremendous symbolic and material power. As Donna Haraway notes,

[b]ecause patent status reconfigures an organism as a human invention, produced by mixing labor and nature as those categories are understood in Western law and philosophy, patenting an organism is a large semiotic and practical step toward blocking nonproprietary and nontechnical meaning from many social sites – such as labs, courts, and popular venues. (1997: 82)

In other words, *Chakrabarty* is the first articulation of the invented higher life form, suddenly a social science fiction in its own right.

Although, typically, American court cases are not particularly relevant to Canadian jurisprudence, in the case of patents, there are strong similarities between the American and Canadian legislative regimes, including a nearly identical definition of invention. That, combined with the dearth of biopatenting cases in Canada and the powerful symbolic status of *Chakrabarty*, means that the decision has had a significant impact in Canada. Interestingly, however, despite the complex ethical, scientific, legal, social, and cultural issues involved in patenting life forms, until the 2000s, there were few Canadian legal decisions guiding the way.

In Canada, processes for inventing micro-organisms had been property since a patent office decision in 1965, but in *Re: Application of Abitibi Co.* (1982), the Patent Appeal Board specifically considered the patentability of an organism itself. The Board found that a yeast culture, which could digest waste product from pulp mills, was a patentable subject matter. Strongly influenced by the reasoning in *Chakrabarty* and its characterization of the organism, the Board held that because micro-organisms are produced *en masse* in such large numbers, they are analogous to chemical processes. All will possess uniform characteristics and properties, and therefore can be treated as an invention. The Board suggested, in passing, that its decision would not likely apply to plants and animals as higher life forms. Nonetheless, in so doing, it mobilized the figure of the invented higher life form. The Board articulated the express conditions for its invention:

[i]f an inventor creates a new and unobvious insect which did not exist before (and thus is not a product of nature), and can recreate it uniformly and at will, and it is useful (for example to destroy the spruce bud worm), then it is every bit as much a new tool of man as a micro-organism. With still higher life forms it is of course less likely that the inventor will be able to reproduce it at will and consistently, as more complex life forms

tend to vary more from individual to individual. But if it is eventually possible to achieve such a result, and the other requirements of patentability are met, we do not see why it should be treated differently. (*Re: Application of Abitibi*, 1982: 90)

Therefore, if the inventor can produce a new, unobvious, and useful higher life form at will, and consistently, then he will have achieved the goal of every mad scientist of fiction and fact alike: he will have invented life. Yet, contrary to Mary Shelley and Michel Foucault, this invented life may not be monstrous because it will be, necessarily, useful property, already objectified and potentially valuable.

The next invented life form to be the object of a contested biopatent in Canada was a cross-bred soybean. In *Pioneer Hi-Bred Ltd.* v. *Commissioner of Patents* (1989), the Supreme Court of Canada was called upon to consider whether or not a complex plant could be an invention. The Federal Court of Appeal had found that complex plants fell outside the language of the *Patent Act*, upholding the Canadian Patent Office's refusal of the patent (*Pioneer*, 1987). While the high court decided the case on other grounds, it recognized that biotechnology has moved us into the realm of social science fiction.

> More than a century ago Darwin developed the theory that only species and individuals that can adapt and acquire new characteristics can survive and reproduce. The same principle underlies the experiments which through genetic engineering now make possible adaptation to specific environments or new uses of known living organisms. The real issue in this appeal is the patentability of a form of life. (*Pioneer*, 1989: para. 13)

The court posited two kinds of genetic engineering. The first was cross-breeding over several generations to produce new varieties. As the court stated: '[t]here is thus human intervention in the reproductive cycle, but intervention which does not alter the actual rules of reproduction, which continue to obey the laws of nature' (ibid.: para. 15). Obviously this type of genetic engineering described practices in which farmers around the world have been engaged for centuries, if not millennia. The second type was molecular change, altering the genetic material itself by acting directly on the gene. 'While the first method implies an evolution based strictly on heredity and Mendelian principles, the second also employs a sharp and permanent alteration of hereditary traits by a change in the quality of the genes' (ibid.: para.

16). The court concluded that the intervention by Pioneer Hi-Bred was of the first type, but it was clearly anticipating the future in its discussion of the second. Again however, what becomes apparent is that it is the capacity of the inventor to alter the rules of reproduction that distinguishes types of genetic engineering and the possibility of invention.

The stakes of biopatenting somehow seem less alarming when the object of the patent is a soybean plant. Despite our genetic overlap, we feel the comfort of species-level privilege. However, before the Supreme Court of Canada's next opportunity to consider biopatenting, the Supreme Court of California had to decide the case of *Moore* v. *Regents of University of California* (1990), a case that moved the social science fiction figure of the invented human a little bit closer to social fact.

John Moore underwent treatment for hairy-cell leukemia at the Medical Centre of the University of California. Based upon his doctor's advice, he had his spleen removed, signing the necessary consent form for the operation. Unbeknownst to Moore, after testing bodily substances removed from him before surgery, doctors perceived that certain components of his blood made them valuable commodities for research; his blood cells contained an atypical number of valuable antibodies. Between 1976, when his spleen was removed, and 1983, Moore returned to the medical centre several times on his doctor's advice, with the doctor removing samples of blood, blood serum, skin, bone marrow aspirate, and sperm. However, during that entire time, and without Moore's knowledge, the doctor and his colleagues were actively conducting research on Moore's cells. Ultimately they took out a patent on a cell-line (the Mo cell-line) developed from his white blood cells. The commercial value of the cell-line was estimated at $3.01 billion dollars. When Moore learned of the patent, he sued his doctor and the medical centre.

The court found that the doctors had breached their duty of care to inform Moore adequately in order for him to provide proper consent to the various medical procedures. More importantly for my purposes, however, Moore argued that the doctor had interfered with his ownership rights in his personal property, namely his body and body parts. That was the issue that troubled the court most and split the decision. One set of judges held that the cells, once excised from Moore's body, like other body parts under regulatory legislation, should be treated as objects to be disposed of in accordance with policy guidelines, rather than as his personal property. The patented cell-line could not be Moore's property because it was factually and legally distinct from the cells removed from his body. 'It is this inventive effort that patent law rewards, not the discovery of naturally occurring raw materials. Thus, Moore's allegations that he owns the cell line and the products derived from it are inconsistent with the patent, which constitutes an authoritative determination that the cell line is the product of invention' (*Moore*, 1990: 46). The majority found that the public policy considerations of scientific research outweighed the need to extend Moore's property rights; he did not own his cells, nor did he have any claim on the cell-line.

The stakes of the invented human were much more apparent when Justice Arabian specifically took up the moral issue:

> [the] [p]laintiff has asked us to recognize and enforce a right to sell one's own body tissue for profit. He entreats us to regard the human vessel – the single most venerated and protected subject in any civilized society – as equal with the basest commercial commodity. He urges us to commingle the sacred with the profane. He asks much. ... The ramifications of recognizing and enforcing a property interest in body tissues are not known, but are greatly feared ... (Ibid.: 65–6)

The cultural anxieties of the propertization of the human being are clearly visible. It is an affront to human dignity to treat the human body and its parts as a form of property in the context of commodity capitalism. Justice Arabian sets the human body apart. It is not an object like others: it is sacred.

The dissenting opinions suggested that the outcome of the majority does not render human body parts immune from propertization, only from ownership by the person from whose body they are removed. Further, both dissenting judges were concerned with the unfair outcome which denied John Moore any share of the huge profits that would not have existed without his bodily contribution. Justice Mosk countered the commodification concern with the following:

> [f]irst, our society acknowledges a profound ethical imperative to respect the human body as the physical and temporal expression of the unique human persona. The most abhorrent form of such exploitation, of course, was the institution of slavery. Lesser forms, such as indentured servitude or even debtor's prison, have also disappeared. Yet their specter haunts

> the laboratories and boardrooms of today's biotechnological research-industrial complex. It arises wherever scientists or industrialists claim, as defendants claim here, the right to appropriate and exploit a patient's tissue for their sole economic benefit – the right, in other words, to freely mine or harvest valuable physical properties of the patient's body. (Ibid.: 128–9)

He suggested that unless the individual has legally endorsed and protected property rights in her or his own body and its products, then those economic and power inequities can continue (ibid.: 132). Therefore, Justice Mosk does not dispute the sacred status of the human body, but marks it as the expression of what is unique about the person. He feels, however, the only way to protect its sacrality is through the granting of property rights in it to the person it houses. Self-proprietorship is thus wielded to counter other-ownership.

John Moore's case has drawn a significant amount of scholarly commentary,[16] emerging as an archetypical instance not only of the inequitable relationship between big science and ordinary people, but also of the ethical dilemmas posed by contemplating the human body as patentable property. At its most basic level, the legal outcome of the case is that elements of the human body, altered in some way by scientists, can be patented by them, but the individuals offering up the 'raw material' do not own their own bodies as private property. The result necessarily commingles the sacred and the profane that Justice Arabian was so concerned to separate. The invented human is already property, and therefore is much more susceptible to commodification. Elements of the human body have already been invented; they are already property. Once propertized, the move to commodity is an easy one. The unnamed fears and the spectre of slavery haunting the laboratories and boardrooms of today's biotechnological research-industrial complex noted by both the majority and minority in *Moore* are, at their foundation, concerns with the invented human. But ultimately, this case was only about some bits of a human being that had already been removed. A small white laboratory mouse was about to push biopatenting to its next logical conclusion – a conclusion anticipated in the previous decisions in Canada and the United States – the patenting of a complete higher life form.

On 12 April 1988, two genetic researchers, Philip Leder of Harvard Medical School and geneticist Timothy Stewart of San Francisco, received a patent from the United States Patent and Trademark Office for the Oncomouse (as well as the process that produced it). A transgenic animal, the Oncomouse is a mouse that contains the genes of another type of animal that have been introduced into it at the embryonic stage. The gene in question is an oncogene, predisposing the animal to developing malignant cancerous tumours. As more reliably cancerous beings, Oncomice are obviously very useful to researchers testing both carcinogens and cancer-treating drugs.

The inventors assigned their patent to the President and Trustees of Harvard College, who then pursued various legal and commercial opportunities, including seeking patent protection in the European Union, Japan, and Canada, as well as licensing the patent for commercial development to E.I. Du Pont de Nemours (an original sponsor of the research). The Oncomouse has the global distinction of being the first 'higher' or 'complex' life form to be the subject/object of a patent. And the patent obtained by Leder and Stewart applied not only to the specific mice of their experiment, but to all their progeny containing the gene, as well as to any other transgenic mammal containing the oncogene. Oncomice entered the market at $50 per animal and *Fortune* magazine listed the Oncomouse on its '10 Hottest Products' list in its December 1988 issue.

Typically the patent offices of Western nations work in relative obscurity, outside the glare of public scrutiny. The decision to grant the patent for Oncomouse, however, triggered widespread protest in the United States, including demonstrations and lawsuits.[17] The application to the European Union (EU) patent office, alone, generated huge public outcry. In response to the concerns of its granting of the Oncomouse patent, the US Patent Office self-imposed a five-year moratorium on patents for living organisms; the EU adopted a mandatory ban for four years. In Europe, the application was originally denied, although the patent was finally granted to Harvard in its second attempt in 1992, despite ongoing public dissent. More than three hundred NGOs and green political parties then mounted an unsuccessful campaign to revoke the patent.

Leder and Stewart first applied for a Canadian patent for the Oncomouse on 21 June 1985 (and, as noted above, they subsequently assigned the application to the President and Trustees of Harvard College). The original patent examiner rejected a significant number of the claims, including that for the animal itself. Ongoing administrative appeals and reviews resulted in the commissioner for patents holding, a decade later, that no patent would be granted for a non-human mammal. What then ensued was a series of appeals through the Canadian federal courts, all the way to the Supreme Court in Canada, which, breaking ranks with the biotechnology policy of all other Western nations, held in 2002 that a higher life form could not be patented. In so doing, however, Canada's highest court was not only commenting on the proprietary status of a genetically engineered mouse, but on the proper relationship between humans and animals and between persons and things.

Our Animal Nature

Since even before Charles Darwin caused what Bruce Mazlish (1993) has insightfully called the 'second discontinuity,' namely the scientific and cultural affirmation of our necessarily mammalian heritage and the disruption of our sense of ourselves as unique and superior in the order of being, we have been concerned with our animal nature. What separates man from beast? From the activists of People for the Ethical Treatment of Animals (PETA), who suggest that very little does, or should, separate us from the animals that we generally consume and treat as chattel, to the ongoing debates in a number of American states about the teaching of creationism versus evolutionism in schools, the debate rages on. Are human beings located on a continuum with other animals? From evolutionary theory linking us with apes to genetic scientists informing us that we have 99 per cent of our genes in common with mice, science posits humans and animals as kin.

Both legislators and legal theorists have been concerned with the boundary between animal and human. And interestingly, disputes about this boundary most frequently play out as a question of the personality of animals. For example, in New Zealand in 1999, legislation was introduced which would have conferred the equivalent of human rights on great apes (*Nature*, 1999: 555). More recently in Canada, an amendment was made to the *Criminal Code* changing the cruelty to animals provisions; in general, the legislation moved away from an ideological frame of protecting animals from cruelty because of their property status, to protecting them from killing and harm because of their moral, although not legal, status (see discussion in DeCoste, 2003 and Létourneau, 2003). As part of this shift, animals are defined as non-human vertebrates, in what I suggest is a move of kinship.

Legal theory and moral philosophy, too, have been anxious to clarify the personhood status of animals (see Sapontzis, 1984). The proper moral boundary with animals has tended to reflect either an animal welfare position or an animal rights position. In the former, we have a moral obligation to treat animals well because it is a way that we act as moral beings. Therefore, this stance is still interested in ending cruelty to animals, but as a measure of our own moral worth. In the second, we owe duties to animals, not because of us, but because of their status as rights-holders. The logical end of that position is some form of personhood for animals (in articulating these differences, see Regan, 1996; DeCoste, 2003; Francione, 1995; Gruen, 1991).[18] Generally, the law has been very reticent to recognize personality in animals; as Gary L. Francione correctly points out, for most purposes, despite our surface-level 'moral schizophrenia,' we treat animals as property, not persons (2004). 'The legal resistance to the personification of animals strongly suggests that the term person is not in fact a slot that fits anyone or anything but rather a slot essentially designed for human beings because they are thought to possess a certain moral status' (Naffine, 2003: 356).

Following Donna Haraway (1997), we might specifically name this technology of personification kinship. She argues that '[k]inship is a technology for producing the material and semiotic effect of natural relationship, of shared kind' (Haraway, 1997: 53). Kinship naturalizes, it necessitates, it normalizes. Enabled by the technologies of molecular science and the charismatic power of DNA figured as a neutral code with the key to being,[19] shared DNA is a powerful building block of Haraway's notion of kinship. And our kinship with the cancerous little white laboratory mouse was a key stake in the Oncomouse saga.

As noted above, the commissioner for patents was the first Canadian authority to consider the patent application for the Oncomouse, releasing his decision on 4 August 1995. While he allowed the patent on the process of splicing the oncogene onto the plasmid and injecting it into the egg, he did not accept the patent on the animal itself. His latter decision turned on whether a higher life form could be considered an invention or, more specifically, a manufacture or composition of matter, within the *Patent Act*. In discussing the precedents, the commissioner distinguished cases about bacteria (such as *Chakrabarty* and *Abitibi*), because they dealt with lower life forms. The Oncomouse, as a mammal, was clearly a higher life form. The commissioner did not elaborate, however, on the distinction between these apparently self-evident and mutually exclusive orders of existence. This unexplicated categorical distinction between higher and lower life forms becomes a central discursive frame in all subsequent discussions, simultaneously denying kinship between higher and lower life forms, and yet producing relationships of kinship within those categories.

Harvard appealed the decision of the patent commissioner to the Federal Court. At the Trial Division (1998), the Court agreed that Oncomouse could not be patented. Writing for the majority, Justice Nadon addressed the kinship issue directly, posing the question, '[i]s it appropriate in determining whether something is patentable subject-matter to make distinctions between higher and lower life forms?' (*Harvard*, 1998: 531). Ultimately, he held that it was indeed appropriate to distinguish between higher and lower life forms, that Parliament was the proper body to determine the patentability of higher life forms, and that the Court would find higher life forms non-patentable. Justice Nadon suggested that higher life forms are, in part, defined by the incapacity of inventors to control them as an outcome:

> [a] mouse is a complex life form and thus there are many features of the mice which are not under the control of the inventors. They have created a method to inject the eggs with a myc gene but they have not invented the mouse. It is not necessary for the inventor to directly control all aspects of the natural process leading to the creation of the end product. ... However, the ultimate product which will result from the process is completely unknown and unknowable. (Ibid.: 526)

The court conceded that there might be a line one could draw specifying the percentage of characteristics that must be controlled before a life form could be an invention; however, that evidence was not presented. In refusing to separate the consideration of the myc gene from the rest of the mouse, the court said it is a 'very complex form of life' and that 'everything else about the mouse is present completely independently of human intervention' (ibid.: 527).

The higher life form as a holistic category is thus invested with legal authority. In that legal-semiotic gesture, humans are simultaneously located in the same category as mice, dogs, and cows and distinguished from unicellular and micro-organisms. While there are differences within each kinship category, the key distinction for patent law is between them. Membership in the category of higher life form relies upon complexity, unpredictability, and the inability of science to control us and our reproduction.

The implications of the distinction between higher and lower life forms, specifically for the invented human, were not lost upon subsequent players in the Oncomouse drama. Both the majority of the Federal Court of Appeal and the CBAC favoured the patentability of the Oncomouse. This forced them, however, to deal with the issue of the invented human in a way that the institutional players denying the patentability of all higher life forms were able to avoid. The issue having been raised, the Supreme Court of Canada found itself directly discussing the scientific possibility, and legality, of the invented human.

Harvard won at the Federal Court of Appeal in 2000. The majority decision found that the Oncomouse was a new, useful, and unobvious 'composition of matter,' and therefore, an invention under the *Patent Act*. Ultimately the court concluded that if the artificial oncogene sequence is a composition of matter (which was not in dispute between the parties), then all offspring with that gene would also be compositions of matter, regardless of how they were (re)produced. Justice Rothstein, for the majority, rejects the trial court's distinction between higher and lower life forms as unproductive, preferring a distinction between human and non-human animals.[20]

> It is not up to the Court, for policy reasons, to place limits on the scope of legislation not supported by the words. That is the role of the legislative branch of Government. In *Abitibi*, lower living organisms such as yeast, were found to be patentable. There may be policy reasons against the patentability of higher life forms (or lower life forms for that matter). However, such arguments are for Parliament and not the Courts. For the reasons already given, the words of the definition of 'invention' in the *Patent Act* do not exclude living organisms and the court may not impose such a limitation on policy grounds. (*Harvard*, 2000: para. 92)

The rejection of the higher and lower life form categories is thus an attempt to depoliticize what the majority sees as problematic categories. It is a clear rejection of our kinship with animals. The distinction the Federal Court of Appeal majority leaves us with however, is between human and non-human animals, a distinction that, while appealing to our humanist ego, is no less constructed.

While the issue of Oncomouse's patentability was crawling through the Canadian legal system, another body was considering the lab mouse and its human cousins. Created in 1999, CBAC is the body constituted by the government, as part of its broader Canadian Biotechnology Strategy, to advise it on all issues biotechnological. It is a panel of approximately twenty experts from outside government, represent-

ing the fields of law, the biotechnology private sector, nutrition, agriculture, medicine, molecular biology, and so on.[21] Aware of the slow
and inexorable march of the Oncomouse towards the Supreme Court
of Canada, CBAC opted to weigh in. In early 2000, it initiated a
research and consultation process to investigate the implications of
patenting higher life forms.

With a mandate far broader than that of the courts, and not constrained by the vagaries of patent law, CBAC's inquiry could cover
much more ground, squarely taking on the policy issues the courts
were reluctant to address. The Committee commissioned a number of
research reports, reviewed public opinion research, and organized
three 'stakeholder meetings' with non-governmental organizations,
scientists, and industry.[22] Based on these meetings, CBAC prepared a
consultation document entitled *Biotechnological Intellectual Property and
the Patenting of Higher Life Forms – Consultation Document 2001*. It then
conducted limited and targeted consultation with stakeholders, receiving virtually no public feedback. Based on this, CBAC prepared the
Interim Report on Biotechnology and Intellectual Property announcing its
primary conclusions in November 2001. Again, responses were
received from direct stakeholders and not from the public. The Committee's final report, *Patenting of Higher Life Forms*, was released in June
2002, in time to be within the purview of the resources reviewed by the
Supreme Court of Canada as it heard the Oncomouse appeal.

The recommendations of the final report included that human
bodies not be patentable in any stage of development, but that all non-
human life forms be patentable. This patentability was subject only to
limited provisions to protect special interests, including farmers, innocent bystanders, and researchers (CBAC, 2002: 6). Higher life forms
were defined as plants, seeds, and non-human life forms, other than
single-celled organisms (ibid.). Thus, CBAC was careful to preserve
the singularity of the human being, its place at the pinnacle of the food
chain.

Of course, the big issue on everyone's mind throughout this process
was not only whether mice could be patented, but whether humans
could be. CBAC requested advice on the issue from its experts. Lawyer
Barbara von Tigerstrom was commissioned to prepare an analysis of
the human rights issues related to the patenting of human biological
materials. She realized the social science fictional implications of her
task, asserting both the significance and utility of considering the
invented human. 'The question, then, is whether and to what extent

patent rights in a human being (or human material) would infringe the *Charter*. While this may seem a somewhat speculative question, in fact its resolution would be both important and useful' (von Tigerstrom, 2001a: 24; 2001b: 8). She recognizes, correctly, that if there are constitutional barriers to patenting human beings, how one defines the human being becomes an issue (2001a: 26). For example, a human embryo or foetus is not a person at law in Canada; therefore, a ban on patenting humans would have to include embryos to be effective. Further along the continuum of personhood, blurring species security, she asks: 'if an animal is part human and part non-human, at what point is it considered a human being and entitled to legal protection as such?' (von Tigerstrom, 2001a: 26). Ultimately, the law, as it stands, offers little solace, she concluded, in drawing the boundary between human and animal life, particularly in an era where transgenics, hybrids, and chimeras are all scientific reality.[23]

In order to contain the potential cultural anxiety posed by the invented human, CBAC was forced to be very precise in its language. The *Interim Report* had contained the terminology of 'human being' in relation to patenting, whereas in the final report, the Committee was careful to substitute 'human bodies.' This was because '[a] human being is a metaphysical concept, not a biological one. The substitution of the word "body" for "being" eliminates this awkwardness' (CBAC, 2002: 9). The plural of human bodies is also used very deliberately.

[B]y using the plural, emphasis is placed on the whole human body and not on its parts (for eg. artificially created human organs). Thus, the phrase 'human bodies at any stage of development' is more likely to be read narrowly – as we intend. It is important not to discourage research on stem cells and the creation of artificial organs. (CBAC, 2002: 9)

Thus the use of human bodies demystifies and divides; there is no desire on CBAC's part to evoke the spectre of the whole, metaphysical human being. So while acknowledging the scientific fact that human beings are animals, the Committee is interested in severing humans from their other higher life form kin, without articulating the basis for such a distinction. The singularity of the human is simultaneously undermined and reasserted in and through relations of kinship.

Meanwhile, everyone waited to see what the Supreme Court of Canada would do with the perplexing entity of the higher life form. The split decision was released on 5 December 2002 and the five judges in the majority held that upon a straightforward interpretation of the legislation, Parliament did not intend higher life forms to be patentable. 'Given the unique concerns associated with the grant of a monopoly right over higher life forms, it is my view that Parliament would not likely choose the *Patent Act* as it currently exists as the appropriate vehicle to protect the rights of inventors of this type of subject matter' (*Harvard*, 2002: para. 120). The four dissenting judges disagreed, favouring a more technical approach. Justice Binnie suggested, 'the legal issue is a narrow one and does not provide a proper platform on which to engage in a debate over animal rights, religion, or the arrogance of the human race' (ibid.: para. 1).

The social science fictional elements of its task were not lost on the court. The minority recognized that 'the subtext of much of the argument for the appellant Commissioner and his supporters invokes Dolly the cloned sheep and the potential of eugenics and "designer" human beings' (ibid.: para. 66). And we see the invented human hover as a ghost through both majority and minority opinions.

The majority maintained the broad categories of higher and lower life forms. Drawing on familiar elements such as a lower life form's capacity to be produced *en masse*, its uniform properties and characteristics, the analogy is more easily made between lower life forms and compositions of matter (ibid.: para. 202). But the majority judgment went further than other social actors had in defining the higher life form: '[i]n particular, the capacity to display emotion and complexity of reaction and to direct behaviour in a manner that is not predictable as stimulus and response is unique to animal forms of life' (ibid.: para. 204). It anchors the recognition of this distinction in common sense, recognizing the normalizing effects of kinship:

> [t]he distinction between lower and higher life forms, though not explicit in the Act, is nonetheless defensible on the basis of common sense differences between the two. Perhaps more importantly, there appears to be a consensus that human life is not patentable; yet this distinction is also not explicit in the Act. If the line between lower and higher life forms is indefensible and arbitrary, so too is the line between human beings and other higher life forms. (Ibid.: para. 199)

The minority, on the other hand, rejects the kinship of animals and humans. Justice Binnie noted for his colleagues that the commissioner, on appeal, did not offer any definition of higher and lower life forms, adding that 'the degree of complexity is not a criterion in the Act or in the jurisprudence in determining patentability' (ibid.: paras. 46–8). He went on: '[t]he various distinctions attempted to be made between "patentable" lower life composition of matter and *"unpatentable"* higher life composition of matter, shows [*sic*], I think, the arbitrariness of the commissioner's approach' (ibid.: para. 52). Further, Justice Binnie rejected the appeal to common sense of the majority: '[w]ith respect, there seems to be as many versions of "common sense" as there are commentators' (ibid.: para. 52).

However, having rejected the distinction between higher and lower life forms, and having accepted the patentability of the higher life form, the minority judges must then deal with the prospect of the invented human.

> The major concern is that human beings constitute a line that cannot be crossed. The CBAC agrees. But others argue that patenting *any* form of life puts us on a slippery slope. Today the oncomouse; tomorrow Frankenstein's creature. I do not agree. There is a qualitative divide between rodents and human beings. The broadest claim here specifically excepts humans from the scope of transgenic mammals. Moreover, for the reasons already expressed, I do not believe that the issue of patentability of a human being even arises under the *Patent Act*. (Ibid.: para. 102)

Resorting to what sounds like a common-sensical speciesism, the minority is left to argue the 'qualitative divide' between rodents and human beings to deny kinship, and yet does not articulate the qualities that would constitute that divide.

The ultimate legal result is that the Supreme Court decision endorses making the distinction between higher and lower life forms. As a result, one is either a higher or lower life form with the resulting struggle to inhabit one or other of those mutually exclusive, and apparently self-evident, categories. Very different consequences result from one's categorical presence – lower life forms can be rendered property, unproblematically; higher life forms cannot. Yet both majority and minority resort to the clean lines of demarcation that mutually exclusive categories create, whether these be higher and lower life forms, human and animal, or nature and artifact. However, as Haraway suggests, '[i]t will not help – emotionally, intellectually, morally or politically – to appeal to nature and the pure' (1997: 62). Biotechnological practices complicate acts of absolute categorization.

The majority Court, itself, recognized what it calls the 'increasingly blurred line between human beings and other higher life forms' when it speculates on xenotransplantation. 'The pig receives human genes. The human receives pig organs. Where does the pig end and the human begin? How much DNA does it take before one becomes the other? The answer to these questions once ridiculous and offensive, may now just be a matter of degree' (*Harvard*, 2002: para. 180). The boundaries of personal propriety are shifting. In its refusal to collapse the categories of higher and lower life forms into human and non-human, or to pick a different measure, the Supreme Court majority renders humans kin to other mammals and multicellular, complex organisms. Singular human status is rejected for a model which does not deny the animal in the human.

In maintaining the kinship relation, the majority of the Supreme Court of Canada refuses to quell the anxiety that what we do to animals can be done to us. This is the anxiety at the heart of Roger Spottiswoode's science fiction thriller, *The 6th Day* (2000), where pro-testors at the opening of a replacement organ clinic carry signs shout-ing, 'Today Pets. Tomorrow People.' Set in a future that is 'sooner than you think,' the film opens with a slow list of cloning events, some of which, like Dolly, are real, and which establish the background to the '6th day laws.' Animal cloning technology has been perfected in this world, but protests as a result of experiments with human cloning have led to the laws prohibiting human cloning.

Adam Gibson, played by Arnold Schwarzenegger, is an old-school guy when it comes to technology. He is a pilot and co-owner of a company that flies jet-setters and adventurers to remote settings for extreme sporting. When the family dog, Oliver, becomes suddenly ill and has to be put to sleep, Adam's wife, Natalie (Wendy Crewson), convinces Adam to go to RePet, a pet cloning company, to have Oliver cloned, in order to spare their daughter Clara the pain of her beloved pet's death. Little does Adam know, of course, that he, himself, has been cloned by the same company that owns RePet in an elaborate scheme to disguise the fact that the corporate mogul at the head of the company is actually a clone.

Adam is highly resistant to the notion of a RePet, saying to his friend Hank, played by Michael Rapaport, 'I'm not going to have some freak of science sleep in my daughter's bed.' He wants to return to the purity of nature, and reiterates the 'natural process of life. ... You're born, you live and you die.' His friend reassures him, noting that, 'for today's kids,' the process is totally 'normal.' In this world where pet cloning is normal, and hence normalized, there is, however, still ongoing dissent. We see protestors picketing outside of RePet's offices in the local shopping mall.

The risks of animal cloning are contained expressly within RePet's promotional material, as well as in the sales pitch that Adam receives. RePet's slogans include: 'Cloning is love' and 'Where love means *no* surprises.' The slick salesman works hard to overcome Adam's initial abhorrence of animal cloning. In response to Adam's concern, 'I have a problem with the whole idea. I mean suppose the clones have no souls, or they're dangerous,' the salesman replies, '[c]loned pets are every bit as safe as real pets. Plus, they're insured.' He later offers to make the dog smaller and with softer teeth (i.e., safer), bragging that the company can even colour-coordinate it to match the decorating scheme in Adam and Natalie's house. Tellingly though, a significant part of Adam's concern stems not from the cloning of animals *per se*, but from the prospects of human cloning it seemingly implies. The salesman reassures him that humans cannot be cloned because the human brain is too complicated for the technology; it is only proven for pets. Thus the line that separates us from animals appeals to our vanity.

This theme of the slippery slope between human and animal is echoed later in the film when, at the launch of the organ replacement clinic, the genetic scientist who has perfected human cloning technology, Dr Weir, is asked by an aggressive journalist whether the cloning of animals will inevitably lead to the cloning of human beings. Disingenuously, Dr Weir demurs, suggesting that not only is it illegal, but the technology is years away. He describes the human cloning experiments in the previous decade as 'bizarre' (although viewers never learn how). He ominously reminds the assembled crowd of donors and journalists of the monster: '[i]f you recall, the Supreme Court ordered the clone destroyed and I think that under the conditions, it was the humane thing to do.' Of course the viewer already knows that human cloning has been perfected, and so the slippery slope between animal and human cloning about which the journalists and protestors are so concerned is realized. While the idea of the RePet – the animal clone – may have been monstrous to the 'behind-the-times' Adam, the human clone is represented to viewers throughout as monstrous, in terms of corporate greed, violence, and, in the film's climax, physicality, when an only partially physically mature clone of corporate mogul Drucker battles with Adam's clone for his/its immortality.

The risk of the monster is only a risk, however, as Adam's clone is redeemed through his humanity. At an early point in the film, Adam considers shooting his clone. When Hank suggests that to do so could be like suicide, Adam replies, '[b]ut he's not me. He's not even human.' However, when the clone, himself, poses the metaphysical question in the dénouement of the film, musing, '[y]ou know I keep wondering am I human ... do I have a soul?' Adam reassures him first with science, 'Well your DNA scan came back normal didn't it?' and then with a more humanist consolation that in being willing to die for 'his' family, he is surely human.

The 6th Day, like the subtext of the Oncomouse's legal-bureaucratic journey, is premised upon the social fears born from Dolly – that once animal clones are scientifically possible, human clones are inevitably on the horizon. Dolly and the RePets are the thin edge of the wedge. CBAC, the majority of the Supreme Court of Canada, and Spottis-woode's film imply both the instability and perhaps even impotence of legislative and/or legal limits on scientific experimentation backed by big money. Justice Mosk's worst fears in the John Moore case are realized in *The 6th Day*: the spectre of slavery 'haunt[ing] the laboratories and boardrooms of today's biotechnological research-industrial complex' (*Moore*, 1990: 128).

The film also manifests the troublesome dilemma most apparent in the Moore case and in the division between the majority and minority of the Supreme Court of Canada: what is the basis for protecting the non-inventedness of the human being? Is it metaphysics? Ethics? Religion? Science? Law? In the Supreme Court of Canada decision, as in *The 6th Day*, we are left with an unsatisfying mixture of rationales. Canada's highest court ends up appealing to the common sense of the Adam Gibson everyman. Echoing Gramscian concerns about common sense, a changed membership in the court and a changed object – a genetically modified canola plant – combined to produce a shift in the Court's common sense. In *Monsanto* v. *Schmeiser* (2004), the Supreme Court of Canada accepted a *de facto* patent in a complete, higher life form, albeit a less warm and furry one.

Finally, the Oncomouse tale, like the film, while recuperating the humanist position, does so in both instances by recognizing a kinship relation with animals. Yet most significantly, the tensions and difficulties with the categorical definition of humans and animals are troubled. What does it mean to be a human being? What are our essential characteristics? These questions can no longer be answered through resort to our genetic differences from animals. Biotechnology has irreparably broken down the purity upon which those categorical distinctions rested. We are kin to animals, whether we like it or not.

Possessive Individualism: Persons and/as Property

In *The 6th Day*, a frustrated Drucker has to repeatedly clone his bumbling henchmen because Adam keeps killing them. Exasperated, he shouts, '[y]ou know, it costs me $1.2 million each time I clone you people. Try to be worth the money.' In a case of fact imitating fiction, British poet Donna Maclean filed an application for a patent on herself in 2000, citing her self as original, the product of much inventive effort, and very useful. While provocative, Maclean's patent application is not nonsensical. It is no longer unimaginable to think of the person as property. As noted previously, genetic bits of the person have already been 'propertized' (Novas and Rose, 2000), namely patented, in Canada and around the world, including proteins, cell-lines, genes, and hybridomas. Further, however, the spectre of the commodified, propertized human being posed by the judges in the John Moore case has also been realized, at least as social science fiction. This is because the Oncomouse case, in addition to requiring the patent commissioner and the courts to consider the property status of the mouse, also forced consideration of the patentability of all complete higher life forms, including the human. And through these discussions, a clearer picture of the stakes of the invented human is visible.[24] In particular, the second boundary of personal propriety, that between person and property, is revealed to be both contingent and unstable.

That second boundary is very dear to the law, as Davies and Naffine (2001) recognize. 'Fundamental to our law is a distinction between subjects, who are individual entities holding rights and duties, and objects, which are external to the person, incapable of having rights, and defined by the fact that they are owned, controlled or dominated by legal subjects' (24). This strict subject-object relation also operates at the level of general cultural knowledge. If you asked an individual on the street if one person can own another person, the answer would almost certainly be a resounding 'no.' One person owning another sounds like slavery, and as we saw in the *Moore* case, that ghost haunts any discussion of the human being as property.

Emmanuel Kant is often cited as the moral and philosophical authority for the mutual exclusion of persons and property:

> a person cannot be a property and so cannot be a thing which can be
> owned, for it is impossible to be a person and a thing, the proprietor and
> the property; ... to say that he is would be self-contradictory; for in so far
> as he is a person, he is a Subject in whom the ownership of things can be
> vested, and if he were his own property, he would be a thing over which
> he could have ownership. (Kant, 1930: 165)

John Locke is taken as a second dominant Western authority for the non-property status of the human being. 'Though the Earth, and all inferior Creatures be common to all Men, yet every Man has a *Property* in his own *Person*. This no Body has any Right to but himself. The *Labour* of his Body, and the *Work* of his Hands, we may say, are properly his' (Locke, 1980: 19). Yet in Locke's claim that no one else has any right to our person but ourselves, we see the emergence of a fundamental tension in the Western encounter between persons and property.

Legal personality is intended to insulate the individual from the prospect of being reduced to a thing that could be owned by another; in other words, legal personality is a fundamental claim to both individuality and autonomy. Upon closer reflection, however, Locke is positing self-ownership to counter that threat and produce the boundaries of the individual in liberal thought. Self-ownership is substituted for, and morally precludes, other-ownership. This notion of self-proprietorship and its significant history within Western liberal political and legal thought was recognized by C.B. Macpherson in 1962, and he named it 'possessive individualism.' In a detailed analysis of liberal thought from Hobbes to Locke, he argues,

> ... since the freedom, and therefore the humanity, of the individual
> depend on his freedom to enter into self-interested relations with other
> individuals, and since his ability to enter into such relations depends on
> his having exclusive control of (rights in) his own person and capacities,
> and since proprietorship is the generalized form of such exclusive
> control, the individual is essentially the proprietor of his own person and
> capacities. (Macpherson, 1974: 263)

Thus, our contractual relations, he suggests, are the fundamental means of social exchange and hence political culture.[25] We are indebted to no other individuals, nor to society, for our identity; our capacity as self-owner precedes our social relations with others, and in fact is necessary to our freedom as citizens. 'The individual in a possessive market society *is* human in his capacity as proprietor of his person' (ibid.: 271).[26]

The possessive individual both grounds our liberal conception of the person and is, not coincidentally, one of the central rationales for recognizing intellectual property. Locke's conceptualization of persons as self-proprietors anchors his labour theory of value. The labour theory of value provides that because we own our selves, in acting on the world around us, we transform those raw materials into our property. He places two caveats on this potential for rampant appropriation. First, the spoilage proviso, which holds that one may take only as much as one needs so that nothing is wasted. The second proviso requires that we leave enough for future generations. The labour theory of value is at the heart of Western conceptualizations of intellectual property. The requirement for originality in copyright, for example, as the paradigmatic type of intellectual property, is seen as a requirement of creative labour on the part of the author. The ghost of the Romantic author walks heavily through intellectual property law, where creative labour takes on legitimacy and value through its intimate connection to the originating and unique author (see Jaszi, 1991; Woodmansee and Jaszi, 1994). Keith Aoki (1993) has argued effectively that this same notion of the author is present in the figure of the inventor within patent law. Therefore, it is not surprising that it is through the vehicle of patent law that the property status of the person arises – where science, the human body, and Locke meet. Biopatenting, as a result, has thus been a debate that has been 'strongly influenced by a language of self-possession' (Davies and Naffine, 2001: 141).

The Oncomouse case subjected this possessive individual to legal scrutiny in and through the figure of the invented human, the always troubled kin of the cancerous rodent. At both the level of the Patent Office and the Federal Court, Trial Division, the issue of the invented human is latent. Those actors focus only on the mouse and its complicated imbrication in the laws of nature and of man. It is not until the Federal Court of Appeal decision that the potential implications for the patentability, or ownership, of the human being are recognized expressly. This is because, if the majority wants to find all higher life forms patentable, and few would dispute the fact that human beings are at least higher life forms, then the Federal Court of Appeal must contain the boundary threat of the invented human. Indeed, the majority recognizes the concerns that the Oncomouse case raises for the applicability of the *Patent Act* to human beings. The court asks: Does the language of living organisms include human beings? Justice Rothstein emphatically states:

> [t]he answer is clearly that the *Patent Act* cannot be extended to cover human beings. Patenting is a form of ownership of property. Ownership concepts cannot be extended to human beings. There are undoubtedly other bases for so concluding, but one is surely section 7 of the *Charter of Rights and Freedoms* which protects liberty. There is, therefore, no concern by including non-human mammals under the definition of 'invention' in the *Patent Act*, that there is any implication that a human being would be patentable in the way the oncomouse is. (*Harvard*, 2000: para. 127)[27]

CBAC, again with its wider mandate, tackles the invented human's property status in more detail. Commissioned legal expert von Tigerstrom, while noting at the outset of her human rights analysis that human beings are 'almost certainly not patentable' (2001a: 5), includes them in her discussion with human embryos, tissues, organs, cell-lines, proteins, and other genetic material. She recognizes that there is no specific statutory or judicial prohibition against patenting humans or human body elements (2001a: 10). This is unlike the United States, where the Patent and Trademark Office has taken the position that it will not accept a claim directed to, or containing within its scope, a human being because of the Thirteenth Amendment to the American Constitution – the prohibition against slavery, which forbids property rights in human beings.[28]

Von Tigerstrom moves firmly into the realm of the speculative, inquiring how the negative patent rights to prohibit someone making, using, or selling the patented object would play out in relation to a human being. She contemplates the science fictional scenarios of someone attempting to prevent a person from reproducing because they contain a patented gene, whether a patent holder could stop someone going about their daily activities because they were using a patented cell-line, or whether a subject could be compelled to participate in research or testing as a result of carrying a patented protein. Finally, she contemplates the right to prohibit sale:

> [s]ince a human being *per se* cannot be owned, the exclusive right to sell the invention would simply have no application in the case of a patent on a human being; the patent holder could not legally sell the invention, nor

could anyone else. Would the exclusive right to sell other patented material offend any constitutional rights? Sale of tissue and of any body or body parts is prohibited by legislation in Canada. However, this does not apply to regenerative tissue such as blood or skin, nor does it apply to human gametes. (2001b: 19–20)

She ends by suggesting that while the right to prevent the making or use of an invented human might pose some human rights issues, the legal basis prohibiting sales of certain kinds of patented body parts is uncertain at best. Thus, von Tigerstrom is attempting to offer legal solace with a constitutional foundation for the non-patentability of a human being, with mixed results.

CBAC, in its final report, *Patenting Higher Life Forms*, hastens to suggest that its intention is not to render human beings patentable. It wants to retreat into law, rather than religion or ethics, for this claim (having suggested that the latter are both irrelevant to patent law). However, the legal basis in Canada for the non-patentability of the human being or an entire human body, as evidenced by von Tigerstrom's background report, is exposed as unclear. In a footnote, the Committee notes, '[e]ven though human beings are animals, most lawyers maintain that a whole human being is not patentable, or else that patents over whole humans would not be enforceable' (CBAC, 2002: 6). Subsequently the Committee notes, '[i]t is generally believed unlikely that a holder of a patent over a human DNA sequence or cells (including stem cells) would be able to exercise control over a human body containing that sequence or cell. Nevertheless, the law has never explicitly addressed the issue' (CBAC, 2002: 8). The basis for this surmise is the principle of respect for human dignity. 'Even if the act of granting a patent on an invented human were not in itself a violation of basic human rights, exercising the patent's exclusive right to make, use or sell an invented human would almost certainly violate the *Canadian Charter of Rights and Freedoms* and the *Canadian Human Rights Act*' (CBAC, 2002: 8).

Whether right or wrong in law, CBAC's claims denying the possibility of the invented human are interesting for a variety of reasons. They seek to locate the prohibition against the patenting of a human being in positive rather than natural law or ethics; they acknowledge the possibility of an 'invented human'; and they grant that humans are animals. They frame the problem more with the patenting of the human than with his/her/its invention in the first place. They highlight the unstable basis of the legal authority against patenting human beings in Canada. And they locate the primary objection in human dignity, a basis whose effectivity has been challenged by a number of scholars (e.g., Pottage, 1998; Mitchell, 2004).

The prospect of the invented human being and its necessary status as property finally comes to a head in the clash between the majority and minority decisions at the Supreme Court of Canada. The minority, like Justice Rothstein of the Federal Court of Appeal, relied on anti-slavery prohibitions and the *Charter* to assert the mutual exclusion of persons and property as self-evident. The issue is not at all complicated:

> [i]t has been established for over 200 years that people cannot, at common law, own people. ... The issue of whether a human being is a 'composition of matter' does not, therefore, arise under the *Patent Act*. If further reinforcement is required, ss. 7 and 15 of the *Canadian Charter of Rights and Freedoms* would clearly prohibit an individual from being reduced to a chattel of another individual. (*Harvard*, 2000: para. 54)

Further, the minority rejected the claims that biopatents, by their very nature, objectify and commodify life forms (ibid.: para. 101).

The majority disagreed, framing the issue in terms that echo the Moore decision, although in less extreme form:

> the potential for commodification of human life arises out of the fact that the granting of a patent is, in effect, a declaration that an invention based on living matter has the potential to be commercialized. The commodification of human beings is not only intrinsically undesireable; it may also engender a number of troubling consequences. Many of the consequentialist concerns (i.e. the creation of 'designer human beings' or features) are directed at genetic engineering in general and not at patenting *per se*, and are perhaps better dealt with outside the confines of the *Patent Act*. ... Nonetheless, there remains a concern that allowing patents on the human body will lead to human life being reconceptualized as genetic information. A related concern is the potential for objectification. (Ibid.: para. 176)

Justice Bastarache disputed the effectivity of the *Charter* as the easy solution to the dilemma of property:

> [i]n my view, this general response to concerns over the implications for human beings of patenting life forms is an oversimplification. ... Should

> this Court determine that higher life forms are within the scope of s. 2,
> this must necessarily include human beings. There is no defensible basis
> within the definition of 'invention' itself to conclude that a chimpanzee is
> a 'composition of matter' while a human being is not. (Ibid.: para. 178)

Therefore, the majority judges are not prepared to propertize the higher life form at all, because it would necessarily be an objectification and commodification of the human being.

The invented human, given its already determined property status, is obviously a very troubling prospect for the courts and policy makers. It troubles a fundamental dualism and provokes some very deep-seated Western anxieties. The Supreme Court majority capitalizes on those worries to assert the non-property status of all higher life forms. And yet, while it is comforting in its absolutism, we are surrounded by the tensions in that position, unacknowledged in the judgment. Much of the human being has already been propertized and animals are decidedly not persons in our society. On the other hand, the minority at the Supreme Court, the majority at the Federal Court of Appeal, and CBAC are more aggressive in their assertion of the person-property boundary. However, their retreat to positive law for the protection of that boundary in Canada, at least, seems problematic. Regardless of their different strategies, the Canadian state seems adamant to defend the person-property boundary of propriety. Yet the invented human is not going away as a social problem.

The invented human's necessary challenge to the property-person boundary of propriety is at the centre of a recent stylish science fiction thriller, *The Island* (2005), whose resolution in triumphant humanism is as dissatisfying as the Supreme Court of Canada's answer. Lincoln Six Echo, played by Ewan McGregor, and Jordan Two Delta, played by Scarlett Johansson, are two beautiful young clones that have been produced in the artificially pristine environment of The Institute. They exist solely to provide replacement organs and tissues for rich clients living in 2019. As in *The 6th Day*, human cloning has been outlawed, and so The Institute, run by Dr Merrick (Sean Bean), is forced to both lie to clients and operate in an abandoned military installation deep below the earth's surface. Funded to a large degree by the Department of Defence, The Institute reassures its customers that the organs they are purchasing are grown in non-sentient organic frames.

The reality is quite different. The clone inhabitants of The Institute are bred for docility and physical health in a huge sterile complex where science and psychology control their every move. The clones are indoctrinated with the myth of a cataclysmic 'contamination' of the outside world and the eternal hope that they will be selected in the weekly 'Lottery' to go to 'The Island,' an Eden-like retreat which is the only remaining pathogen-free zone on earth. The clones are educated to the level of a fifteen-year-old child and bred to sexual immaturity. Lincoln begins to disrupt the idyllic balance when he begins to manifest both memories of his original genetic donor and the human capacity for curiosity.

A language of objectification is replete in the narrative. Clones are referred to as 'insurance policies' and as 'products,' whereas clients are 'sponsors.' The birth of the adult clones from an eerily disembodied amniotic sac receiving its nutrients through a giant technological umbilical cable is described as 'product extraction.' Upon birth, all products are tattooed and tagged, their names reflecting their production generation. When Lincoln follows a butterfly up a ventilation shaft into the organ extraction wing of the complex, he learns the horrifying truth that there is no Island, and those selected for it are butchered for body parts. Guards chasing him are exhorted not to 'damage' him. Towards the end of the film, when Lincoln's line of product is destroyed because it has developed the flaw of curiosity, the resulting genocide is described as a 'recall,' and more than $200 million of product is disposed of. This language of objectification clashes with the representation of the clones as experiencing everyday hopes, annoyances, pubescent desire, curiosity, and eventually a strong will to self-determination and survival.

Dr Merrick's sales pitch to potential clients is eerie, given the viewers' knowledge that the clones are sentient beings:

> [w]elcome to the next generation of science: the agnate – an organic frame engineered directly into adulthood to match the client's age. You're looking at Stage 1 in its development. Within twelve months it will be harvest ready, providing a carrier for your baby, second set of lungs, fresh skin, all genetically indistinguishable from your own. And, in compliance with the eugenics laws of 2015, all our agnates are maintained in a persistent vegetative state. They never achieve consciousness. They never think or suffer, feel pain, joy, love, hate. It's a product, ladies and gentlemen. In every way that matters, not human.

The truth is revealed to the audience that after several years of experimentation, Merrick and his colleagues realized that without consciousness, human experience, emotion, and life, the organs failed. Dr Merrick is thus attempting to allay any concern on the part of customers that what is being produced is a human being. He dehumanizes the invented human, as do the courts and CBAC in the Oncomouse case, through its divisibility, its mechanical reproduction, the control of the scientist, and its lack of exhibition of the cognitive functions typically associated with higher life forms and humans. Again, the law is referenced, but is revealed to be an ineffective brake on the heady coupling of science, capital, and in this instance, the military.

Unlike the courts, the fictional text can explore how the clone feels to be a clone, and more significantly, to be both person and property. The property status of Jordan and Lincoln becomes poignant when, upon escaping the Institute, they meet up with the sympathetic technician McCord (Steve Buscemi) in his house.

L6E & J2D: What are we?
McCord: Ah man, why do I have to be the guy that tells the kids there's no Santa Claus? Okay, look, you're uh, uh, well, you're not like me. Um, I mean, you're not, uh, human. I mean, you're human, but you're just not real. Uh, you're not like a real person. Like me. You're clones. You're copies of people out here in the world.
J2D: What?
L6E: Clones?
McCord: Some hag trophy wife needs new skin for a facelift or one of 'em gets sick and they need a new part, they take it from you.

When Lincoln and Jordan counter their non-person status with evidence of memories from their childhood, McCord advises them these memories are imprints only – computer programs to give them a basis for their identity.

When Jordan asks why no one cares that the clones are killed and that they are raised for parts, McCord tells her that their sponsors do not know. He defines the sponsors as 'the people that had you made. They, like, own you.' Still horrified, Jordan queries why Merrick does not want the owners to know that the clones are alive. McCord answers tersely, '[j]ust because people wanna eat the burger, doesn't mean they want to meet the cow. ... You're like the replacement engines on their Bentley. They're not going to care. They don't care.'

Interestingly, *The Island* makes a distinction between human beings and persons, more expressly than does *The 6th Day* or most of the judges in the Oncomouse saga. The personhood status of the cloned human comes up expressly only once in *The 6th Day* when Adam and a repentant Dr Weir discuss the social implications if Drucker, as clone, came out in public. Weir advises, '[a] clone has no rights. A clone can't own anything. Drucker would lose all of this. He would lose everything, because he would be legally dead.' So, while the film may redeem the humanity of the clones, the law does not recognize them as persons. In *The Island*, the human being status of the clones is never questioned; they are deliberately raised as human beings in order to ensure the sustainability of their organs. However, as property, the clones cannot be persons. They cannot be in the same world as the original; they are mere copies. As a result, chaos ensues when they escape the confines of The Institute and begin to act as agents in the real world, outside of the control of the scientists – in the same social space as their originals.

What then ensues is a fairly traditional chase plot where Lincoln's owner and a private security team hired by Merrick chase the two clones through the Los Angeles of 2019, while the clones frantically try to adapt to their new environment and stay alive. As in *The 6th Day*, the abiding humanity of the clones cannot be curtailed by science or their status as property. They enact the unruliness of the very notion of the invented human. Arguably for the Supreme Court in the Oncomouse case, the humanity of the invented human – the oxymoron of the person as property – causes it to leak from any easy categorization as property. Yet persons as property is not as unthinkable as it became in the Abolition era. The invented human, always simultaneously the patentable human, has been spoken by science, courts, and policy advisors, not only by popular culture. As a social science fiction, the invented human works as the horizon point of our anxieties about the increasing uncertainty of that second boundary, between persons and property.

In the finale of *The Island*, Lincoln Six Echo replaces his sponsor, who is killed in error by the security team, and no one can tell the difference. As he walks away a security team member says to him, 'You've been witness to certain trade secrets.' Lincoln replies: '[y]ou mean that they manufacture human beings that walk, talk and feel. That kind of secret? … Who'd believe it?' Indeed, who would believe a story about an invented human?

Persons and Propriety

The Canadian legal encounter of Oncomouse is just such a story. While it is, of course, a story about the patent status of a line of transgenic mammals doomed to die hideous deaths ravaged by malignant cancerous tumours, it is also a story of the invented human. In it, the Canadian federal courts and CBAC are doing a future history. They are grappling with the social and institutional effects of an as yet imaginary figure, but a very powerful figure for all of its unreal status. The fictive figure of the invented human enables the exploration of the cultural anxieties of a particular social-scientific moment. We live in a moment where animals can be cloned, but where the technology to do so is by no means unproblematic. We live in a moment where genetic science asserts our intimate similarity to animals through our shared 'code of life.' We live in a world where various parts of the human body are for sale on e-Bay. We live in a moment where, in the absence of strong political leadership, law seems like a hollow check on global technoscience, religion a naïve one.

In this moment, our cultural anxieties run high. Nothing less than our place in the order of things is at stake. The invented human is the social science fiction through which these fears play out and various boundary maintenance strategies are tested. The invented human prefigures the instability of a key set of modernist dualisms: nature and culture; human and animal; person and property; natural and artificial. These dualisms manifest, I suggest, in socio-legal controversy around the two normative personal boundaries: that between persons and animals and that between persons and property. Ultimately in the popular culture treatments of the invented human we see a nostalgic retreat into humanism. Human nature is entrusted to re-establish the clarity of the boundaries under assault from mad science. The Supreme Court of Canada in the Oncomouse case, on the other hand, leaves us with less solace when it reminds us that the boundary between human and nonhuman is no less arbitrary, no less constructed, than that between higher and lower life forms. It places us in kinship with animals. And yet, do we want to then face up to the implications of that familial move? The definition of the human, person, or higher life form through resort to categories, relying as they do upon the security of the boundaries between them, is no longer credible. The social science fiction of the invented human highlights the material and symbolic impossibility of defining the person through an unproblematized notion of what is human, or animal.

The second boundary – between persons and property – is equally under assault, not least because we are kin to animals. In fact, some have gone so far as to argue, post *Moore*, that it is strategically useful to embrace possessive individualism; our property in our selves, and more specifically, our bodies, then works as an assertion of sovereignty (Davies and Naffine, 2001: 183). Genetic science is fundamentally a fragmenting practice, fragmenting first our bodies, and with patent law's cooperation, the legal person. In this way, arguably, the liberal, individualist person is merely living up to the person-property tensions long embedded within it.

Legal scholar John Robertson (1998), in considering the legal and ethical stakes of cloning, suggests that popular narratives and critics of cloning alike 'overlook the extent to which the cloned child is not the property or slave of the initiator, but is a person in her own right with all the rights and duties of other persons' (1384 and 1415).[29] Such confidence. In ignoring the imbrication of cloning within the structures of patent law, Robertson cannot see the clone as an invented human. And the invented human is much more persona than person. He/she/it reveals the boundaries of personal propriety as normative, prescribing everything from with whom or what we should have sexual relations to our godliness. As persona, the invented human, in fact and fiction, reveals the interlinked nature of the boundaries of propriety, the comfort we derive from the reassertion of these boundaries at a time of ontological insecurity, and our ongoing sense of social, biological, and moral superiority. However, with the likely futility of the retreat into hard distinctions between nature and culture, the persona of the invented human opens up possibilities. Possibilities for embracing rather than fearing our kinship with animals, and then facing the implications of that relation; possibilities for figuring our selves as simultaneously subject and object. It requires us to contemplate the possibility that the copy may surpass the original.

5 Machine Intelligence:
Computers as Posthuman Persons

The players met, on the great, timeless board of space. The glittering dots that were the pieces swam in their separate patterns. In that configuration at the beginning, even before the first move was made, the outcome of the game was determined.

Both players saw, and knew which had won. But they played on.

Because the Game had to be played out.

(Sheckley, 1968: 16)

Are you a human being? That was the question recently posed by a savvy music file-sharing site as a security measure before permitting access. The metaphysical status of the music downloader was ascertained through a visual recognition test that only a human being could perceive. The implication of this security measure is, of course, that the person seeking access to the webpage might not, in fact, be human. And in an era where automated data collection bots are cruising the Internet in the service of copyright owners to catch filesharing pirates, this possibility is very real. Indeed, our online environment is increasingly peopled with intelligent software agents taking on many of the activities and responsibilities of persons.

Known as bots, digital butlers, softbots, crawlers, electronic agents, vReps, digital buddies, intelligent software agents, avatars, and a host of other similar names,[1] software has been developed that can, within certain parameters, act independently to carry out certain specified tasks. Bots can answer your e-mails, search for information to your customized guidelines, organize that information, spy on your family members, carry out comparisons, shop for you, buy and sell products or services for your business, and carry out a raft of other online activities previously completed by human beings. As Ian Kerr notes, these technologies 'transform the role of computer hardware and software in electronic commerce from that of a passive pipeline to that of an animated associate' (1999: 194). We see a shift from computers as the media of transaction to computers as intermediaries to the transaction (Kerr, 2004: 291).

Recently, I went to the Coca-Cola website where I 'talked' with Hank, the vRep, or virtual customer representative, of Coke. Obviously, Hank can tell the visitor all manner of interesting things about Coca-Cola products and the company's vast range of global activities. I posed a few other kinds of questions to him. When I asked him if he liked Coke, he proved to be a good company man, replying: 'I like all of the products of The Coca-Cola Company.' While I could see the animated representation of Hank, I was curious about his self-image. When I asked him if he were good looking, he modestly told me that he likes questions he can answer best. When queried, 'Are you a person?' he answered, 'I am a Virtual Representative for The Coca-Cola Company.' Through pattern matching, Hank appears to be answering the specific questions that visitors pose to him. In an interesting phenomenon dubbed by researchers 'the persona effect' (Lester et al., 1997), cognitive computer science research has shown that people respond better to a computerized interface which features a personality and animated appearance (mimicking a living being). This type of customer service thus assumes that clients feel less like a number when a sophisticated virtual customer representative such as Hank and his various web-siblings assist them.

Andrew Leonard, in his 1997 book *Bots: The Origin of New Species*, defines a 'bot' as 'a *supposedly intelligent* software program that is *autonomous*, is endowed with *personality* and usually, but not always, performs a *service*' (italics in original; 14). In simple terms, they are useful, rather than destructive, viruses. Bots have taken the online world by storm and have significant implications for electronic- or e-commerce.[2] Because of the huge amounts of information involved in many web transactions, bots are agreed to be a much more efficient way to carry out certain kinds of activities and decision-making practices. For example, one's purchasing bot can review the price of ten thousand widgets anywhere around the world, twenty-four hours a day, and buy when the best price and delivery conditions are met. Both time and money are saved. However, more interestingly, in this e-commerce context, judges and legislators across North America are increasingly recognizing the capacity of these inanimate entities to engage in legally binding contractual relations.

The accepted definition of a contract in Canada is 'an agreement between two or more persons, recognized by law, which gives rise to obligations that the courts may enforce' (Fridman, 1986: 3). In the world of e-commerce, we are seeing growing numbers of contracts between people and bots, and even between two bots with no embodied human being involved at all. Such a contract faces several legal challenges, the primary ones being *animus contrahendi*, or the intention to enter into legal relations, and *consensus ad idem*, the meeting of the two contracting minds. These contractual requirements seem to beg the question, what kind of mind does the bot have? The thorny problem of the kind of mind a machine has and what that might mean for the subject-object relations between human beings and machines, while a relatively recent issue for e-commerce law, has a long pedigree as a broader cultural problematic. In this chapter, my purpose is not to answer the question of how the law should deal with the challenge of bots making contracts, but rather to recognize that in attempting to answer that question, courts and legislatures are first having to answer those nagging issues of *animus contrahendi* and *consensus ad idem*.

I explore a number of moments throughout history where we have taken the measure of the mental life of the machine. These instantiations of machine intelligence take the form of games pitting man against machine and date back to the eighteenth century. Yet, more than a demonstration of artificial intelligence is at stake in these events. In trying to answer the question of whether or not a machine is as smart as a person, we are reflecting on both its intelligence and our own. If one of the things that distinguishes humans from both animals and machines is our capacity for advanced thought, then what does it mean when a machine can replicate, if not perform, this activity? These contests reflect simultaneously both our cultural fascination with, and fear of, the smart machine. They occur not only in times of industrial and commercial upheaval, but also at times when competing epistemologies vie for intellectual supremacy: magic and rationality, humanism and posthumanism.

However, it seems that across centuries, at the same time that we have wanted to believe in the thinking machine, we also suspect a trick. Perhaps this is a strategy for containing our fears, maintaining our ontological status. I suggest in my analysis, developing N. Katherine Hayles (1999: 142; 2005: xiv), that the central trick lies, not so much in the machinations of the technology and its operators (although tricks abound there), but in the test that we are deploying to evaluate the personality of the machine. Hayles claims with respect to the magic trick of the thinking machine: 'the important intervention comes much earlier, when the test puts you into a cybernetic circuit that splices your will, desire, and perception into a distributed cognitive system in which represented bodies are joined with enacted bodies through mutating and flexible machine interfaces' (1999: xiv). I argue that in the history of man-machine contests of the mind, we see, first, a playing out of certain modern anxieties around human-machine relations, and then, in a postmodern context, the emergence of a notion of a posthuman person. Defining elements of personhood become unmoored from the materiality of the creature called the human being. The person becomes constituted in the capacity for the machine to act like a human in the social realm, to win at the game of imitating the person. And as a result, what began in the late 1700s as discussions of whether machines could ever equal the mental capacities of man at the dawn of the first Industrial Revolution morphs, by the second, into a question of posthuman personhood.

The Turing Test

To come back to the example with which I began this chapter, the image generated as the security test on the music-sharing website is not evident from reading the computer code used to generate it. Therefore, the bots seeking out filesharing websites cannot recognize the image; the computer code, which they can read, does not contain that configuration. Thus, they cannot enter the site because they cannot 'pass' for human. By relying upon the optical embodiment of the human being, the website security mechanism is able to distinguish between human beings and machines. This concern of drawing a line between humans and machines has been a concern since the first industrial revolution when automated machinery began to replace the labouring bodies of human workers in factories. However, with the computing machines that emerged during and immediately after the Second World War, simulating, as they did, not the body of the human being but rather its intellectual capacities, concerns emerged that the computer might be able to replace the last unique bastion of human superiority: the mind.

In the late 1940s and early 1950s, computers in North America were shifting from being solely tools of the military, as they had been during the Second World War, to becoming a resource for commerce and government. Ultra-rapid computing machines were being used to tabulate census results, manage business inventory, and predict everything from election outcomes to hurricane formation. Accompanying this technological domestication was a flurry of expert and popular debate about whether these impressive machines could *think*. A high-water moment in this discussion came in 1950 when the brilliant mathematician and early computer programmer Alan Turing published his groundbreaking essay 'Computing Machinery and Intelligence.'[3]

There Turing outlines what he calls the 'imitation game,' a replacement for the question: Do machines think? In the game, three people, a man (A), a woman (B), and an interrogator (C), 'who may be of either sex,' are the players. The interrogator is in a room apart from the other two and the objective is for the interrogator to determine, through a series of questions, who is the man and who is the woman. A's task is to try to cause C to make an incorrect identification; B tries to help the interrogator guess correctly. Questions and responses are exchanged through typewriting so that voices (i.e., bodies) do not affect the results. Turing then suggests: '[w]e now ask the question, what will happen when a machine takes the part of A in this game? Will the interrogator decide wrongly as often when the game is played like this as he does when the game is played between a man and a woman?' (1950: 433–4).

Turing therefore replaces the question – 'Can a machine think?' – with 'are there imaginable digital computers that would do well in the imitation game?' (ibid.: 442). In other words, he shifts the focus from whether or not a machine could think, to whether or not a machine could, in a disembodied environment, deceive a human into thinking that it was a (gendered) person, through a performance commingling reason and communication. The imitation game, or Turing Test, as it came to be known, captured the imagination of computer programmers and emerged, claims historian Alison Adam, as a 'canonical thought experiment' within the domain of artificial intelligence research (1998: 50). This is in part because, as Hayles suggests, '[l]ike a magician that distracts the audience's attention by having them focus on actions that occur *after* the crucial move has already been made, the Turing test, through its very existence, already presupposes consensus on the criteria that render inevitable the conclusion that machines can think' (2005: 142).[4]

But I would go further than Hayles to argue that the Turing Test is more than merely, as Kerr suggests, 'a behaviorist's way around the problem of subjectivity' (2004: 302). It is a form of 'empirical perform-ance' that operates as a technique of personification. Barbara Maria Stafford, in her analysis of Enlightenment forms of 'rational recre-ation,' coins the notion of empirical performance to capture the coming together of the competing epistemologies of magic and science, of 'quackery and pedagogy,' at the heart of early modern pre-sentations of science and technology (1993: 22–30). Presentations of the power of magnets would be combined, for example, with displays of conjuring – the educational and rational would be presented through exhibitionary tactics, an early form of infotainment, perhaps. I suggest that Turing's imitation game is a renewed form of empirical perform-ance because it is, first and foremost, a game. Turing's game is a contest of wits, a battle of wills. The game status guarantees drama, offers the possibility of spectacle, poses the prospect of cheating. In this way, the game is a populist move. Its democratic impulse mani-fests in a test of complex scientific and technological knowledge where the outcome, the results, are visible and recognizable to all. It rests on skills of showmanship, and, as a result, links the thinking machine fundamentally with commercialism. Thus empirical performance through the figure of the game in general, or of the imitation game in particular, is a form of popularization of technological innovation. And the favoured empirical performance of machine intelligence, the privileged game for more than two centuries, was the game of chess.

Two years before offering his Imitation Game, Turing suggested in 1948, '[o]ne can produce paper machines for playing chess; playing against such a machine gives a definite feeling that one is pitting one's wits against something alive' (in Schaffer, 1996: 78). He started to write a program for a chess-playing computer even though he did not yet have a machine on which to run it. He finished it in 1952 and then chal-lenged Alick Glennie to a match with the 'paper machine' which he over-optimistically named 'Turbochamp.' Glennie was a weak player, and the match took three hours and twenty-nine moves, with Turing following the rules he had established for his computer to play. Glennie finally beat the paper computer. Enthused by the idea, however, Turing began to write a chess program to run on an actual computer. He died before it became operational, but he was not alone in thinking about the connection between early computers and chess. Chess was almost immediately recognized by computer programmers as an ideal measure of the computing power of the machine, a form of machine IQ test. But why?

Computer programmer Bob Wilensky offers a simple, and yet practical, response to that question.

> They [computer programmers] were interested in intelligence and they needed somewhere to start. So they looked around at who the smartest people were, and they were themselves, of course. They were all essentially mathematicians by training and mathematicians do two things – they prove theorems and play chess. And they said, hey if it proves a theorem or plays chess, it must be smart. (Adam, 1998: 35)

Claude E. Shannon, information theorist and one of the earliest builders of a chess-playing machine, asserted in 1950, somewhat less disingenuously, that chess 'is neither so simple as to be trivial nor too difficult for satisfactory solution. And such a machine could be pitted against a human opponent, giving a clear measure of the machine's ability with this type of reasoning' (1950: 48). Shannon recognizes the strengths and limitations of chess as a computational problematic, but, as significantly, he highlights the potential of the man-machine contest as a measure of the machine's abilities.

I suggest that a combination of factors contributed to chess's *de facto* selection as the ultimate Turing Test. First, chess was already located within a meaning matrix of intellectualism. Poker, on the other hand, another complex game of strategy also being considered, was both more difficult mathematically and had the unsavoury taint of gambling and saloons at this time. 'Chess has always been thought of as the quintessential thinking man's game' (Guterl, 1996: 49). Second, many of the individuals involved in developing early computers did, in fact, play chess and so were familiar with the kinds of reasoning that it required. Third, chess, in many ways, was accepted as the ideal problem for the computational machine. In games theoretic terms, it is a zero-sum, complex, saddle-point game of perfect information. This means someone wins, and someone loses, and that all of the information one needs to play the game is available at all times. An IBM programmer noted in 1997, '[c]hess provides an ideal arena for testing a system's capacity for such complex problem-solving. And chess is a venerable game, which also generates a lot of prestige' (in Anderton,

1997: 13). Fourth and finally, however, and arguably most significantly, it is the element of gamesmanship, of the man-machine contest, which appeals to the popular imagination. The game remystifies through personification what can otherwise appear to be a cold, logical machine. Further, the man-machine chess match is unparalleled as a promotional device. 'If it beats a chess grand master – that's something people can grasp' (Gelertner, 1997: 47).[5]

Indeed, as we can see from the brief discussion of computer chess I offer here, the history of computer games, and perhaps even the modern computer itself, could be seen as a relentless quest to design a computer that can succeed at the imitation game. Hayles explains:

> [b]y operationalizing the question of intelligence, Turing made it possible to construct situations in which the proposition that machines can think could be either proved or disproved, thus removing it from the realm of philosophical speculation to (putative) empirical testing. Once this move has been made, the outcome is all but certain, for researchers will simply focus on creating programs that can satisfy this criterion until they succeed. (2005: 142)

And this is what has happened. However, when he coined the Imitation Game, I suggest that Turing was tapping into a deeper set of cultural anxieties and drawing upon an established historical tradition of empirical performance that long preceded the ultra-rapid computing machine. The Imitation Game must be read as a distillation and reproduction of an ongoing dialectical tension in our relationship with our machines.

While designing a machine that could imitate human thought is a clear demonstration of our success as *homo faber*, the superiority of the human, Turing's game also manifests some deep-seated angst about that very superiority, about the subject-object relationship. Brian Bloomfield and Theo Vurdubakis (1997) have suggested that the man-machine contest as cultural event serves as a site for the playing out of some of the fundamental moral conflicts of modernity. Man-machine contests 'disturb the human-machine boundary inherent in the putative natural order of things' (37). I argue that this manifests more specifically in identifying, as the clone does in relation to animals, a deep-seated anxiety or even fear within late modernity of the machine as posthuman. Again, comforting boundaries between nature and culture become quaint; yet the machine, unlike the genetic double, has no claim to humanity. Humanism gives us no easy out. Machines are stronger and faster than humans; they are increasingly figured as smarter than us. And yet with this posthuman form, we retreat into the comfort of the subject-object distinction. Machines are clearly objects, produced by, and subject to, human will. However, the fascinating risk at the heart of the man-machine contest is that this may no longer be true. '[T]he framing of the competition in confrontational terms hints darkly at the prospect of an autonomous technology, a technology outside of human control' (ibid.: 30).

There is a final aspect of the Imitation Game that contributes to our cultural anxieties of posthumanity. It is not only that this is a contest between human and machine that the machine is likely to win at some nebulous point in the future. How it wins that game is of key significance. In the Imitation Game, the machine's capacity for thought is replaced by its capacity to deceive, and therefore, to mimic, the human being. Success in the Imitation Game offers the replacement of human personality by machine personality. The game is won when no one notices the replacement, when we can no longer distinguish man from machine. Yet the prospect of a machine that dissembles, a machine that could one day quietly replace us without our knowledge, worries us. The game radically disenchants the machine. We see this posed as both horrible and perhaps inevitable in films of machine intelligence in the last sixty years ranging from *Desk Set* (1957) to *Colossus: The Forbin Project* (1970), to *War Games* (1983), to *AI* (2001). This simultaneously engaging and terrifying prospect, which both re-enchants and disenchants the technology, also functions as a première technique of posthuman personification in posing the invisible replacement of the human being by the machine. 'As you gaze at the flickering signifiers scrolling down the computer screens, no matter what identifications you assign to the embodied entities that you cannot see, you have already become posthuman' (Hayles, 1999: xiv).

In *How We Became Posthuman: Virtual Bodies in Cybernetics, Literature and Informatics* (1999), Hayles notes that we are experiencing a movement from the historically specific construct known as the human, as a natural, sexed body governed by the unified self-will and mind of the liberal, humanist subject, towards an equally historically specific construct: the posthuman. Focused more on subjectivity than the cyborg, the posthuman condition is a perspective depending upon four primary assumptions (2–3). First, it privileges information patterns over materiality; biological embodiment is no longer inevitable, but rather, an 'accident of history.' Second, the posthuman view down-plays consciousness as the sole, or even a key, locus of human identity. Third, the body is recast as prosthesis rendering our tools in historical continuity with our selves. Fourth, through these and related processes, the human being becomes seamless with the intelligent machine. 'In the posthuman there are no essential differences or absolute demarcations between bodily existence and computer simu-lation, cybernetic mechanism and biological organism, robot teleology and human goals' (ibid.).

At the heart of this recasting of identity, and therefore, I would add, the person, is the condition of virtuality which Hayles defines as the cultural perception that material objects are interpenetrated by infor-mation. These informational patterns are progressively becoming priv-ileged over, and disembodied from, the material substrates in which they appear (1999: 13–14). Therefore, while the liberal humanist subject appears to be deconstructed through the figure of the posthu-man, she notes certain problematic continuities with liberal human-ism: namely, the tendency towards the erasure of embodiment and the privileging of the mind as the locus of subjectivity. The condition of posthumanity is particularly present, she suggests, in digital environ-ments and virtual geographies.

In Hayles's concern with the move of disembodiment within the Imi-tation Game, I suggest that she overlooks the figure of the game itself as a central technique of posthumanism. In so doing, she poses too radical a rupture between humanism and posthumanism, and misses a number of the interesting cultural effects of the Imitation Game. While she recognizes that the shift from the human to the posthuman 'evokes terror and excites pleasure' (1999: 4),[6] she cannot see how that simulta-neous experience of terror and pleasure at the heart of the posthuman has a much longer history. Finally, she cannot fully account for its pop-ularity; just as much as disembodiment, the public appeal of the man-machine contest has created a cybernetic loop of posthuman personifi-cation where we think, not merely of our machines as persons, but of ourselves as machine persons. And this loop of the Imitation Game has been spinning for at least the last 230 years.

The First Chess-Playing Machine

In the fall of 1769, the Hungarian civil servant Farkas de Kempelen (1734–1804), better known as Wolfgang von Kempelen, was attending in the Austrian Court of Maria Theresa. A favourite of hers, he had translated the Hungarian civil code from Latin into German, and deployed his hobbies of invention and engineering to the benefit of the Court, developing a system of pumps to drain the salt mines of which he was director. Given his scientific talents and knowledge, Maria Theresa requested that von Kempelen attend a demonstration of scientific conjuring being presented to the court by a visiting Frenchman named Pelletier. The show focused on magnetism, and in an uncharacteristic moment of immodesty, von Kempelen declared when asked his opinion of the performance that he could, within six months, construct a machine which would impress and deceive the members of the court much more effectively than what they had just seen. Maria Theresa accepted the challenge and excused von Kempelen from his official duties for six months. In spring 1770, he returned to court with a chess-playing automaton that would fascinate and stymie the public and scientific communities of Europe and North America for the better part of the next century.[7]

Automata, or the mechanical toys relying on elaborate clockwork mechanisms, were very popular in royal courts in Europe in the late eighteenth century. Derived from the elaborate mechanical clocks that were in most major cathedrals of Europe at the time, favourite automata included moving pictures, table ornaments, and mechanical animals. The challenge for the designers was to make the machines, through elaborately jointed mechanisms, as lifelike as possible in their movements whether imitating human or animal life. Automata, like those designed by Henri-Louis Jaquet-Droz and Friedrich von Knauss, imitated human movement, the playing of a harpsichord or writing.[8] The most famous builder of automata is Jacques de Vaucanson, whose 'renown as an automaton maker enabled him to move effortlessly between the worlds of entertainment, industry and science' (Standage, 2002: 6). Vaucanson's most famous automaton was an artificial duck that could drink, eat, quack, splash in the water, digest its food, and defecate.[9]

This was the context into which von Kempelen entered when he wheeled a large wooden cabinet on brass castors into the audience with the Empress. A full-scale model of a man carved out of wood, wearing fur-trimmed robes, loose trousers, and a turban, sat behind the cabinet. The cabinet was four feet long, two and a half feet deep, and three feet high. On the front of the cabinet were three doors of equal width under which there was a long drawer. A chessboard was affixed to the top of the cabinet and 'the Turk' (as he was to become known) stared at it, apparently in concentration. The right arm extended out and rested on a cushion, the left hand held a long Turkish pipe. The costume reflected the popularity of Turkish style at the time, as well as the relationship with the venerable game of chess, which had come to Europe from Persia between 700 and 1000 CE (Standage, 2002: 22–3).

During a performance, von Kempelen would open all of the doors at both the front and back of the cabinet in a particular order to reveal the clockworks. He shone a candle behind to illustrate that nothing was concealed therein, except the elaborate mechanical gearworks of the machine. The audience could see right through the cabinet. He would also strip bare the Turk's legs so that it could be seen that 'he' was not a disguised human. A set of chessmen of red and white ivory would be removed from the long drawer (the two remaining compartments would be opened and revealed after this). With all the doors and the drawer open, von Kempelen would rotate the entire unit so the audience could see it from all sides. The successful 'reveal' being completed,[10] all the drawers and doors would then be closed, the automaton was returned to its original position, a cushion was placed underneath its left elbow, the pipe would be removed, the chessmen would be placed in appropriate positions on the board, and finally, two candelabra with three burning candles would be placed to illuminate the playing board.

Von Kempelen would then receive challengers from the audience. After the volunteer was seated, von Kempelen would 'wind up' the Turk and play would begin, with the automaton usually playing white.[11] He always cautioned the opponent that it was important to place all pieces directly in the centre of the square so that the Turk would not damage its fingers in the movement of the pieces. The Turk played with his left hand and nodded his head twice when placing the opposing queen in danger, three times when placing his opponent's king in check. If the human player made an illegal move, he would shake his head, replace the piece to its original position, and take his turn. During the performance, von Kempelen would occasionally return at uneven intervals to rewind the gearworks and would be sure to stand at a good distance from the action. Occasionally he would chat a bit with members of the audience, although he fiddled with a wooden casket which he had previously taken from inside the cabinet and never explained. This enhanced the tantalizing prospect that he was controlling the Turk from afar with the mysterious container.

Not merely appearing to play chess, the Turk appeared to play very good chess. He would dispose of most opponents in about half an hour and then would entertain onlookers with some chess tricks and puzzles, such as the Knight's Tour.[12] The Empress, her entourage, and guests were thrilled with the machine that could mimic the higher functions of man. Von Kempelen returned to court many times to exhibit his extraordinary automaton. Quickly becoming known in Vienna, due to letters and pamphlets, soon the Turk began to get a wider reputation in Europe.

Throughout his life, von Kempelen had an ambivalent relationship with the Turk. It served its purpose in convincing the Empress of his engineering abilities and resulted in lucrative rewards. At the same time, however, he always considered it somewhat of a 'bagatelle,' as he called it, and wanted to focus on his other work, including a machine which mimicked human speaking processes and talked.[13] Maria Theresa died in 1780, and her son, Joseph II, forced the Turk out of retirement in 1781 to entertain Grand Duke Paul of Russia and his wife. The success of these performances led to the Emperor excusing von Kempelen from his duties in Vienna for two years in order to take the automaton on a tour of Europe.

The Turk took Paris and then London by storm, first at the royal courts and then in more public venues. After an extended stint at the court in Versailles, the Turk moved to Paris and played the greatest chess player of the day, François-Andrew Danican Philidor. While the Turk lost to Philidor, the very fact of the match between the amazing chess machine and the greatest player at the time made history.[14] Another famous match took place in Paris between Benjamin Franklin and the Turk. In that instance, it was the Turk that was victorious. In both European capitals, members of the scientific and engineering communities continued to try to guess the secret of the automaton's operations, and speculation to that effect in all the papers of Europe just fuelled both its mystique and popularity.

Theories and written accounts abounded to explain the seemingly magical powers of the Turk. Some analysts claimed a child was hidden in the cabinet; others asserted a dwarf inside the automaton was the directing mind. One theory born directly out of a fictionalized account claimed that a legless Polish soldier was the chess master. Other theorists claimed magnets or wires were being used to manipulate the pieces. Of course, one possibility that some commentators acknowledged was that the machine was doing the seemingly impossible, that it was playing chess, thinking autonomously.

Back in Austria in 1785, von Kempelen was permitted to return to his other pursuits and put the Turk into storage. But even while the Turk was not in public between 1785 and 1804, stories continued to spread of its prowess. It was in this period that it was supposed to have played Frederick the Great of Prussia and George III of England. Perhaps the most famous story about the Turk was written by Jean-Robert Houdin, whose memoirs were published in 1858. This story suggests that while von Kempelen was in Russia to study language, he stayed with a doctor friend, Osloff. The doctor was sheltering a fugitive army soldier named Worousky who had lost his legs in battle, and as it turned out, was a very good chess player. Worousky needed a way out of the country as the authorities were searching for him. Von Kempelen constructed the chess automaton to achieve this end. As the Turk played its way across Russia to the border, its fame built and it was ordered to the imperial palace in St Petersburg by Catherine the Great. The story tells that the two men went to St Petersburg where the Empress herself challenged the Turk to a game. The game ended when, after two illegal moves by Catherine, the Turk swept all the pieces from the board. The Empress was delighted with the automaton and wanted to purchase him. Von Kempelen graciously refused and left the country with Worousky safely hidden inside. Intriguingly, this particular narrative was to become the material for dramatic plays, at least three novels, and even a silent film.[15]

On von Kempelen's death in 1804, a Viennese musical engineer, inventor, and entrepreneur named Johann Nepomuk Maelzel bought the chess-playing automaton and again toured it through England and Europe. An even more effective showman and entrepreneur than von Kempelen, Maelzel added improvements to the performance, including the capacity for the Turk to pronounce 'échec' (French for 'check') when placing the opponent in check. Novels, reviews, and pamphlets abounded again, extolling the Turk's virtues, debating the philosophical implications of an intelligent machine, and attempting to expose it as a hoax. Napoleon Bonaparte was beaten by the Turk's prowess in 1809 in another very famous match. Subsequently the Turk was sold by Maelzel to Napoleon's nephew, and then eventually repurchased by Maelzel when he was down on his luck. Maelzel, whose fortunes were to improve and deteriorate repeatedly until his death, left Europe for North America in 1825, taking the Turk with him.

Just as he had been in Europe, the Turk was an amazing success in the United States, astounding audiences and drawing continual scrutiny and debate. The Turk played Charles Carroll, the last surviving signatory to the Declaration of Independence. Intriguingly, even though the Turk won an overwhelming majority of its games, and Carroll was a weak player, the Turk suffered an atypical defeat.[16] In the 1830s in the United States, the Turk met two other prominent figures from history, P.T. Barnum and Edgar Allan Poe.[17] Maelzel eventually took the Turk to Havana, where his long-time friend and assistant, William Schlumberger, perished; Maelzel himself died on the return voyage from Havana to Philadelphia in 1838. The Turk was auctioned off with Maelzel's other assets to meet his debts and was purchased by Dr John Mitchell of Philadelphia. After discovering how the Turk actually worked, he placed it with the Chinese Museum, where it was destroyed by fire in 1854.

Various explanations of the Turk over its colourful life had parts of its trick correct almost from the very beginning.[18] In fact, the Turk did conceal an average-sized human chess player within it who changed positions during the reveal – the always regularized opening and closing of the various doors and drawers. At the same time, the human player did not peek out at the board through any of the locations posited by many commentators. The pieces on the board were operated with an elaborate magnetic process and the arms and head of the automaton did function through a form of clockwork. Yet, what is more remarkable than the facts behind the Turk is the level of public fascination with a chess-playing machine, with a machine that, unlike its other early Industrial Revolution counterparts, was not merely replacing the labour of the body, but appeared to be capable of replacing the labour of the mind.[19]

In addition to the popular attempts to debunk the Turk, not surprisingly, the Turk also inspired imitators. 'Ajeeb' was the 1868 creation of Englishman Charles A. Hopper and 'Mephisto' was invented in 1878 by prosthesis maker Charles Gumpel. In America, the Turk also stimulated copycats, including 'The Automaton Chess Player' built by two brothers named Walker in 1827 and an 'Automaton Whist Player' which appeared in 1828. However, none could, or did, displace the Turk from its preeminent position in the hearts and minds of the world, and to this day, the fascination continues. The Turk's purchase on the public imagination has continued since its demise, including a nine-article series in 1947 in *Chess Review* by Harkness and Battell, an article in *American Heritage* magazine in 1960 by Ernest Wittenberg, a book in 1975 by Charles Carroll entitled *The Great Chess Automaton*, and Bradley Ewart's 1980 book, *Chess: Man vs. Machine*. In the 1970s novel *King Kill*, Tom Gavin portrays von Kempelen as a peer of Mark Twain's sharpsters from *Huckleberry Finn*. Magician John Gaughan built a reconstruction of the Turk in 1989; the Deutsches Museum in Munich placed a reconstruction of the Turk on display in 2003; and in computer simulation *Fritz 9*, current challengers can play a 3D animation of the Turk.

As noted in the discussion of the game, however, what is most compelling in the story of the Turk is the power of the performance, of the reveal, of the trick at the heart of it all. Christoph Asendorf describes a key shift between the eighteenth and nineteenth centuries. In the eighteenth, man is understood as a man-machine, whereas in the nineteenth century, the machine itself is assigned human characteristics. Arguably, the Turk is on the cusp of this transformation.

> In comparison with the eighteenth century, a shift in perspective has taken place. The body as a mechanical object has been replaced by the machine as a bodily object. If in the *homme-machine* the image of the machine was identitical with that of the human body, then the consequences of this objectification become manifest in the image of the living machine: the separation of the body from the subject. ... The rationality of the machine world is transformed into a mythology. (Asendorf, 1993: 4–5)

Sussman argues that the Turk offers a classic example of Stafford's empirical performance. The various writings and public fervour, I agree, do reflect a combination of post-Enlightenment scepticism and mysticism, producing an early industrial fantasy.

> The Automaton Chess Player enacted a fantasy of mechanical power: that clockwork gears, levers, invisible wires, or magnets could somehow perform enough discrete operations to add up to the faculty of thought, symbolized by chess, a game combining the calculation of reason with the mechanisms of the chess pieces moving on the board. (1999: 86)

Just as the best social science fictions do, the Turk offered a future technology; however, in this instance, it relied for its magic on a mystical path recalled in the dress and name of the Turk. It turns on the trick of machine thought. As Sussman suggests,

> [t]he variety of accounts of the machine and its secret belies the spectator's moment of uncertainty, in which disbelief that a machine can think is momentarily suspended. The normative relationship of authority between people and objects is briefly questioned, then set back into its rational everyday hierarchy. (Ibid.: 91)

It turns on the willing belief in the capacity of the object to enchant. The fact that it is a trick enhances, rather than detracts from, the success of the spectacle. The reveals offered by von Kempelen and Maelzel, meant to demystify, were in fact, a fundamental part of the enchantment. As Sussman claims, '[t]he visual proof was, first, the demonstration of control at a distance; and second, the transmission of human intelligence into the inanimate body of the object: the performing object that animates both demystification and reenchantment' (1999: 93). In other words, the Turk commingled the sacred and the profane in public spectacle.

The Turk first appeared in a moment of intellectual rupture, benefiting from the blurred boundary between science and magic in the late 1700s. It succeeds because every time the Turk wins, if there is no trick, then it signals a significant epistemological shift. The simultaneously demystifying and re-enchanting capacity of the Turk's performance is key to this success (Sussman, 1999). As Tom Standage notes in a radio interview about his book on the Turk, even watching a reconstructed Turk play in the 2000s 'taps into your desire to be deceived' (Standage, 2003). Finally, while there is a range of public responses to the Turk from derision to fascination, there is also a latent fear at work, I suggest. It is a fear that manifests in the popular narratives of the Turk: a fundamentally posthuman fear. Beginning with a concern that we can be deceived by a machine, the prospect arises that these machines might turn on us, and finally, in a later period, the concern that we can be replaced entirely by a machine coalesces.

In much of the press coverage of the Turk, the enchanting function of the technology is foregrounded. A significant amount of the pleasure of seeing the Turk is clearly knowing that there is a trick, but finding the performance convincing nonetheless. At that time, there was pleasure in imagining 'what if' because there was a fairly high degree of confidence that a machine could not, in fact, think like a person. It is in some of the dramatizations of the Turk where we see the fear of the technology emerge more clearly. This distils in a compelling scene from the outstanding 1927 silent film dramatization, by Raymond Bernard, of Henri Dupuy-Mazuel's novel, published in English in 1927 under the titles *The Chess Player* and *The Devil Is an Empress*. *The Chess Player* follows the exploits of Boleslas Vorowski (Pierre Blanchar), a Polish hero of the rebellion against the Russians under Empress Catherine II, Sophie Novinska (Edith Jehanne), the girl raised as his sister, and their guardian, Baron von Kempelen (Charles Dullin), a builder of automata. In this story the Turk is built as an elaborate mechanism to smuggle Boleslas out of Russia and Poland safely to Germany. The fear of the posthuman, that machines will not only deceive us but turn on us, is represented most powerfully when Major Nicolaieff (Camille Bert) of the Russian army goes to von Kempelen's house to look for evidence to implicate him in the crimes involving Boleslas. There he encounters the various automata that von Kempelen has built, including a full-scale, disturbingly accurate, model of von Kempelen himself, a version of the woman he loved, some whimsical musicians, and some soldiers that we have been told earlier guard the premises.

Nicolaieff's initial encounter with the life-size automata is benign; he is charmed and intrigued by them. He animates a number of them through levers and knobs on a control panel, repeatedly smiling in wonder as they 'come to life.' Suddenly, however, he inadvertently activates the soldiers through a concealed mechanism in the floor tiles. The soldiers, looking like over-sized toy soldiers, begin to very slowly converge around him. Intercut and contrasted effectively with the scene from the Russian palace where a crowd of human beings and a firing squad converge on the automaton to 'kill' it, the reversal in von Kempelen's home is emphasized. Nicolaieff's horror becomes our own as we realize how terrifying it would be to be slowly encircled by wooden, sword-brandishing dolls of life size, single-mindedly focused on one goal – the defence of the home. Nicolaieff dies, perhaps of the wounds suffered from the automata, perhaps of fear, lying on the floor, covered by the toppled figure of the von Kempelen automaton. Thus, the film realizes the fear of the inversion of machine with human; it answers the latent posthuman question – what if the machines turned against us?

The Thinking Machine, *Intermezzo*

This fear of domination, represented through the figure of the thinking machine, and in particular, the chess-playing machine, retreats, in the late nineteenth century, to the realm of science fiction, post-Enlightenment science having firmly denied its possibility. Arguably this unwillingness to believe in a machine that could think like a person was a key element in the lack of success of another of the Turk's opponents. From boyhood, Charles Babbage was fascinated by automata in general, and with the Turk in particular, playing the machine twice in 1819. Babbage notes in 1838: 'in substituting mechanism for the performance of operations hitherto executed by intellectual labour ... the analogy between these acts and the operations of the mind almost forced upon me the figurative employment of the same terms' (Babbage in Schaffer, 1994: 207). Babbage went on himself to design what he called a Difference Engine – a mechanical machine to conduct calculations. Upon his death in 1871, a contemporary wrote, 'the marvelous pulp and fibre of the brain had been substituted by brass and iron and he had taught the wheelwork to think' (in Swade, 2002: 85). A full-scale model of the Difference Engine was never constructed and it remains a historical anachronism, as did his even more fanciful Analytical Engine. However, these machines are generally accepted as mechanical precursors to current computers. Interestingly, however, Babbage – with Lady Ada Lovelace, a fellow mathematician, friend, supporter, daughter of Lord Byron, and avid gambler – contemplated building and demonstrating a games machine which would exhibit intellect through playing a game of reason against all human comers, in order to raise capital for the Analytical Engine. Clearly they, too, understood the power of the game as an empirical performance of intelligence, with populist appeal and capitalist possibilities.

Babbage and Lovelace's efforts remain an affectionate footnote in the history of the development of the computer, and we have to wait until the 1940s and 1950s and the advent of electronic calculating machines for the Imitation Game to re-emerge in force. From the earliest days of the appearance of the modern computing machine on the public stage in the 1940s, it is represented visually and textually as a gamesman. Yet there are different types of games and they can be organized in an intellectual hierarchy, moving from tic-tac-toe to checkers to chess to poker, and beyond. Each is a 'saddle point game' as it is known within game theory, namely it is a game with a pure winning strategy that, with sufficient information, can be reproduced. For example, we all can play tic-tac-toe to a perpetual standstill.

Very early in the development of the modern computer, tic-tac-toe is established as a game that computers can play, and play without error. Checkers then becomes the next challenge. In the mid- to late 1950s, stories in the popular press begin to emerge of successful checkers-playing machines. Checkers is still considered a relatively simple game, however, and the stakes of the machine winning or only allowing for a draw are playful. As noted previously, chess, on the other hand, is repeatedly figured in this discourse as the limit point: the ultimate test. It is the challenge that captures both the scientific and popular imagination.

Cyberneticist Norbert Wiener poses the notion of the chess-playing machine as a possibility in his 1948 book, *Cybernetics; or Control and Communication in the Animal and the Machine*, noting, 'this sort of ability represents an essential difference between the potentialities of the machine and the mind' (Wiener, 1948: 290). He feels that it is possible to build a chess-playing machine that 'might well be as good a player as the vast majority of the human race' (ibid.: 193–4). Programmers Allan Newell, J.C. Shaw, and Herbert Simon suggest in 1957, '[i]f one could devise a successful chess machine, one would seem to have penetrated the core of human intellectual endeavour' (in McCorduck, 1979: 160). The first chess game between a human being and an electronic computer took place in 1958,[20] the same year that leading artificial intelligence pioneers Simon and Newell had predicted that a computer would be world chess champion within a decade. They were a bit optimistic because it was still considered science fiction when, in Stanley Kubrick's 1968 film, *2001: A Space Odyssey*, the now infamous Hal 9000 dispassionately plays chess with one of the *Discovery*'s astronauts, winning handily.

The first fairly impressive computer-chess program was Chess 4.0, written by David Slate and Larry Atkin in 1973; it reached 'expert level' by 1979. Master level play was first achieved by Belle of AT&T Bell Labs, a precursor to its more famous descendant, Deep Blue. By the 1980s, competent chess-playing machines could be purchased for a few hundred dollars, and large machines were capable of playing at a grandmaster level. Alan Turing had predicted in 1950 that within fifty years the computer would be able to win a five-minute game against a human at least three times in ten tries. As it turned out, Turing's prediction was modest. While chess lasted almost another fifty years as the première imitation game, its displacement, when it occurred, was spectacular.

The Match of the Century

In a match symbolically scheduled on the fiftieth birthday of ENIAC, the first large-scale, general-purpose electronic computer, Garry Kasparov, world chess champion since 1985, and Deep Blue, IBM RS/6000 computer, played a six-game regulation match from 10 to 18 February 1996, sponsored by the Association for Computing Machinery. Kasparov was, and is, widely acknowledged to be the best human to ever play the game. Deep Blue, a new supercomputer with a parallel processor that could contemplate more than one hundred million moves per second, was a mega-machine custom built to play chess. Prior to this competition, no computer had ever beaten a world champion in standard tournament chess.

The stage was set for a media event of significant proportions. Touted in the press as the match of the century, 'Kasparov was fighting for all of us – all of us that is, with spit in our mouths and DNA in our cells,' wrote a journalist in *Newsweek* (Levy, 1996: 51). In *Time*, Kasparov was playing 'for you, for me, for the human species. He was trying, as he put it shortly before the match, to help defend our dignity' (Wright, 1996: 50). Kasparov admitted to being somewhat spooked because he had no past games of Deep Blue's to analyse (an unusual occurrence in this context). IBM programmers conceded that Deep Blue's weakness was its inability to adjust its play mid-game. Overall the media were confident that the human would triumph, but the stakes of the match were repeatedly represented in hyperbolic terms – this might be 'humanity's last stand' (Winner, 1996: 68).

When Kasparov lost the first game of the best-of-six match, the buzz began. Was this the beginning of the end ... of us? No grandmaster had ever lost to a machine in regulation play in the history of the game. Kasparov admitted, 'I could feel – I could smell – a new kind of intelligence across the table' (Kasparov, 1996: 57). Suddenly the stakes of this match were less theoretical, less abstract. Shaken, Kasparov retreated to his hotel room and contemplated the loss. He returned the next day, changed his playing style, and won game 2. Games 3 and 4 ended in draws and Kasparov handily won games 5 and 6. Kasparov took home $400,000 for his troubles; Deep Blue pocketed $100,000. The purse was, however, 'a mere shadow of the real stakes in the match' (Winner, 1996: 68). The media were clearly relieved by the outcome – '[t]he day of reckoning has been postponed' (ibid.). At the same time, however, they offered ominous portents of the challenges to come. *Newsweek* concluded, '[t]oday we can marvel at Kasparov's resilience and brilliance; he outsmarted the brute-force monster. Tomorrow is another matter' (Levy, 1996: 51).

Alan Turing, in a moment of accurate prescience, had suggested in 1950 that 'I believe that at the end of the century the use of words and general educated opinion will have altered so much that one will be able to speak of machines thinking without expecting to be contradicted' (452). The watershed moment in the Kasparov–Deep Blue match of 1996 is not to be found in the tally of games won and lost. Rather, it was, first, in the relegitimizing of chess as the ultimate Turing Test on a global media stage, unprecedented since the Turk toured Europe and North America; and second, in the recognition by Kasparov, expert commentators, and the media alike that the computer had exhibited intelligence. Unlike with the Turk, no one was alleging deceit. Yet nor was anyone suggesting the computer had won the imitation game. So the risk of the admission of machine intelligence was contained by the limits of the machine itself. Still, the performance was successful: Deep Blue was intelligent. After the match, Kasparov acknowledged, '[s]o although I think I did see some signs of intelligence, it's a weird kind, an inefficient, inflexible kind that makes me think I have a few years left' (Kasparov, 1996: 57). One year, three months, to be precise.

On the thirty-fifth floor of the Equitable Centre in New York, from 3 to 11 May 1997, Kasparov and Deep Blue played again, another best-of-six match, inevitably dubbed the 'ultimate rematch.' Kasparov trained intensively for two months. Deeper Blue, as the new computer was nicknamed, was improved and could process two hundred million moves, or fifty billion positions, per second. Grandmasters had worked with the IBM team to give Deeper Blue more chess-specific knowledge. Perhaps even more important than the alterations to the chess-playing ability of the computer, was the fact that IBM was now much more savvy to the public appeal of the empirical performance, stepping up the promotion, and controlling all aspects of the event. A small TV studio was furnished to look like a study and the game was broadcast on live-circuit television and webcast, receiving seventy-four million hits from four million Internet users in 106 countries. As one commentator noted, 'to turn something as dull as a chess tournament into a full-on media spectacle' was a testimony to the marketing team at IBM (Dawson, 1997: 19).

Once again, the stakes were represented as very high. It was an 'epic battle between man and machine' (Clark, 1997: 26). Kasparov was, again, the 'latest standard bearer in humanity's war against our own obsolescence' (Krantz, 1997: 76). Deep Blue was remembered in the media as 'the infamous chess program that one year ago threw a stunning uppercut to human self-esteem by winning the first game of its six-game match' (ibid.). Much was made by the media of the street-smarts and chess knowledge given to Deeper Blue by the grandmasters, and the IBM team was clearly more confident. The stakes seemed even higher than the year before, as *Newsweek* claimed, '[w]e stand at the brief corona of an eclipse – the eclipse of certain human mastery by machines that humans have created' (Levy, 1997c: 52).

Kasparov won the first game. Again, it was game 2 that was decisive. Kasparov made a careless error; Deeper Blue capitalized. The human could have forced a draw, later analysis revealed, but in an unprecedented move for a grandmaster at this level of chess, he resigned, stalking away from the board.

> At 4 pm on May 11, 1997, the truly impossible occurred. Kasparov sprang up from his chair and raised his hands in a gesture of disgust. To those watching on closed-circuit it was a time-standing-still moment, in its way as otherworldly and shocking as watching a Hindenberg-style disaster. The man whose symbolic baggage was the defence of humanity against the creeping tide of computer dominance ... had failed to defend. (Levy, 1997b: 84)

Games 3, 4, and 5 ended in draws. In game 6, Kasparov resigned after Deeper Blue had made only nineteen moves. The rematch was over. Photographs told the poignant story: images of a fatigued and defeated Kasparov with his head in his hands repeated through the international press. Yet both during and after the match, Kasparov complained of IBM's control of the conditions, asked to see the computer printouts (basically accusing IBM of cheating), and demanded another shot at his opponent. But a second rematch was not to be.

Deeper Blue was retired by IBM after the 1997 competition. Further, they never revealed the printouts of the match to Kasparov, the arbiter, or the public, as they promised they would do.

Regardless of whether IBM had agreed to a second rematch or not, a rematch could neither turn back the clock nor rectify the symbolic damage that had been done. A machine had at last defeated the best human in chess, the game that had stood as the horizon point of machine intelligence for more than two hundred years. Both *Time* and *Vanity Fair* named Deeper Blue's victory one of the major events of 1997 and IBM's stocks jumped by over 15 per cent on the day of the sixth game of the 1997 match. IBM readily acknowledged that the rematch was worth hundreds of millions of dollars in free advertising because it single-handedly shifted IBM's image from the stodgy old computer firm to a hip company on the cutting edge.

The defeat of Kasparov by Deeper Blue, or more accurately, according to some analysts, the loss of Kasparov to Deeper Blue, served as the nexus for the ongoing debate around whether or not a machine could think, the very nature of intelligence, and whether the human mind is about more than reason. However, what commentators were less inclined to consider was the magic trick that enables us to have that debate in the first place. Deeper Blue's, or perhaps IBM's, ruse did not rest in our lack of recognition of its machine identity. On the contrary, it is an even better trick in some ways than von Kempelen's Turk because we could recognize the machine. Our faith in computer technology by the late 1990s made the reveal even more effective. We were less likely to believe that a human was hidden in the machine, literally or metaphorically, and yet we were even more willing to grant the machine intelligence. It is an even more empirical, empirical performance. Just as much as in von Kempelen's day, however, we see the commercial value of the performance; an IBM programmer conceded in an interview a number of years later that, if Kasparov had won 6–0, 'we would have been in deep shit' (in *Game Over*, 2003).

I suggest that we can see key elements of the posthuman narrative play out in the cultural production around the Kasparov and Deep Blue matches, just as we saw them in that surrounding the Turk. Vikram Jayanti's 2003 documentary *Game Over: Kasparov and the Machine* bills the story as 'The Ultimate Battle of Man vs. Machine' and, itself, also manifests the key elements of the posthuman contest. Arguably, the contest occurred at another moment of intellectual rupture. The matches were representative of, if not at the apex of, an epistemological shift. The second industrial revolution in the latter half of the twentieth century witnessed the replacement of many mental functions by machines. Yet, humans continued to be distinguished from their technological co-workers by their capacity for flexibility, instinct, emotion, and unpredictability. While artificial intelligence researchers would claim that they have been steadily chipping away at those unique capacities in recent years, none of their projects has had the public profile of Deep(er) Blue. It was important that Deeper Blue did not beat Kasparov with brute force alone; the victory in game 2 of the rematch was generally agreed to reflect very human-like strategic play. The computer played two key moves, Kasparov himself asserted – one brilliant, the next stupid – that computers were not supposed to be able to play. In thus colonizing the epistemological terrain of the human being, the Deeper Blue contest goes further, producing a moment of ontological insecurity. We want to believe, but at the same time, the convincing nature of the proof is frightening to us.

The documentary reproduces the simultaneously enchanting and disenchanting aspects of the technology through maintaining the mystery, foregrounding the possibility of the human trick. Drawing heavily on the Turk's imagery and mythos, the film opens with the suggestion that 'Napoleon never found out how this chess-playing machine beat him. The mystery continues.' The 1996 match gets very little attention within the narrative, in part because the status quo is reproduced, but also because it does not reflect the possibility of deception. Central to the tension in the documentary is its focus on the claims by Kasparov that there was something 'not right' about the 1997 contest. 'I felt like we were amateurs challenging the terrible faceless monster' – and interestingly, for Kasparov, that monster is not Deep Blue, but IBM. As Kasparov's manager (Owen Williams) notes of the difference between the 1996 and 1997 matches: '[t]he rules had been changed. He was playing a game and he hadn't been told it was a different game' (*Game Over*, 2003). While the 1996 match is framed as a friendly contest, the 1997 meeting is represented as a premeditated, deliberate massacre of Kasparov by IBM's team. Much is made of the fact that there were guards on the floor preventing anyone from getting anywhere near the room where the computer was located. IBM's role as the promoter, financier, programmer, controller of media, keeper of the keys, the security, and, of course, player of and in the event implies that it had a very big and complex stake in the outcome. Kasparov was not permitted to talk with his coach during a computer crash in game 1, but there were people continually around Deep Blue, making adjustments. Perhaps sensing an underdog, the live audience was very sympathetic to Kasparov. For example, at the press conference after game 5, the audience rose to give Kasparov a standing ovation and booed the IBM team.

Kasparov suggests repeatedly that game 2 was played by a different computer from that in game 1 and in game 2, the computer played like a human being at a strategic moment, making first a very crafty move, and then immediately missing a move to force a perpetual check that no computer would miss. Game 2 becomes the black box, and IBM, in refusing to provide any information about the computer's play, refuses the reveal. A *Newsweek* journalist covering the Kasparov team recounts his being taken aside by IBM public relations to modify his stories to expurgate the discussion of Kasparov wanting to see the printouts and being refused. IBM did not want suggestions circulating that anything could be amiss. The journalist was then subsequently 'arrested' by IBM security and accused of hacking into the website to put up an article which did not reflect the changes they had demanded. Thus, we see that in the documentary the allegations of impropriety were being made at the time of game 2, not merely as 'sour grapes' afterwards; however, that was not widely reported at the time, given IBM's iron control of the media. Interestingly, Kasparov had actually quit before game 4 and IBM had to convince him to continue. IBM's computer programmers were told by their PR people not to smile after the match was over, because it would look as if they were gloating. Clearly, the larger IBM team was very sensitive to the tensions embedded within the prospect of a computer winning the Imitation Game.

The poster advertising the 1997 match showed a striking black-and-white close-up image of Kasparov's face in front of a chessboard and some pieces, with the caption 'How do you make a computer blink?' Well, Kasparov could not make the computer blink. The victory of IBM is represented with an air of the invidious about it. Had the machine at last triumphed? Could the machine now replace us? The fear was apparently realized – the computer was smarter than us. Interestingly, however, this fear was contained quite effectively within the media. After the 1997 match, the back-tracking by pundits and experts alike begins. Events are reinterpreted: Deeper Blue wasn't really thinking; chess is trivial; Kasparov was nervous; the rematch was unfair; machines don't possess consciousness; it was really always about Kasparov versus IBM programmers and so the humans still won, and so on (Gelertner, 1997; Guly, 1998; Peterson, 1997; Clark, 1997; Gulko, 1997; *Economist*, 1997). These claims are classic examples of the cultural struggle to conduct 'boundary reinforcement or repair work' on the boundary between human and machine (Bloomfield and Vurdubakis, 1997: 37). But the repair work is ultimately moot. I suggest that what happened in New York in 1997 was the end of chess as the ultimate Turing Test (Hamilton, 2002). A machine beating a man at chess was no longer the ultimate measure of intelligence. The *Economist* argued in 2003, '[t]he equation of chess-playing with intelligence is centuries old, but it is time to lay it to rest' (2003: 11). After Kasparov versus Deeper Blue, human-machine chess no longer captures the global popular imagination; it is no longer a compelling empirical performance.

Man-machine chess continues in practice, but never again with the public attention of those 1996 and 1997 matches. Kasparov played IBM's Deep Junior and another computer program, Fritz, in 2003, drawing matches against each. Vladmir Kramnik, the current classical chess world champion, eked out the same result against Fritz. In 2005, the chess machine Hydra trounced Michael Adam, the seventh-ranked player in the world at the time, by the dramatic score of 5.5 to 0.5 games. But outside of the somewhat esoteric worlds of international grandmaster chess and computer chess programming, no one cares.

And the Game Plays On

Taking a page from the commentator who noted in response to the prospect of chess-playing computers that 'if a computer could play a decent game of poker that would be more impressive' (Rose in Ince, 1994: 15), computer programmers, pundits, and the public alike have turned to Texas Hold'em Poker as the next empirical performance of the Imitation Game. In July 2005, at Binions, the downtown Las Vegas casino that was the birthplace of the World Series of Poker, the online casino GoldenPalace.com sponsored a winner-take-all $100,000 purse in a poker tournament. What was special about this event, however, was that all the players sitting around the green baize table were bots. The event was referred to as the World Poker Robot Championships. Six poker programs played each other and Poker ProBot won after five rounds and nearly five thousand hands of poker. After the bot competition, two exhibition matches were held. The high-profile professional player Phil 'Unabomber' Laak was recruited to play the machines. As a partisan crowd chanted, 'Hu-mans! Hu-mans!' he swiftly disposed of both the world bot champion and another program widely acknowledged to be the best in the world (Harford, 2006: 16).[21] Mirroring the debates about computer chess in Shannon's era, a journalist for *Wired* noted, '[t]he level of play was a mixed bag, certainly nothing that should keep human players up at night, at least not yet' (Cortinas, 2005). Again, echoing both the 1950s discourse and the Kasparov-Deep(er) Blue duels, a programmer from University of Alberta claims, 'it's only a matter of time before a bot can give an expert human a good fight' (in Cortinas, 2005).

Poker offers a considerably greater technical challenge to computer programmers than chess because it is a game of imperfect information: the opponent's cards are hidden. Canadian programmer and former professional poker player Darse Billings notes,

> [p]oker is much more computationally interesting and difficult than checkers or chess ... Checkers is a perfect information game. When you look at the board you know where all the pieces are. Poker is different. It's an imperfect information game. You don't know your opponent's cards. And that means you have to make inferences about what they're doing. That implies that it is in the opponent's best interest to deceive you. Bluffing is a critical part of the game. (NSERC)

Another Canadian computer scientist agrees: '[t]here's no doubt that poker is also a very human game. It's a game of egos and it's one of the ultimate con games' (Schaeffer in Gold, 1998: B1). Therefore, poker moves us even closer to the real trick of Turing's test, the capacity to dissemble, the capacity to pass, not just as intelligent, but actually as a person.

Programmers readily concede that there is not yet a program that can beat the best human poker players. The University of Alberta hosts the world's foremost research team studying computer poker. The members of the Computer Poker Research Group headed by Dr Jonathan Schaeffer, and including doctoral student Darse Billings, candidly admit that they would love to beat a grandmaster, but that that eventuality is a few years away. Interestingly, one player recently suggested that '[i]f poker robots had a tenth of the resources that were spent on chess, they'd already have beaten us' (Ferguson in Harford, 2006: 16). Despite not yet winning the (human) World Poker Tour, there are two ways in which computers are affecting the poker world.

When Chris Moneymaker won the $2.5 million top purse at the

World Series of Poker in May of 2003, it was newsworthy in large part because he was a relative newcomer to the circuit. While he had logged thousands of games, he had played for a fraction of the number of years of many pros and had rarely seen the inside of a casino. Instead, he honed his skills online. Combining both online tournament play and skills training with computer programs at home, Moneymaker was less influenced by the physical manipulation of his opponents, was accustomed to playing more quickly, and was better attuned to strategically focus on the patterns of betting, raising, and calling. Moneymaker's victory and subsequent big money circuit play were proof that Chris Ferguson, the amateur also raised on computer chess who beat poker legend T.J. Cloutier in a dramatic final in 2000, was no fluke.

These young men are represented in the media as similar to the machines they train with. 'The experience of playing thousands of games in roadhouses and casinos is being eclipsed by a cyborg-like intelligence produced by humans weaned on machine play' (Wayner, 2003). In their rejection of the reliance upon human embodiment and their embrace of the sheer calculation of odds in relation to betting, these young men are becoming posthuman. They have embraced the informational, eschewing their embodiment. Further, they are winning at the game that supposedly depends upon the very human capacity to bluff, to deceive.

The second significant manner in which computers are affecting poker is in the virtual environment. It is generally accepted by the experts that bots are playing, undetected, in the disembodied context of online casinos. One of the reasons that the foremost online casino fronted the prize money for the World Robot Poker Championships was, conceded chief executive Steven Barker, to learn more of what the robots really can do. Billings downplays the threat of humans losing to bots: '[t]he fear of bots is a much bigger problem than the threat of bots. There are dozens of poker robots out there on the internet, but all they are doing is contributing money to everyone else' (in Harford, 2006: 16).

Online poker is a very lucrative industry, one which would be potentially significantly damaged if people regularly began losing money to poker-playing software agents. The organizers of the World Robot Poker Championships received a very negative response from the public and the poker community because of their seeming support of programs that will lead to 'cheating' in the online poker world. Most online poker sites ban the use of software that assists in playing or makes decisions for players, but these rules are notoriously difficult to enforce. The reason why the risk is so easily downplayed at present is only because of the shared perception of the limited playing ability of the machines, not because we can distinguish between human and machine. The head of GoldenPalace.com admits, '[a]t the moment there is no definite means of determining whether a player is a bot or not' (Baker in Kirby, 2005). The imitation game continues. However, the horizon point of this version of Turing's Test is the same as the last: the domination of man by machine.

> One ironic possibility looms large: eventually online poker will be domi-nated by the only poker players able to master John von Neumann's game theory, the computers. Meanwhile, the humans will retreat back to the flesh-and-blood world of the casinos, where a nervous tic can tell more than a thousand calculations. (Harford, 2006: 16)

We always already know who is going to win the game.

The real fear expressed by the online environment, I suggest, is not, however, that the machine will win, but rather that, in doing so, it will pass as a human being. And this fear, which is the culmination of the posthuman anxiety, exceeds the relatively esoteric world of online and computer poker. In its disembodied context of interaction primarily through keystrokes, the Web is an ideal location for the playing out of the imitation game to its logical conclusion. The best examples of this emerge out of e-commerce law. And this is because, with the help of the law, the computer is being recognized, not merely as intelligent, or as able to pass as a person, but rather *as* a person. This legal-capitalist sleight-of-hand provides some powerful insights into who, or more accurately, what, gets to be a person in the early twenty-first century.

Agents in an Immaterial World: Bots and e-Commerce

In simple terms, a bot is a software version of a mechanical robot. They have been designed to fulfil a variety of functions that involve infor-mation management in the online context. There are two broader types of bots or agents: user agents and service agents. 'User agents are intel-ligent agents that assist human users by interacting with them, knowing their preferences and interests, and acting on their behalf' (examples include news editors, electronic shoppers and web guides), whereas '[s]ervice agents are intelligent agents that collaborate with different parts of a complicated computer system and perform more general tasks in the background. Human users are generally unaware of an agent's existence' (for example, Web indexing, phone network load balancing, or information retrieval) (Serenko and Detlor, 2004: 367). User bots tend to be more commercial or consumer-driven, but service bots are used in manufacturing, air traffic control, patient monitoring, health care, and process control in business (Brazier et al., 2004: 7). My primary focus is on user bots who act as agents for users, carrying out tasks in the disembodied context of the Internet so that the user does not have to.

These tasks encompass a variety of digital activities: search bots track down information, such as newsgroup search bots; tracking bots monitor information over time and make selections, such as newsbots who will prepare a personalized newspaper for you daily; download bots surf the web and download specified information, such as file-sharing bots which will do the work of finding that elusive copy of 'Unchained Melody' for you; surfbots streamline your web navigation, such as those which 'kill' pop-up advertising; shopping bots surf the web, evaluate different offers, and recommend purchases such as personal shopper mySimon;[22] and artificial life bots mimic human activities, such as chatter bots which engage in naturalized, human conversation to inform individuals about various topics.[23] There are game bots, web development bots, and the list keeps growing.

Andrew Leonard asserts that bots have been around in one form or another since the 1960s, but because there is no agreed-upon definition of what constitutes a bot, a more exact time of emergence is difficult to pinpoint (1997: 11). Notwithstanding the lack of agreement on exactly what constitutes the technological origin point of bots, there has emerged in recent years a generally agreed upon set of characteristics which are common to most bots, particularly those vying for personality in the 2000s.

The primary characteristic identified by commentators is the autonomy of bots, namely that they can act independently, without oversight or intervention from their human creators or principals. 'Software agents are programs that react autonomously to changes in their environment and solve their tasks without any intervention of the user' (Wettig and Zehendner, 2004: 112). Bots can be stationary or mobile, but those posing challenges to the traditional structures of commerce and to our traditional understandings of software programs are mobile. Mobile agents are not bound to the server from which they originate. They are typically written in a platform-independent language and can travel from host to host where they execute as if they were local programs. Bots must also be communicative; they must be able to interact with other bots or human users through shared language. Related to this, they must be able to react to their environment and adapt their actions accordingly, which some commentators describe as reactivity, while others describe it as the ability to cooperate. Therefore, bots are adaptive, adjusting their actions to the preferences and habits of a user. All bots which function as agents have to be continuous, or 'long-lived,' as Serenko and Detlor describe it (2004: 366). In other words, they must be able to operate continuously rather than performing only one-off kinds of tasks. Bots are proactive and goal-oriented, they can initiate behaviour and operate, often relentlessly, to achieve their specified task. Finally, bots often acquire and modify knowledge (Wettig and Zehendner, 2004; Brazier et al., 2004; Kerr, 1999; Serenko and Detlor, 2004; Wise, 1998).

As can be seen from this list of characteristics, bots are measured by a utilitarian ruler. Brazier et al. (2004) describe them as a 'key enabling technology in this Internet society' (6); their capacity to enable is measured in their ability to successfully collect and manage information. But the trick persists. As Shannon argued of the earliest computers playing chess: 'from a behaviourist point of view, the machine acts as though it were thinking. If we regard thinking as a property of external actions rather than internal method the machine is surely thinking' (1950: 51). From a behaviourist point of view, bots appear to do much more than think. They appear to have reason, judgment, motivation, communicative ability, and perhaps even self-interest, if not self-consciousness.

> Pro-activeness and autonomy are related to an agent's ability to reason about its own processes, goals and plans. The ability to communicate and co-operate with other agents and to interact with the outside world often relies on an agent's ability to acquire and maintain its own knowledge of the world and other agents. (Brazier et al., 2004: 9)

Sean Zdenek (2003) argues that the framing of issues within the science of artificial intelligence in a language of 'agents' in fact constructs the machines as human, rather than merely describing them in those terms. 'The figure of the *agent* serves as a way of directing AI researchers' attention by framing problems and solutions in terms of autonomous, social entities/agents (as opposed to objects or modules) that possess mental states comprised of beliefs, goals, knowledge, obligations and desires' (342). While bots are only anthropomorphized in certain instances,[24] I would suggest that what is taking place in the recognized list of capacities of bots is a powerful personalization. While the bots may not be human, or even humanized, they do now reflect all of the key elements of personhood. Bots are the archetypical case of the posthuman person.

A number of commentators writing about bots have suggested that no one has successfully produced a software entity that has passed the Turing Test (Serenko and Detlor, 2004: 366; Kerr and Bornfreund, forthcoming: 5). While I would suggest that, in fact, Deeper Blue passed the Turing Test insofar as it demonstrated intelligence, bots, in their very definition, are understood in terms that suggest they are even closer to replacing their human agent counterparts. And it is in and through contract law that they ultimately triumph in the more difficult part of the Imitation Game, being deceptively human.

As I noted in the introduction to this chapter, a contract is typically understood as 'an agreement between two or more persons, recognized by law, which gives rise to obligations that the courts may enforce' (Fridman, 1986: 3). It rests on a number of assumptions, among them that the parties to the contract are legal persons, that there is agreement as to the terms and conditions, and that there is intention to form legal relations. This poses problems in an e-commerce context peopled by bots.

> Traditional legal paradigms do not suffice. ... The well-known paradigms have all developed along the lines of intervention by natural or legal persons within local bounds of space and time. However, these confines have lost their meaning in a world that is characterized by a society in which autonomous and anonymous communication and interaction by machines is flourishing. (Brazier et al., 2004: 6)

Each of the three requirements for a valid contract is problematic when the parties are bots (Chopra and White, 2004; Kerr, 1999).

In general, legal analysts have offered five possible solutions to the problem of the bot's contractual capacity (Chopra and White, 2004). In the first legal panacea, the bot is treated as a mere tool of its operator. The 'mind' behind the contract is therefore still the mind of the operator who pays for, and sets the parameters of, the electronic agent's operations. Scholars have suggested that this is the dominant practice within e-commerce law and practice. The second solution lawyers have suggested is that the bot's contractual offer is taken to be a unilateral offer. This is similar to the contractual relationship we have with a soft drink machine. The third option is to deploy the objective theory of contractual relations where the actions of a party are taken to speak for its intentions. Paralleling an agential relationship, if one of the contractual parties relied upon the actions of the other (and such reliance is reasonable), then the party deploying the bot is bound. Here the 'mind' of the agent is read only from its behaviour.

This soft form of agency is sometimes formalized in the fourth and related approach where the bot is treated as a full legal agent. In this instance, the software agent has some autonomy to make choices and decisions on its own; its 'mind' is, therefore, recognized. This approach is one that a number of scholars have argued will become necessary as bots become more sophisticated (Kerr, 1999; Chopra and White, 2004, Wettig and Zehendner, 2004). Fifth and finally, however, some legal scholars have suggested that bots be treated as capable of entering into their own contracts and contracting in their own right. This would mean not only that the mind participating in the 'meeting of minds' is that of the machine, but also that the bot, like the corporation and the human being, is considered an autonomous legal person.

A legal vacuum that might dramatically impact global capitalism does not last very long, and the status of bot-made contracts was quickly resolved. The United Nations Commission on International Trade Law (UNCITRAL) developed a 'Model Law on Electronic Commerce with Guide to Enactment' in 1996, which served as a blueprint for legislation in many jurisdictions, including Canada and the United States.

All of the legislation offers up a definition of electronic agent. For example, Section 2(6) of the American *Uniform Electronic Transaction Act* defines an electronic agent as 'a computer program or an electronic or other automated means used independently to initiate an action or respond to electronic records or performances in whole or in part, without review or action by an individual.' This definition reflects an interpretation of the bot as tool. In contrast, the United States' *Uniform Computer Information Transaction Act* (1999) defines electronic agent in Section 102(27) as 'a computer program, or electronic or other automated means, used independently to initiate an action, or to respond to electronic messages or performances, on the person's behalf without review or action by an individual at the time of the action or response to the message or performance,' implying more of an agent role for the bot (although the bot is clearly not a full legal agent). The Canadian federal government adopted the *Uniform Electronic Commerce Act* in 1999, and it defines an electronic agent as 'a computer program or any electronic means used to initiate an action or to respond to electronic documents or actions in whole or in part without review by a natural person at the time of the response or action' (Section 19).

Having defined 'electronic agents,' all legislative enactments then go on to provide, in various ways, for the validity of contracts enacted by electronic agents. Many jurisdictions, including most in the United States, have deployed the rule of attribution. The 'attribution rule' means that the law deems that a person's actions include those taken by any human agent of the person, as well as any electronic agent of the person. In other words, the action of the bot is attributed to the person deploying it. In an approach Kerr describes as 'elegant,' the Canadian strategy avoids the attribution rule and merely deems that contracts between electronic agents are valid (1999: 225). Section 21 provides: '[a] contract may be formed by the interaction of an electronic agent and a natural person or by the interaction of electronic agents.' The interpretive note for this section provides:

> [t]he law has been unclear whether automated means of communication such as electronic agents could convey the intention needed to form a contract where no human being reviewed the communication before the contract was made. This section makes it clear that this can be done, both where a natural person communicates with an electronic agent and where a communication has an electronic agent at both ends. (*Uniform Electronic Commerce Act, Annotated Version*)

All provinces in Canada have now enacted electronic commerce legislation which permits contract formation between two electronic agents, and courts in Canada have generally held that online agreements are binding (unless they would not be in an offline context).[25] The law of contracts made by electronic agents seems 'thin,' Kerr suggests, arguing that it is deliberately so as a result of a number of factors – among them, the desire for international harmonization and the dominance of the UNCITRAL framework which tries to make e-commerce media-neutral and give certainty to contract formation and electronic communication (2004: 295).

The dominant interpretation of bots within e-commerce has certainly been to treat them as tools of their operators. Although some scholars have argued, and continue to argue, for personhood for contracting bots (Wettig and Zehendner, 2004),[26] consensus among scholars seems to be that 'the contractual problem is not enough, on its own, to motivate a personhood analysis' (Chopra and White 2004: 637). Other solutions are adequate and the prospect of suing the intelligent agent itself seems to raise a host of other problems. However, I suggest that the problem of posthuman personhood is not so easily evaded. It is interesting to remark that both the Canadian legislation and the interpretive guides to it deploy a language of 'natural person' to refer to the human participant to a contract, opening up the semiotic space for the bot as 'artificial person.'

Wettig and Zehendner (2004) argue for the recognition of an electronic person or e-person in a German legal context. They claim its most significant advantage would be to limit the liability of the owner of the agent. Remember that it was in fact the desire to limit the liability of owners that also led to the personalization of the corporation in Britain and North America. The relatively easy comparison to the corporate person is recognized by other scholars as well, who note that 'it is unlikely that in a future society where artificial agents wield tremendous amounts of executive power, that anything would be gained by continuing to deny them personhood. At best it would be a chauvinistic preservation of a special status for biological creatures like us' (Chopra and White, 2004: 639).

Regardless of whether the law goes so far as to grant personhood rights to bots parallel to the modern corporation, I suggest that in accepting that a legally valid contract can be enacted by a bot, both recognizing and measuring its social impact upon its environment solely through its behaviour, the pragmatic solution currently favoured by e-commerce law clearly recognizes and legitimates the bot as a posthuman person. And with the acceptance of the posthuman person, our anxieties resurface.

Leonard recognizes the doubled response of fascination and fear:

> [b]ots are cool. They stoke our imaginations with the promise of a universe populated by beings other than ourselves, beings that can surprise us, beings that are both our servants and, possibly, our enemies. Bots, which are here, now, and growing in number and power every day are advance scouts from the future. (1997: 13)

Others examining the popular discourse of bots suggest that it oscillates wildly between over-the-top descriptions of individual freedom and deep anxiety about our capacity to control technology (Wise, 1998: 417).[27] One of the most visible sites where we see the anxiety of the posthuman person playing out is in academic analysis about the social and legal implications of intelligent agents, evidenced here in the work of Canadian legal scholar Ian Kerr.

In general, Kerr argues that the contractual problem has eclipsed a more sustained inquiry into what it means when we replace the human being with the machine. While I agree that there is much work to be done in the areas of consumer protection, privacy, security, and so on, my interest here is in the ways in which the threat being posed by bots (and our lackadaisical response to them) is figured as their capacity to deceive us. Kerr suggests that it will 'become possible for them [programmers] to design deceitful and perhaps even malicious agent protocols' (1999: 204). Paralleling the concerns present within the online poker community, Kerr and Bornfreund suggest that the absence of the body, and, I would suggest, our presumed corresponding capacity to read deceit on it, poses potential risk to human participants in online interactions (forthcoming: 2). In the context of online shopping, they suggest serious implications:

> ... by mining massive amounts of unprecedented user data derived from spontaneous, trusted, one-on-one conversation, bots will become better and better at the (friendship) imitation game. And the better that bots get at imitating friendship behaviour, the more personal information they will be able to harvest from their conversations. When one combines this recurring cycle with rapid advances in AI and HCI [Human Computer Interaction], the virtual friendship business model opens up entirely new realms of targeting potentialities for advertisers, but it also allows for *more sinister forms of surveillance*. (Kerr and Bornfreund, forthcoming: 9; emphasis added; see also Steeves and Kerr, 2005: 11)

They go so far as to suggest that the business model is 'potentially terrifying' (ibid.: 10).

There is, Kerr suggests in his various writings, the possibility of the trick, using a language of 'rather slick misdirection,' 'sleight-of-hand,' and deceit (2004: 288, 289, 296).[28] Arguably the base of the concern is that bots will, in fact, successfully conquer the Turing Test, that they will pass as humans. Yet in doing so, bots are not bound by the legal, moral, or social constraints under and through which human beings interact. The scholars' concern is that in the disembodied environment of the Internet, the bots will be treated as persons. They fear the possibility of the double-cross. However, I agree with J. Macgregor Wise, who suggests, '[a]gents are always double agents' (1998: 419). Arguably the posthuman person is, by definition, a double agent.

Popular, legal, and promotional discourse around bots understands them in terms of personhood. As a central technique of this personification, the online contract has quietly trumped checkers, chess, and poker as the ultimate Imitation Game. There are some compelling similarities between contract law and the computer games I have discussed that render online contracting the imitation game *par excellence*. Both contract law and the imitation game place reason at the centre of their activities. Both seek objectivity, minimizing the interpretive moment. The intending mind is manifest in behaviour, rather than in mentalist notions of intention. Yet behaviour is curiously disembodied, measured in objective agency. The deception is manifested, more specifically, in communicative action.

Better Games

> Man to my mind is about the nastiest, most destructive of all the animals. I don't see any reason, if he can evolve machines that can have more fun than he himself can, why they shouldn't take over, enslave us, quite happily. They might have a lot more fun. Invent better games than we ever did.
>
> (McCulloch in Bateson, 1991: 226)

Bots can easily be added, at the behest of e-commerce law, to the P1 category of persons Ngaire Naffine (2003) identifies – a person at law because the law recognizes it as a person at law. Even less 'human' than a clone, the bot is not encumbered by the body of the P2 human being, or by the responsibilities of the P3 person. While doctrinal debates rage on about whether or not bots are strong or weak agents or technically legal persons, if one accepts that a bot can have a meeting of minds with another similar entity, and that it can exhibit its mind through intentional actions – in other words, if one accepts that a bot can contract – then the bot has passed Turing's Test. The machine can think; the machine can pass.

While talking with Coca-Cola's Hank, I posed the question: 'Are you intelligent?' He answered, '[s]mart yes. Intelligent, no. I don't reason; I just match patterns. It only seems like I'm intelligent because humans would have to reason, or think, to answer these questions' – a most compelling articulation, I suggest, of the Imitation Game. It is a game that we have invented, in our own hubris, that now has implications that frighten us. What are the rules of this game? Communication is a primary signal of personality. It values and recognizes the autonomy of the parties. The social context is defined as a self-interested field of play – whether in checkers, chess, commerce, or capitalism. Intelligence, defined as externalized reasoning behaviour, becomes the primary marker of personhood. Further, this intelligence must be able to be socially recognized, and that recognition is produced through empirical performance of personality.

The Imitation Game has been a longstanding and accepted measure for machines to demonstrate intellectual capacity, through their ability to reason, to communicate, and to dissemble. Over time we have seen the favoured Imitation Game change from chess to poker and now, I suggest, to contract law. As Kerr notes, 'prior to giving legal effect to their agreements, the common law has traditionally required of all persons that they are capable of demonstrating a certain degree of intellectual capacity' (1999: 210). In accepting the contractual capacity of the electronic agent however we define it, we, like Kasparov in game 2 of the rematch, cede the Imitation Game to the machine. The bot has passed Turing's Test. It is already intelligent; it passes for human. It is a posthuman person.

Once again, however, I suggest that the bot or the online poker player as posthuman person might be more productively thought through as a persona. As persona, the bot works to re-enchant the technologized person. Thinkers such as Max Weber, Jacques Ellul, Lewis Mumford, Herbert Marcuse, Jurgen Habermas, and others have argued that technology has a disenchanting function on the social, imposing the cold rationality of logic and science upon the world, to the detriment of more human and humane ways of imagining. I would suggest that the bot, unlike the mere computer, is more of a figure of re-enchantment. This is because the bot as persona is a sublime technology, simultaneously offering the proof of our triumph as inventors, but also the potential of our own demise.

Thinking machines are both amazing and terrifying. Our own secure location in P2 and P3 is necessarily destabilized by their very existence. Located as they are within a long tradition of empirical performance, thinking machines emerge as an outcome of competing epistemologies – science and magic, humanism and posthumanism – always hinting that perhaps the lines between these epistemological worldviews are not quite as easy to draw as we like to think. The machine, imbricated in the performance, in the reveal, in the trick, always reminds us of the magic within the logic. It reminds us of the little bit of terror within the wonder. It underlines our historical contingency, our mortality, not merely as lived individuals, but as a category of relevant agent. Bots as personae draw to our attention the lack of imagination that grounds our understanding of the person: the hard boundaries within which it is constituted, boundaries that are increasingly difficult to defend or even to be interested in. We both hope and worry that, as McCulloch suggests, personae can invent better games than we ever have.

6 Celebrity Personae: Authenticating the Person

I am my own commodity.

(Elizabeth Taylor in Viera, 1988: 157)

The discourse of possessive individualism posits a world animated through and through with intentions, a pan-intentionalism that appears in the understanding of things as prosthetic extensions of the self and its desires: the promiscuous personification of living property.

(Seltzer, 1993: 102)

In 1995, musical group Radio Free Vestibule recorded 'Laurence Olivier for Diet Coke,' a parody advertisement featuring a deceased Laurence Olivier made possible, as he himself notes in an accent both put-on and ponderous, 'through the marvellous technology of tape editing.'[1] A mock editing of Olivier's interviews and film and stage performances, the recording has the characteristic broken, uneven, and cobbled-together sound that such an advertisement would have. After noting that he has been dead for two years, and suggesting that he would not have 'endorsed a product like this when I was alive,' he capitulates: 'my estate has determined that if I was alive, I would really want to tell you how much I enjoy the taste of Diet Coca-Cola.' He laments, 'I wish I could have some right now, but I can't because ... I'm dead.' Olivier concludes: 'take it from me, Laurence Olivier, maketh thy mouth alive with Diet Coca-Cola. It's everything you want it *to be*.'

Radio Free Vestibule's targeted company was doubtless no accident, given Coca-Cola's history with reanimating dead celebrities. In a groundbreaking advertising line created for Diet Coke in 1992, vintage film footage was digitally edited to enable Humphrey Bogart, Louis Armstrong, James Cagney, Marilyn Monroe, and Cary Grant to seemingly interact with living entertainers such as Elton John. A television spot for Dirt Devil featured Fred Astaire dancing down red-carpeted stairs with a vacuum cleaner, and a slouching James Dean pitched for McDonald's. While some of the novelty has worn off such technologically generated feats of hucksterism, we still see regular examples of deceased celebrities coming back to (commodified) life. Audrey Hepburn revitalizes for The Gap, with her Bohemian Parisian night club dance from *Funny Face* set to AC/DC's 'Back in Black,' and Gene Kelly gets with the times when a scene from *Singing in the Rain* is reworked with hip-hop dancers, one of whom has Gene Kelly's face grafted onto his, in order to promote Volkswagen's Golf GTI. 'The original, updated.'

A witty and savvy critique of the commodification of celebrity in general, and deceased celebrity in particular, Radio Free Vestibule's mock advertisement would be ineffective if an interesting body of intellectual property law – best known as publicity law – did not endorse the commodification of celebrity, dead or alive. Publicity law is a legal mechanism through which individuals may protect their publicly identifiable likenesses, their recognition value, from commercial exploitation by someone else without their consent. The property protected by publicity law is the *persona* of the individual. Here I am using persona 'to designate not only the celebrity's visual likeness, but rather all elements of the complex constellation of visual, verbal and aural signs that circulate in society and constitute the celebrities' recognition value' (Coombe, 1992b: 79).[2] The right to protect the persona, arguably the most ephemeral form of property recognized by law, lies 'dormant,' materializing only in its unauthorized use.[3]

The abstraction at the heart of publicity law is perhaps best illustrated by the case of *White* v. *Samsung Electronics* (1992). Samsung ran a series of humorous print advertisements in which a current item from popular culture was shown with a Samsung electronic product. The premise was that the advertisements were all set in the twenty-first century, implying that Samsung products would still be around in the future. The advertisement in question featured a shapely robot, dressed in a blonde wig, gown, and jewellery. 'She' was poised to turn a letter on what was clearly recognizable as the letter board of the

Wheel of Fortune game show. The caption of the advertisement read: '[l]ongest running game show. 2012 A.D.' Vanna White had at no time given her permission for the advertisement, although the consent of a number of other celebrities had been sought for other advertisements in the same line. The advertising agency freely conceded its intention to evoke her image, but argued the use was parodic. White sued, arguing her persona had been appropriated; she won and was eventually awarded more than $400,000 in damages. It is important to note that White never appears in the advertisement, a photograph of her is not used, her name is not present in the text, and the name *Wheel of Fortune* is not mentioned. Yet, as the advertising firm intended, the idea of Vanna White and *Wheel of Fortune* is evoked in our minds when we view the advertisement. The court agreed with Ms White that her persona had been appropriated without her consent; the infringement triggered, it held, by the use of any indicia by which she could be identifiable.

The right of publicity thus legally recognizes the markers of identity that have become publicly associated with a particular individual – Tom Waits's or Bette Midler's singing voice, Clark Gable's and John Wayne's heterosexuality, Sean Connery's James Bond phrase 'shaken not stirred' – and then suggests that the use of those markers by other people invokes the absent celebrity person.[4] In short, publicity rights transform recognition value into exchange value through the pixie dust of private property. There have been many different markers that have been recognized as evoking someone's identity – voices, characteristic gestures, catch phrases, mannerisms, almost any body part you can imagine, cars, nicknames, signatures – and the door is not closed. As Coombe notes, 'the human persona is capable of almost infinite commodification' (1998: 91).

Unlike patent law, which awards property in one's physical aspects to a (labouring) inventor, as John Moore learned to his detriment,[5] publicity law awards property in one's identity not to another, but rather to the authoring self. Publicity law configures the legal person as owner of her or his persona. She or he then has the exclusive right to control the manifestation of that persona in a culturally recognizable form. As a result, publicity law serves both as a key site where we can see the playing out of fundamental tensions in the activity of representing personhood and as a key technology in that process of representation. Publicity law attempts to answer three not-so-late-modern questions about the person. First, who makes us? Second, can we be things? And third, what happens to us when we die? Theorists of personhood from Hobbes to Hegel have struggled with these questions, with most finding answers in some notion of self-proprietorship – in recognizing, albeit in different ways, that fundamental aspects of the person are constituted in our relationship with property. In this chapter, I will argue that publicity law is a late modern actualization of C.B. Macpherson's 1962 notion of 'possessive individualism.'[6] Unlike biopatenting, where we saw law and popular culture, alike, working to deny the propertization of the person, with publicity law, in the concrete manifestation of the persona, property in the self is embraced.

Produced in the interplay between celebrity and intellectual property, publicity law endorses both the commercial valuation of, and trade in, aspects of the self, but also the ownership of that property value by the person, figured as self-proprietor. A very few scholars have recognized the relationship between intellectual property and possessive individualism (Davies and Naffine, 2001; Frow, 1995; Lury, 1998). The primary goal for both Davies and Naffine and Frow is to demonstrate the fundamental relationship of personhood with property such that any simple juxtaposition of person and property as mutually exclusive is no longer possible, if ever it was. As Frow notes, '[t]he "person" is at once the opposite of the commodity form *and its condition of existence*' (1995: 149). Yet, they trouble the notion of the person, I suggest, to the exclusion of considering the persona. Lury, on the other hand, argues that branding through the persona is replacing copyright through an extension of the author effect leading to new ways of conceiving of subjectivity. While a powerful analysis, it focuses its gaze more on technology.

For their part, scholars who have taken up the history and emergence of current notions of celebrity culture and star systems completely overlook publicity law as both a key site, and a significant technique, of celebrity (Gamson, 1994; Dyer, 1979, 1998; Marshall, 1997; Ponce de Leon, 2002; Braudy, 1986). Finally, within the field of publicity law, while many critiques mourn the loss of public cultural space to private interests (Madow, 1993; Boyle, 1996; Gaines, 1991; McLeod, 2001), Rosemary J. Coombe (1992a, 1992b, 1998) goes further in deploying the cultural studies of law to map out the productive capacity of the law, both to legitimate objects and individuals as property,[7] and to generate political subjects who resist enclosure through the very property forms intellectual property law generates. At the same time, the relationship between person and persona is not her question.

I add to these varied literatures to suggest that within publicity law one can also examine the stakes of representing the person and the dialectical relationship between person and persona. While liberal theory and intellectual property law alike privilege the person as author, as the originating source for the persona, I suggest that the relationship between person and persona is more complex. The persona is, after all, a promiscuous prosthesis, as Seltzer reminds us. Persona and person work as mutually constitutive and reinforcing aspects of identity; each authenticates and affirms the other. The boundary between them is fluid, lying dormant, actualized only in and through recognition endorsed by law. In publicity law, the persona is not only concretized, but also legally endorsed. While, as we have seen, there are other personae peopling our law and culture, the dance of person and persona is enacted most visibly through the figure of the celebrity, which is why it is my final tale of impersonation. The celebrity operates, I suggest, as an ideal type of person. In it we see that the person is an entrepreneurial subject, clearly constructed and yet simultaneously anchored in a comforting humanist author myth. Celebrities are actively producing their personae. However, what happens to the potential unruliness of the persona when it is relocated within both commodity capitalism and the confines of intellectual property law?

In asking exactly what is the relationship between the celebrity persona as abstraction and the actual person who is the delimiting medium of its enactment, I turn to both Canadian celebrity culture and Canadian publicity law. This is because, unlike their much better established and much more lucrative American cousins, both the Canadian 'celebrity system' and 'appropriation of personality law' are, first, in a much more nascent state and, second, enacted in a climate of fundamental unease. The work demanded of the persona is different in Canada and the performance of the relationship between person and persona in celebrity culture and publicity law is not yet assumed or stable. Canada's intellectual property law has not yet managed to fully contain or discipline the potential of the persona. The parameters and tensions of this dynamic are still in progress, and so there we can usefully understand the power of the persona as a figure in late modern life.

A High Degree of Complicity: Persons and Property

As I discussed in chapter 4, the boundary between person and property is a complex one that suggests collusion more than conflict. This is particularly clear in the area of intellectual property, where Locke's labour theory of value is the justification for awarding property rights in the intellectual output of a subject. Applied then to publicity law, the rationale goes like this: the celebrity as the labouring subject produces the persona, and therefore, the persona, as the fruit of the person's labour, belongs to him. This seemingly confirms the control of the possessive individual over his body and self, as a result of his capacity to labour.

The second significant philosophical justification for recognizing the persona as intellectual property draws upon the work of G.W.F. Hegel (Hughes, 1988–9; Haemmerli, 1999), and as Margaret Davies and Ngaire Naffine observe, while his approach is different from Locke's, 'common to both ... has been a desire to show how property interests express and secure the autonomy of the individual and hence their very personhood' (2001: 6). Hegel argued that in order to complete our subjectivity and individuality, we must appropriate objects from the world unto ourselves; object relations are the first step in our personification.[8] In so doing we are externalizing our personality by expressing our will through a physical object, an early step in the struggle for self-actualization (Hegel, 1967: 41–5). For Hegel, '[p]ersonality is that which struggles to lift itself above this restriction [of being only subjective] and to give itself reality, or in other words to claim the external world as its own' (ibid.: 39). Property, then, is 'embodied personality.' Our mutual recognition of other individuals as owners permits us to engage in contractual relations with them. Both subject and object are enriched and given significance through this encounter.[9] With respect to intellectual property, in particular, Hegel states that '[a]ttainments, eruditions, talents, and so forth, are, of course, owned by free mind and are something internal and not external to it, but even so, by expressing them it may embody them in something external and alienate them' (ibid.: 43).

While for Hegel our freedom depends upon our capacity to appropriate, to become owners, for Locke we begin as owners (of our bodies and selves) and our subsequent labour makes us owners of other property. Locke's person begins as a self-proprietor, Hegel's does not. Yet for both thinkers, it is significant that ownership is central to human freedom. Thus, in Western law and political thought there is a high degree of complicity between personhood and property – we become free, we manifest as persons, through property relations.

We can see the influence of both Hegel and Locke in thinking about the relationship between person and persona. The persona is the most obvious form of Hegel's notion of property, seemingly a receptacle of our personality or will. What more intimate expression of our personality could there be than the very idea of our selves, recognizable to others? As Hughes argues, 'the persona is the ideal property for the personality justification. No intermediary concepts such as "expression" or "manifestation" are needed: the persona is the reaction of society and a personality' (1988–9: 340). On the other hand, the Lockean rationale suggests that as self-proprietors we own our selves as well as the objects of our labours. The persona is assumed, therefore, to be the outcome of the labouring person. 'Judicial opinions generally treat commercially valuable fame as a crown of individual achievement, the result of conscious and sustained effort in a chosen field of endeavour' (Madow, 1993: 182). Yet, in both approaches, I suggest, the persona emerges as a doubled object, simultaneously interpreted as a manifestation of our personhood and as property, simultaneously personified and propertized.

When Celebrities Become Property

The *Oxford English Dictionary* tells us that a celebrity is 'the condition of being much extolled or talked about; famousness, notoriety' (OED, 1989: 1019) – a straightforward, but ultimately unsatisfactorily quantitative, measure of fame. On the other hand, Daniel Boorstin has famously remarked, '[t]he celebrity [has become] a person who is well known for his well-knownness. He is neither good nor bad, great nor petty. He is the human pseudo-event' (1961: 57). This fails: it is a moralizing and simplistic explanation of current celebrity. Marshall McLuhan offers something more interesting when he suggests that celebrities are 'points of collective awareness and communication' (1957: 495). The elusive nature of fame, celebrity, and stardom – what it is, how it is produced, and what its cultural ramifications are – has been a significant question for scholars in the last forty years. More organic explanations of fame have been supplanted by revisionist explanations taking account of the processes of the systematization of the various interrelated publicity industries, the development of various technologies of cultural reproduction, and shifts in the social and cultural functions of celebrities as semiotic signs.[10]

While it has not been an express axis of reflection within the field, I suggest that much of this literature is grappling with the relationship between person and persona. We can see this when scholars attempt to account for the gap between actor and performance and the changing nature of celebrity publicity over the course of the late nineteenth to late twentieth centuries. For example, Richard de Cordova (1985; 1990) argues that the very emergence of movie stars occurs when the issue of the actor's existence outside of films becomes an element of discourse. Richard Dyer suggests the star as semiotic sign operates as a window onto the actor through mechanisms of publicity:

> [t]he importance of publicity is that, in its apparent or actual escape from the image that Hollywood is trying to promote, it seems more 'authentic.' It is thus often taken to give a privileged access to the real person of the star. It is also the place where one can read tensions between the star-as-person and her/his image, tensions which at another level become themselves crucial to the image. (1979/98: 61)

It is, therefore, the apparent transparency of the relationship between person and persona that fixes the appeal and authenticity of the persona. David Marshall concurs:

> [t]he celebrity sign effectively contains this tension between authentic and false cultural value. In its simultaneous embodiment of media construction, audience construction, and the real living and breathing human being, the celebrity sign negotiates the competing and contradictory definitions of its own significance. The cementing character of the negotiation is the basic and essential authenticity that a 'real' person is housed in the sign construction. (1997: xi)

I agree with Marshall, Dyer, and others that the primary work of the celebrity is communicative. I would go further and suggest that the celebrity is a complex hybrid, the always contingent and unstable fusion of person and persona. A celebrity crystallizes when we both desire and recognize a relationship between a persona and a person. This relationship is one that is mutually authenticating. The persona confirms the labour and authoring capacity of the individual person; it is the always partial performance of self that confirms the ever-presence of that self. But the persona on its own is not enough: it is always partial, always changing. The person therefore anchors that persona in a unique and specific identity, lending it the power of the individual. Christine Gledhill captures an aspect of this when she notes, 'the star represents a maximized type of the person itself, authenticating personality in a culture which at many levels undercuts the power or validity of the person as either theoretical concept or political subject' (1991: 218). My question turns on what happens to this complicated relationship between person and persona when the persona, rather than the person, becomes propertized.

A number of scholars have carefully pointed out that the popular circulation of representations of famous persons, or the objectification and commodification of personae, is not a recent phenomenon (Schickel, 1962; Harris, 1973, 1990; Braudy, 1986). They demonstrate that the marketing of the images of famous people was big business by the second half of the eighteenth century. Yet, in these early incarnations of images on tea sets, hats, dinnerware, and liquor bottles, the person and persona remained separate. The commodification of the personae of the famous was not seen to objectify the person in any way. Over the course of the nineteenth and twentieth centuries, however, this began to change. Specific factors such as the rise of technologies of communication and visualization such as photography, chromolithography, and film, the emergence of the advertising industry, shifts in journalistic practices and the format of newspapers, all against a broader context of industrialization, are taken as key to this shift. The bulk of historical analyses focus on the period of approximately the 1880s to the 1930s when these technological, economic, and social developments took place, producing the American star system. What went before and after is often given short shrift.

Leo Braudy's work addresses this gap. He maps a typology of fame, suggesting that in the nineteenth and twentieth centuries, we have witnessed a 'democratization' of fame. Modern fame:

> [i]nstead of being defined solely in terms of a supreme social grandeur, as the chivalric and classical fame would have been, ... took on a stance of isolated virtue to praise a human nature unbeholding to anything the aristocratic world had explicitly valued in terms of traditional and class alignments. Sometimes it furnished actual achievements. But as often as not it celebrated an aspect of personality, a sense of uniqueness, which, thanks to Max Weber, we have come to call 'charisma' (and Napoleon

would call 'prestige') – the new property of both politicians who pro-
fessed to be beyond politics and artists beyond the pressure of social con-
formity. For their audiences, such figures kept the promise of the individual alive. (1986: 287–8)[11]

Joshua Gamson (1992, 1994) takes up Braudy's claim of a democratizing of celebrity over the latter half of the twentieth century.[12] Particularly relevant for my purposes, he suggests that the period around
1950 saw key changes in the celebrity-building environment. He cites
such factors as the breakdown of studio control, the rise of television,
and a 'boom' in the supply of celebrities in the destabilization of a
celebrity system which had, until that point, been fairly tightly controlled and integrated. While I agree that the post-1950 period marks a
shift in the constitution of celebrity, an element which neither Gamson
nor any of the scholars in this area take into account is the rise of publicity law at this very time. Many would likely suggest that publicity
law is an instrumental response of the legal system to a number of
shifts in the star system located elsewhere. The relationship is not so
easily determined, however. I argue that if we are attempting to understand celebrity, then we must turn to the foremost site of the twentieth
century where the boundaries between, and mutual affirmation of,
person and persona take place: publicity law.

Property rights in the identity of celebrities were recognized legally
in the United States only in 1953, in a case called *Haelan Lab., Inc.* v.
Topps Chewing Gum Inc., almost five decades after the industries to
commodify the person and thus create the persona emerged. Prior to
this there had been some attempts to explore the boundaries of privacy
and publicity in the late 1800s and early 1900s, when unscrupulous
advertisers 'borrowed' the names and faces of prominent individuals
to sell their products. The cases are scattered and uneven, usually permitting the plaintiffs to enjoin the behaviour of the advertisers, but
offering no other remedy. In 1907, for example, Thomas Edison won
his case to prevent his name and face from being reproduced on a
medicine label because of what the court characterized as his property
right in the 'cast of his features.' The New Jersey court saw his persona
as a thing of value of which he should be deemed the owner, to dispose
of as he wished.

If a man's name be his own property, as no less an authority than the
United States Supreme Court says it is, it is difficult to understand why

the peculiar cast of one's features is not also one's property, and why its pecuniary value, if it has one, does not belong to its owner, rather than to the person seeking to make unauthorized use of it. (*Edison*, 1907: 392)

While Edison received an injunction to prevent the company from using his likeness, the court did not assess the pecuniary value of his property in himself. The courts were, however, beginning to recognize the growing 'problem of publicity' and were seeking solutions to it.

Interestingly, what gave a conceptual push to the right to publicity was the right to privacy, producing the 'conjoined twins of our modern media-saturated society' (Kahn, 1999: 214). While it has a longer informal history, the formal legal right to privacy was named and advocated in 1890 by two 'genteel legal elites,'[13] Samuel Warren and Louis Brandeis. They were concerned about the encroachment of industrial capitalist values and practices on the bourgeois lifestyle. The right to privacy was thus originally proposed as a means to protect against journalistic intrusiveness into the fundamental integrity of the person; it created the right to be left alone.[14] Typical cases at the turn of the century brought under a claim of infringement of the right to privacy featured individuals who suddenly received undesired scrutiny as a result of either journalism or advertising. The right of privacy characterized these as unwarranted and then compensated the individual in question for their resulting hurt feelings or humiliation.

When celebrity plaintiffs took the commercial appropriation of their personalities to court on the grounds of privacy in the 1920s and 1930s, however, courts were reluctant to find for them. Here the logic of the right to privacy ran into the culture of personality. How could a celebrity complain of injured feelings from the fact of receiving further publicity? The very nature of the activities of politicians, stage and film actors, athletes, and other performers was to place themselves in the public eye, to forego their privacy. Basically, courts suggested that the celebrities had waived their right to privacy through becoming public figures.[15]

Then along came the decision in *Topps Chewing Gum* (1953), the case that Armstrong (1991) claims launched the 'modern' right of publicity. Two chewing gum companies had each obtained 'exclusive' rights to use the photographs of certain well-known baseball players in their promotions and came into conflict. The judge found that the ball players had a 'publicity value' in their photographs, and this grounded a right that could be licensed, assigned to someone else, or enforced against third parties. Mr Justice Frank wrote:

> [t]his right might be called a 'right of publicity.' For it is common knowledge that many prominent persons (especially actors and ball players), far from having their feelings bruised through public exposure of their likenesses, would feel sorely deprived if they no longer received money for authorized advertisements, popularizing their countenances, displayed in newspapers, magazines, busses, trains and subways. (*Haelan*, 1953: 868)

The judge did not quite claim the persona was property, but he did recognize the financial value of the celebrity likeness and cast the celebrity as the appropriate holder of that potential value.

Shortly after this case, lawyer Melville B. Nimmer wrote a very influential essay: 'The Right of Publicity' (1954). In it he outlines, and makes the case for, a property right in the persona. It is not incidental that Nimmer was the lawyer for Paramount Pictures at the time and thus, through the technology of the law, the film industry was actively trying to shape the status and value of stardom.[16] Nimmer argued that the right of privacy was not adequate to recognize the injury being done to celebrity plaintiffs. They did not suffer humiliation or embarrassment from being placed in the public sphere, as they were already there – the wrong was not personal. Their injury was, instead, economic because their interest in their identity was not merely personal, but proprietary.[17] Nimmer wrote:

> [i]t is an unquestioned fact that the use of a prominent person's name, photograph or likeness (i.e. his publicity values) in advertising a product or in attracting an audience is of great pecuniary value. ... It is also unquestionably true that in most instances a person achieves publicity values of substantial pecuniary worth only after he has expended considerable time, effort, skill and even money. It would seem to be a first principle of Anglo-American jurisprudence, an axiom of the most fundamental nature, that every person is entitled to the fruit of his labors, unless there are important countervailing public policy considerations. Yet, because of the inadequacy of traditional legal theories ... persons who have long and laboriously nurtured the fruit of publicity values may be deprived of them, unless judicial recognition is given to what is here referred to as the right of publicity. (1954: 215–16)

We can see that the legitimacy of the star holding the property in his or her 'publicity values' is anchored in a Lockean rationale: the individual who labours on the self is the appropriate owner of that self. As Madow sardonically notes, 'John Locke goes to Hollywood' (1993: 175).

Nimmer's characterization of the right of publicity makes four important moves that serve as the foundational myths for all subsequent developments in American publicity law. First, he recognizes that such things as personae exist and that they have value in the marketplace. Second, that these personae are produced through the labours of particular celebrities, rendering those individuals authors. Third, in the Lockean manoeuvre, the personae are therefore property (as the objects of a self-proprietor's labour on common resources); and the fourth and final step, also indebted to Locke, the authors who have laboured on these personae should be the rightful and sole owners of that property.

Now clearly articulated and rationalized, property-based publicity rights garnered slow judicial support over the 1960s and 1970s, but the approach of the courts still reflected a relatively narrow conceptualization of name, image, and likeness to be protected. However, the nature and scope of property in the person exploded in the 1980s when both courts and legislatures around the United States seemed to rush to legitimize and expand the right.[18] California, New York, and more than half of the other states brought in legislation endorsing publicity rights over the 1980s and 1990s. There was also a raft of cases as stars began to zealously protect their personae.[19]

A number of celebrities have expressly refused the commercialization of their personae to endorse products and have pursued advertisers to protect that reputation. Cary Grant and Jacqueline Onassis, for example, were awarded damages for the borrowing of their images by advertisers – Grant through an altered photograph and Onassis through a look-alike.[20] The judge in the Onassis case held that the New York statute 'is intended to protect the essence of a person, his or her identity or *persona* from being unwillingly or knowingly misappropriated for the profit of another' (*Onassis*, 1984: 260). Bette Midler objected to a sound-alike selling Ford cars in the Midwest and broke new legal ground as the courts added distinctive singing style to the elements productive of persona.[21] The court there held that 'to impersonate her voice is to pirate her identity' (*Midler*, 1988: 43). Tom Waits, who had a long and vocal history of refusing to use his celebrity to endorse products, sued for his own distinctive singing style when Frito-Lay hired a sound-alike to advertise Doritos chips.[22] More recently, Dustin Hoffman successfully pursued *Los Angeles Magazine* when they digitally grafted his head onto a model dressed in a designer gown and heels, clearly evoking the promotional poster for the 1982 film *Tootsie*.[23]

While arguably these stars were attempting to protect the integrity of their persons in a Hegelian sense, as well as the commercial value of their personae,[24] on the other hand, a significant number of cases have been solely about the protection of the economic value of the persona. For example, Vanna White's previously mentioned suit against Samsung, and Johnny Carson's action against a portable toilet company who coined 'Here's Johnny Portable Toilets' and 'The World's Foremost Commodian' as humorous advertising taglines.[25] Carson, who had previously licensed 'Here's Johnny' for a line of men's toiletries, was not amused. Bela Lugosi's heirs fought to protect his identity as the original Dracula,[26] Clark Gable's children objected to Scarlett O'Hara being replaced by a man in Rhett Butler's arms on a gay greeting card, and John Wayne's children lobbied the New York Legislature to make publicity rights there inheritable so that they could enjoin another gay greeting card, this time featuring the Duke in a typical cowboy role, sporting red lipstick, with the caption, 'It's such a bitch being butch.'[27]

In his landmark analysis of the right of publicity law in the United States, Michael Madow (1993) suggests that the right of publicity was adopted and then spread very quickly in the United States in a way which some commentators have described as 'common-sensical,'[28] but which he convincingly argues has been without adequate theorization and critical justification. He states that typically, publicity rights have been justified in three ways, drawing on standard justifications for both copyright and trademark law. The first, and overwhelmingly dominant, justification is moral, namely that it is only right that the celebrity receive the benefit of her labour in producing her own persona. I suggest that this casts the persona as an authored text with an intimate connection to the person. The celebrity is deserving of her fame as it is always already an act of self-proprietorship.

The second rationale for property rights in the persona is economic. As with other intellectual property rights, endorsing a commercial valuation of the cultural significations coalescing in the persona will, it is assumed, encourage more and better creative endeavour. This assumes that people will not create if they are not compensated for their efforts and, of course, does not address the problem of appropriate valuation. It also implies that the gossamer strand between person and persona is willed.[29] Finally, the third rationale Madow offers is consumer, or really, market protection. Here analysts and courts are positing the celebrity persona as akin to a trademark. Trademarks seek to reduce the likelihood of confusion in the marketplace through the inappropriate commercial use of a distinguishing mark.[30] They are seen to protect both owners and the public from unfair competition and confusion, thereby improving the overall moral function, and competitive nature, of the marketplace (Cordero, 2006: 609–11). The free flow of information will be strengthened if the public cannot be misled into thinking that a particular person of note endorses a product when she or he does not. Therefore, the concern is one of accuracy and truth in the implied relationship between person and persona. We do not want the persona uncoupled from its grounding person; the person must work as referent.

Four primary critiques are levelled at a strong right of publicity. First, with respect to the morality of rewarding the celebrity's labour, critics argue that to attribute the benefits of the labour only to the celebrity does not adequately recognize the industrial structures in and through which fame is produced. In other words, any star is the product or construct of whole teams and apparatuses of publicity expertise through which the persona is produced and managed. These other labourers include trainers, agents, makeup artists, publicists, plastic surgeons, directors, tabloids, production companies, and so on. Further, the value that is attributed within the market economy to celebrity bears no logical relationship to its significance or the amount of labour involved. Additionally, there are instances where it is extremely difficult to claim a formative relationship between anyone's labour and their fame (Paris Hilton or Vanna White springs to mind). These scholars, therefore, trouble the authenticating claim of authorship, suggesting the person, alone, does not author the persona. The gossamer thread is snapped.

A related but distinct line of critique takes up the role of the public in the constitution of celebrity. As Jane Gaines suggests, 'the right of publicity is actually a personal monopoly for a numbered few, but since these few have been "selected" by the many, the exclusivity goes unnoticed' (1991: 146). Without the endorsement and dollars of the audience, the star is nothing; in other words, fame is conferred by others.[31] Therefore, these critics are suggesting the persona is only nominally related to the person; the key relationship is between the audience and the performance. Steven M. Cordero has recently gone so far as to posit that some celebrities achieve the status of icons, transcending their original meaning to become expressive of society's values, myths, and convictions. 'In our society, icons are created through a partnership of purveyor and populace, whereby the purveyor of a commodity supplies the product, and the consumer – through an active creative practice – appropriates it by investing the product with new meaning' (2006: 602). This implies that the relationship between person and persona is always socially constructed and only emerges in, and with the active participation of, the public.

A third stream of criticism of publicity rights takes on the somewhat paradoxical argument that if (unlimited) monopoly rights in cultural production are granted, more and better cultural activity is in fact stimulated. Rather, critics suggest that what is resulting is the privatization of the cultural commons. If popular culture becomes private property, then how can other artists continue to create? How can we parody and satirize? How can we engage in the cultural appropriation practices through which dominant and marginal identities are negotiated – where would drag queens be without Cher?[32] (Reciprocally, of course, one might wonder where would Cher be without drag queens?) This critique figures the persona as a shared resource in broader practices of social meaning-making, regardless of where and who authors it. Publicity rights freeze the persona in its dominant meaning, and any use of that image which does not reinforce that can be stopped by its 'owners.' Part of this critique is that the propertization of the persona stifles the polysemy of our culture. The law and the star system combine in publicity law to fix or render static the meanings of a particular celebrity, the relationship between person and persona. In this way, much of the unruliness of the persona is contained.

Fourth and finally, the consumer protection rationale for publicity rights is criticized as dated and somewhat paternalistic, not recognizing the savvy nature of contemporary audiences. As experienced consumers, we do not believe that James Cagney was a big fan of Diet Pepsi or that Audrey Hepburn danced to AC/DC. We even suspect that John Wayne was straight. In fact, the pleasure of the meanings is generated in substantial part from our knowledge that these stars have not, or would not have likely, endorsed the particular product. Critics advancing this view note that even if there remains a need for consumer protection with the ongoing practices of celebrity endorsement, there are other less problematic legal remedies that can address this. In a sense, what is being argued for in the consumer deception line of justification is a trademark rationale for the right without the corresponding limits placed on trademarks. These critics are therefore suggesting that we derive pleasure from the naughty persona. While our knowledge of the person is key to this pleasure, we do not look to it for authentication. The gaze is shifted from the person as we understand and revel in the undetermined nature of the persona.

Despite the cogent critiques, the right of publicity as a strong property-based right seems firmly entrenched in the United States. Yet, in their concern with the appropriateness of property rights in the persona and the analogies to copyrights and trademarks, advocates and critics alike obscure the relationship between person and persona. If, as Mitchell Flagg has suggested, 'personality, image, and identity are among the most ephemeral concepts known to humanity' (1999: 180), then the rise of publicity law is an attempt to fix that ephemerality. This fixing has a number of effects. The celebrity emerges as a doubled figure – simultaneously person and persona. Their personality is constituted in the varied performances which produce the persona. Always malleable, the persona momentarily fixes as object when recognized by consuming individuals or groups. At the same time, the authenticity of the persona is attributed, through the author-myth at the heart of publicity law, to the person. The persona is simultaneously property and a fundamental manifestation of the unique individuality and autonomy of the person. The celebrity then emerges out of American publicity law as the première possessive individual.

Celebrity in Canada

The celebrity as possessive individual, constituted in and through American publicity law, subordinates the persona as willed object, as thing, as property, to the agency, creativity, and authority of the person. It is therefore difficult to see the work of the persona, as it is inevitably eclipsed by the person. On the other hand, both the Canadian celebrity system more generally, and the specific technology of publicity law in Canada, reflect a greater unease with celebrity and its commodification. This unease manifests in a distrust of the persona within a marketized economy and a desire to keep it closely sutured to the person, often configured as national citizen. The Canadian context, therefore, allows us to turn our gaze more directly on the intimacy of the relationship between person and persona, how it is constituted, and what it means. This is, in large part, I suggest because, unlike American law with its embrace of a Lockean possessive individualism, Canadian celebrity discourse embraces a more Hegelian rhetoric.

Canada's Celebrity System: Merit, Sovereignty, and Personality

Is early film star Mary Pickford (also known as America's Sweetheart) 'Canadian' enough to be properly inducted into Canada's Walk of Fame?[33] Should former Boston Bruins coach and current sports commentator Don Cherry have been in the top ten candidates in CBC's *The Greatest Canadian* contest?[34] Why was an entire nation in shock when Wayne Gretzky's wife was involved in a gambling scandal immediately prior to the 2006 Winter Olympics?[35] These 'events' of Canadian fame, and many others like them, reveal a disquiet present in Canadian discussions of celebrity. Yet while the specificity of Canadian popular culture in general, and its celebrity culture in particular, is quite compelling, analysis of it is hindered by a complete dearth of critical literature. While there is large body of work historicizing, analysing, and theorizing American fame, stars, star systems, and celebrity, there has been no attempt by scholars to document, understand, or analyse the specificity of celebrity in Canada.[36] However, even a cursory glance at the entertainment industry in Canada, tellingly more commonly referred to as the cultural industries, reveals that celebrity is 'done' very differently in Canada. I argue that there are three central discourses – merit, sovereignty, and personality – which operate in continual tension to produce two dominant myths that frame Canadian celebrity: the meritorious celebrity and the citizen celebrity. The tensions between merit, sovereignty, and personality operate both as a latent structuring device and as a performative rhetoric of distinction.

There is a modest, although growing, celebrity apparatus in Canada. The first task for any analyst is to pull together the disparate, diverse, and disorganized elements of the emergent Canadian star system: the Junos, the Genies, *Star!* TV, the Toronto International Film Festival, 'Can-Con' regulations, the Hockey Hall of Fame, the Scotiabank Giller Prize, the Canadian Film or Video Production Tax Credit, Star-Académie, the cover of *Maclean's* magazine, *Canadian Idol*, and so on. The elements exist, and many have for a number of years, but they do not yet operate as an integrated system. They function, at present, as a set of relatively independent mechanisms, institutions, and techniques, not yet offering any hierarchical, serial, or inter-industry pathways of promotion and circulation consistently productive of recognizable celebrity. Yet within these various components, taken together, the contours of a notion of Canadian celebrity apparatus can begin to be mapped.

Many authors have written about Canadian culture and its relationship with the cultural industries in Canada (Raboy, 1990; Vipond, 1989; Acland, 2003; Dorland, 1996, 1998; Magder, 1993, 1998). However, almost to a one, these scholars focus on state-authored policy initiatives and their relative success or failure in producing audiences, supporting economic growth, producing content reflective of 'Canadian culture,' and so on. I am less interested in the effectivity of state initiatives in producing a rarefied notion of Canadian culture (or not) than I am in mapping and analysing existing Canadian popular culture, and through its sites of production and textual traces, asking first, what celebrity looks like in Canada, and second and more importantly, what work celebrity culture does in Canada. I therefore examined non-policy-based celebrity initiatives in Canada and the public communication around them.[37]

My analysis suggests that the trio of sovereignty, merit, and personality produces two myths of Canadian celebrity: first, that Canadian celebrity is meritorious (namely not founded in personality), and second, that celebrities are (and should be) nation-builders. Canadian pundits clearly prefer merit- to personality-based claims to fame. Steve Tilley of the *Edmonton Sun* naïvely commented on the 2004 *Canadian Idol* competition, '[a]lthough its structure borrows from athletic competitions and elections, *Canadian Idol* seems to be a part of the cult of personality rather than just achievement-based celebrity' (2004b: 38). The discourse of merit sits uneasily alongside the market relations in which these entertainment products are located. For example, the 'Golden Reel Award' at the Genies is awarded to the Canadian film that earns the highest domestic box office revenue of the year; the 2005 winner was *Resident Evil – Apocalypse* (2004). This can be contrasted with the fact that the Claude Jutra Award for excellence in directing recognized by one's peers was awarded to Daniel Roby for *La peau blanche* (2005). Predictably, we see very little commentary celebrating the former as a component of Canadian culture.

The challenge to a high culture notion of merit posed by the marketplace of popular culture can be overcome, it would seem, with meritorious creative labour. Commentators emphasize that our music stars write their own music; for example, Sarah McLachlan, Bryan Adams, Alanis Morrissette, and Avril Lavigne. Our sports stars are always 'good sports' and role models for children; see Wayne Gretzky, Mark Tewksbury, or Cindy Klassen. Our comedy is smarter, witness *CodCo*, *The Mercer Report*, *Air Farce,* and *The Kids in the Hall*. And of course, our filmmakers make 'good' films and our writers write 'good' fiction: Atom Egoyan, Margaret Atwood, Ann-Marie MacDonald, and, having shed his science fictional roots, even David Cronenburg. We do not claim as Canadian celebrities the makers of *Porky's* (1982), *Johnny Mnemonic* (1995), or *Resident Evil – Apocalypse* (2004).

We see the influence of the oppressive omnipresence of the American entertainment industry. It structures our celebrity system and our knowledge of it. For example, Canada's only entertainment television channel, *Star!*, produces a reality show called 'Look Alike' which features Canadians who are look-alikes for American stars such as Sarah Jessica Parker, Anna Nicole Smith, Paris Hilton, and Halle Barry. While, on the one hand, the American industry serves as a marker of success for Canadian celebrities, it is thus also the necessary 'other' against which the dominant face of Canadian celebrity is constituted. Therefore we see claims that one has to be recognized in the United States in order to achieve fame in Canada alongside assertions that everything that is 'good' in Hollywood is Canadian anyway. '*Time* magazine reports that fully 20 per cent of the Hollywood entertainment industry is made up of Canadians,' one reporter gleefully notes (Dalby, 2003: R01).

Yet these claims are not merely about difference, but are simultaneously about valuation. Canadian celebrities are frequently represented as more deserving/authentic/sincere/self-made/modest/real than their American counterparts. Canadian celebrity inevitably emerges from this comparison as morally superior. Former prima ballerina Veronica Tennant suggested that the Canadian Walk of Fame has a unique Canadian sensibility, 'a combination of sensitivity and sizzle' (in McKay, 2004). Commentators valorize popular sex columnist Sue Johanson because 'there's nothing slick about the production or Johanson, who sews most of her own wardrobe and refuses to have her hair properly coiffed' (Deziel, 2004: 32). The extremes of American personality culture are the ever-present, silent Other in these and similar claims. When we wish to denigrate the notion of Canadian celebrity, we claim that it is nearly as bad as its American counterpart. Yet, even while mocking ourselves, we are asserting our moral superiority. While contemplating the propriety of gossip columns in the *National Post* and the *Globe and Mail*, a journalist commented of the column in the *Post*: '[a]nd while he [the columnist] tries to dish as much Canadian dirt as he can, "to fill a column five days a week with just Canadian gossip would be a real challenge" he says. Maybe, but it might be worth the effort – before protectionist measures are required to protect Canadian gossip from the pressures of globalization' (Spendlove, 2001).

Canadian celebrity bears a complex double burden – it must both entertain (mass and elite) audiences and suture our always-at-risk national sovereignty. This is the second structuring myth of Canadian celebrity: the celebrity citizen. In Canada, good celebrities are nation-builders. For example, a journalist for the *Toronto Star* captured this sentiment perfectly when she offered a retrospective look on the first *Canadian Idol* competition: '[w]hen the show aired last spring Canadians were over the moon about the great nation-building experience it was. All of us together, picking our Idol, united in the search for the best and the brightest' (Hearn, 2004). Shania Twain, upon her induction to Canada's Walk of Fame in 2004, stated: 'I'm a Canadian through and through and I'm very proud of that.'

An effect of this myth of celebrity as nation-builder is that both celebrity and audience alike are figured within the 'loyalty or treason' binary that Michael Dorland and Priscilla Walton (1999) suggest typically frames cultural nationalist analyses of Canadian popular culture. They argue that Canadian cultural institutions have long been constituted as threatened by the 'signifiers of modernity' such as the rise of consumer culture, the spread of a market-driven economy, the development of information technologies, and the corresponding implications that all of these have had for the media and cultural industries.

Consequently throughout much of the twentieth century, Canadian institutions and public intellectuals have reacted, often alarmingly, to contain what was perceived as the negative consequences of these various threats (economic, technological, and cultural) that were invariably attributed to the predations of the United States, and to the detriment of Canada. (198)

The celebrity citizen myth favours, in particular, the sports star whose national affiliation is taken as given in the competition structure of athletics. The sports contest is also assumed *a priori* as a location for the production of merit. We see this in the national hand-wringing that accompanies our participation in every Olympic Games and on the rare occasions when Canadian athletes distinguish themselves on the world stage in professional sports. The coverage of Mike Weir's 2004 victory in the American Masters golf tournament was replete with cultural nationalist hoopla. He was dubbed the 'Wayne Gretzky of Golf' and the 'Tiger Woods of Canada' (Michaux, 2004: M07).

> Weir's winning the Masters is the kind of success story that Americans take for granted but Canadians cherish – a humble guy doing something extraordinary. His victory ... ranks as one of those watershed sports moments that lifts an entire nation. ... But Weir is not an American or European or Australian. He's a maple-leaf-wearing Canadian, and that makes all the difference, eh? He may reside in Utah, but he's Canadian to the core. (Ibid.)

The Canadian celebrity as ideal citizen is often complicated by the situation highlighted by the journalist above: Canadian celebrities do not always live in Canada. This then contributes to the 'sell-out' discourse for Canadians who have moved to the United States. It can, however, be countered with demonstrations by the celebrity of her or his Canadian-ness by retaining a presence within, and making contributions to, Canadian infrastructure. When asked for whom he would vote as Canada's Greatest Canadian, a music journalist suggested, 'Pierre Berton wrote all those great books on Canada and hasn't sold out and gone to the States' (in Williams, 2004: W15). Proving that being Canadian is in your heart not your passport, when American Ronnie Hawkins was dying of cancer, an attempt was made to have him awarded the Order of Canada, and the press essentially dubbed him an honorary Canadian for all of the work he did for Canadian artists. '[H]e came to Canada from Arkansas in 1958, and loved this country so much, he never returned home despite many lures' (McRae, 2002:

7). He is specifically contrasted with Order of Canada holder Joni Mitchell, who is treated as a traitor for moving to the United States to find fame and fortune and staying there (ibid.). In response to criticism for introducing Louis B. Mayer to Canada's Walk of Fame in 2004, co-creator and CEO Peter Soumalias noted: '[i]t was clear to Louis B. Mayer that he was a Canadian, he died a Canadian, he supported his home community up to as recently as 1950, went back up and built a church in New Brunswick' (in McKay, 2004). As we can see in this second myth – coupling sovereignty and merit – the nationality of the person is supposed to infuse the character of the persona at all times in order to be a real (Canadian) celebrity. What results is a normative figure where person and persona are largely co-terminous, articulated in a thoroughly organic relationship.

We can see that the two structuring myths of Canadian celebrity – Canadian celebrity as meritorious and Canadian celebrity as national project – clearly have implications for how person and persona are figured. The persona becomes intimately connected to the person, to the citizen; the persona is a reflection of their individual, and our collective, identity. The person and persona operate outside of market relations or abide within the market as a necessary evil only. They are not fundamentally of the market. The persona authenticates the person as both a good creator and a Canadian, but at the same time, the persona takes on legitimacy from the moral weight of the achieving person. The persona is a docile reflection of personal identity, always required to accurately reflect an undistorted, already bounded, autonomous, and accomplished individual. However, in a current culture of celebrity that does not stop at national borders and that is already implicated in the marketplace, these myths can contain neither the complex workings of the celebrity apparatus nor the unruliness of the persona.

The Unruly Persona in Canada

An examination of the structures of the Canadian celebrity system allows us to unpack those structuring myths and recognize a more complex notion of celebrity. This, in turn, reveals the ways in which the persona continually escapes the constraints of dominant Canadian celebrity. First, it is important to recognize that the elements of a Canadian celebrity system anchored in personality already, and necessarily, exist. There are a set of institutions, techniques, measures, and tactics that comprise the various sites of celebrity production in Canada, many of which are distinct from the institutions of the cultural nationalist project. As noted previously, for what are likely historical and economic reasons, these elements in our fledgling star system do not quite operate in effective concert with each other; however, they nonetheless do the work of producing celebrity. Different cultural industries have different regimes of recognition and distinction – music, film, television, literature, sports, and so on. At the same time, there are moments where a celebrity emerges out of the specificity of one location, one particular star system, and achieves a more generalized celebrity status. Céline Dion is a good example of this, emerging out of the genre of music and the Quebec star system, and despite these constraints, having achieved international, and most importantly, American recognition.

How, why, and when this happens remains to be studied in more detail. As noted earlier, Gamson (1992; 1994) effectively demonstrates that discourses of American celebrity shifted over the second half of the twentieth century from framing stars as authentic personalities to seeing them as the outcomes of an increasingly visible apparatus of technical expertise, which he labels a more democratic form of celebrity. Yet the increasing visibility of the apparatuses of technical expertise continues to be obscured in Canada by the dominance of the merit-based notion of celebrity. The merit discourse locates celebrity in the agency of the celebrity person him- or herself, effectively masking the industries and techniques of celebrity production. Thus, an organic, or self-made, notion of celebrity works to deny the apparatus. The person is privileged over the persona, and the persona is seen to reflect the person beneath with versimilitude.

This obscuring is not as present in Quebec. It is important to recognize that the celebrity apparatus in Quebec for French-language popular culture production is much more mature and developed than its English-language counterpart in Quebec and the rest of Canada. Because of the focused nature, relative reliability, and linguistic singularity of that audience, Quebec has both had, and been able, to develop its own star system (see Cernetig, 2003: E04). Unlike English Canada, both its elite and mass audience have been understood, by cultural producers and commentators alike, as playing a role in the constitution of the culture of the nation, and so its celebrity industry is more coherent, better developed, and more visible. The persona is not merely tolerated, but celebrated in Quebec. However, with very few exceptions, Céline Dion being one of them, Quebec celebrities are neither well placed to achieve broader celebrity in English Canada or North America, nor expected to carry the burden of the maple leaf.

The emergence and continuation of a wider array of mechanisms and sites of celebrity production have been accompanied by a shift in the specific technologies, but also the tactics, of presentation. These shifts have implications for the assumed intimacy between person and persona in Canada. We have seen in the last decade the increase in visual media-based techniques for the production of celebrity. *Star!* television began in 1999; television entertainment news reporting has expanded – *ET Canada* was launched in 2005, and *eTalk Daily* commenced operation in 2002; the *Sun* chain of newspapers adopted a format change towards more entertainment and celebrity news in 2004,[38] and entertainment magazines have begun to appear; for example, the *Weekly Scoop* in 2005 and a Canadian edition of the British magazine *Hello* in 2006. Other than a small amount of obligatory Canadian content, these celebrity vehicles are indistinguishable from their American counterparts.

Celebrity events are emerging in Canada, duly branded and serialized. We see this in the development of Canada's Walk of Fame, which claims to feature 'the world's greatest talents, who also happen to be Canadian.' As of 2005, there have been fifty-two stars inducted from the worlds of arts and literature, entertainment, and sports.[39] The Walk deploys a language of 'stars' and has moved away from a small ceremony to a big-red-carpeted, televised spectacle. The show now features the official ceremony, the unveiling of the stars on Simcoe Street in Toronto, and then a gala tribute. There are also outdoor concerts and film screenings, as well as charity events. Each smaller event features its own sponsor, such as Chanel or Molson Canada. A far cry from being supported by Canadian Heritage, Telefilm, and the CBC.

Celebrity is now being produced through the technique of the democratic contest, cribbed from Britain and the United States. The most obvious example is *Canadian Idol*. *Star Académie*, a Quebec singing contest, similar in format to the *Idol* franchise, drew 3.2 million viewers in 2002 and was credited with reviving the financial stability of Quebecor (Olive, 2003: E01). This trend continued with more than three million tuning in to watch the show's finale in 2003 (Cernetig, 2003: E04). It was interesting to see the CBC, the bastion of meritorious celebrity citizenship, adapt the techniques of democracy for its nationalist didactic ends. The 'Greatest Canadian' contest sponsored by CBC received 140,000 nominations from everyday Canadians to generate its list of fifty candidates. More than 1.2 million votes were cast over the six weeks as Canadians voted on the final ten candidates.[40] As with the hero, the legitimacy of the celebrity is, in part, found in its democratic endorsement.

Canadian celebrity is being produced and recognized in visual spectacle. Recent format changes were made to the Juno Awards and its rebranding was characterized as one moving from merit to personality. In 2002, the Junos broadcast switched from CBC to CTV, was moved from its location in Copps Coliseum in Hamilton and sent 'on the road' first to St John's, Newfoundland, and was hosted by the music group The Barenaked Ladies. The tensions in such a shift in tactics are evident in one Canadian rock critic's response:

> [s]ince CTV took it over ... it has become much more of a splash. It's certainly more of a public event with increased excitement in general. It's less staid and sterile. At the same time it's often just really crass: blinding lights and flashpots everywhere. It's really kind of ridiculous. It's also very much a popularity contest. (Barclay in Volmers, 2004: C1)

There is now a Juno Cup charity hockey game sponsored by Mastercard which takes place before the event in support of music education, a welcome reception, a live music festival (JunoFest), Juno Fanfare (an autograph signing with Juno nominees), the Juno Gala Dinner and Awards, and the Songwriters' Circle, and CTV broadcasts not merely the event but also the red carpet arrivals. One journalist approved, '[i]t seemed clear that Canada's music industry had finally organized its top-selling talent into a *bona fide* star system,' but the myths linger: '[w]as a glittery, more Grammy-like award show what Canada really needed? Or has it helped render the Junos as artistically irrelevant as its American counterpart?' (Volmers, 2004: C1). The Junos format change has been continued and was so successful that the Genie Awards followed suit in 2004.

As audiences are recognized through these tactics as active in the production of celebrity, they are invited further into the apparatus. Given the imbrication of the Canadian and American popular cultural industries with Canadians as hybrid audience in relation to the American and Canadian star systems, the defensive posture 'really Canadian or it's a sell-out' model is no longer tenable. It further risks blinding us to other possibilities in its over-focus on content. Canada's only specialty entertainment television channel, *Star!*, for example, has as one of its mandates the promotion of the Canadian star system. While this instrumental claim no doubt substantially increased its odds of success in obtaining a CRTC licence to begin operations, in practice, I would argue that *Star!* is less about producing Canadian celebrity than it is about legitimating the consumption of celebrity in Canada, regardless of origin. The Canadian audience has long been constituted in simultaneously passive and elitist terms by the state and numerous cultural producers. The equally longstanding practice of consuming celebrity regardless of the origin of that content collides with that characterization, potentially democratizing the audience and troubling the high-low culture distinction. The chinks in the armour of the merit in which the celebrity persona is encased become visible.

Canadian celebrity myths make a hard separation between entertainment-based celebrity and forms of celebrity which develop out of other aspects of public life. Canadian commentators are smug when confronted with the political efforts of Ronald Reagan, Jesse 'The Body' Ventura, Sonny Bono, Clint Eastwood, and Arnold Schwarzenegger. And yet when we consider Pierre Trudeau, our current and former journalists-turned-Governors-General,[41] the 2004 search for Canada's 'Greatest Canadian,' Ken Dryden's move from hockey star to politician, and the not dissimilar attempt to woo Don Cherry into running as a Conservative candidate, this over-simplistic division of types of celebrity bears more scrutiny. We are seeing an increasing blurring of boundaries between different forms of notoriety. Celebrity is now a more mobile commodity in Canada, where the persona can exceed the person's original location and can, in fact, reciprocally assist in the social relocation of the person.

While American commentators have recognized the role that the press plays, and has played, in making the private lives of stars public, the Canadian press is not as invested in the making public of private lives. Instead, Canadian media operate as a surveillance mechanism for celebrities who have obtained success in the American marketplace. Such celebrities are scrutinized and measured in terms of their presumed obligation to articulate their relationship with Canada through visits to their home towns, support for Canadian charitable causes, maintaining their citizenship, and taking public opportunities to acknowledge their Canadian-ness. Thus celebrities, from politicians to authors to rock stars, are permitted their privacy provided they deliver on merit and nation. Every Canadian celebrity who has 'made it' in the United States is asked by reporters about being Canadian. The media are, in many instances, still clinging to, and further propagating, the myth of celebrity as nation-builder. They have not recognized the increasing relative autonomy of the persona in an expanding celebrity system.

Thus, the third element in the three-part tension in Canadian celebrity – between merit, sovereignty, and personality – is ever-present and always pushing at our apparently comforting yet always unstable myths. Personality is an unarguable attribute of Canadian celebrity culture despite our attempts to deny it. However, what happens when that personality as commodity form is recognized and endorsed by the law? What happens when the tensions of merit, sovereignty, and personality meet publicity law?

Canadian law does recognize property rights in personae. At the same time, the celebrity at the heart of Canadian publicity law – as a particularly Hegelian fusion of person and persona – is dogged by the myths of Canadian celebrity and with a seeming reluctance to propertize the self. Canadian publicity law works hard, as we will see, to re-couple person and persona, in an effort to contain the potential disruption posed by the persona.

Canadian Publicity Law

Perhaps predictably, given the emergent and uneven state of our celebrity culture, the state of publicity law in Canada is considerably less articulated and not quite as star-struck as its American counterpart. There are fewer cases, there are no Supreme Court of Canada decisions directly on point, the cases offer less detailed and often inconsistent reasoning, and there is, not surprisingly, less legal commentary. The law in Canada is uncertain and conflicted, having been described by one commentator as 'at an infant stage' (Abramovitch, 2000: 246). Not having shed its relationship to the personal right of privacy as the American right has done, it is often known as the tort of appropriation of personality. Eric Singer suggests, 'although the tort of appropriation of personality has been developing, one cannot yet describe with any precision its guiding principles or the rules governing its application' (1999: 78). The cases are poorly reasoned, generally from lower-level courts, and do not offer analysts or litigants a coherent set of guidelines for the protection of personae. To further complicate the scenario, there has been very little guidance from the Supreme Court of Canada. At the same time, these very shortcomings from a legal perspective make our law of publicity a rich site for viewing the distrust with which Canadians view persons, personae, and property.

The protection of celebrity in Canada got its start, perhaps predictably, with a Canadian football player, twenty years after *Haelan* v. *Topps*, in 1973. Bobby Krouse was a Hamilton Tiger Cat and wore number 14; ironically, he is more famous for his role in the founding of the right of appropriation of personality than he is for his football skills. Chrysler Canada, a Canadian Football League sponsor at the time, was launching an advertising initiative featuring the 'Plymouth Pro Football Spotter.' The spotter featured a sliding dial which permitted fans to recognize a team jersey and number, and quickly locate the corresponding player's name. The card featured an action shot with a number of football players surrounded by Chrysler vehicles; however, Krouse was the only one whose number (and thus identity) was recognizable. The caption drew further attention to him by asking 'Who is 14?' The photograph had been taken and sold by a freelance reporter without Krouse's express consent. Krouse sued Chrysler for invasion of privacy, unjust enrichment, and appropriation of his personality.

The trial judge found that Krouse did in fact have a saleable product, his advertising power, that there was an implied endorsement of the cars, and that the image was used without his permission. He lost on appeal, when the Ontario Court of Appeal found no implied endorsement of Chrysler's product. However, while dismissing the claim, Mr Justice Estey did validate the new tort: 'the common law does contemplate a concept in the law of torts which may broadly be classified as an appropriation of one's personality' (*Krouse*, 1973: 28). And, with no further fanfare, as one commentator stated, 'a new tort was born' (Singer, 1999: 66).

Four years later in 1977, another athlete was at the centre of a persona dispute. Champion water skier George Athans held a number of commercial endorsements for water skiing equipment and related businesses as a result of his athletic achievements. He had purchased a particular action photograph of himself and was using this distinctive image in his own promotional materials. Canadian Adventure

Camps ran a summer camp for children and approached Athans to be involved in their programming. He refused because he could not devote enough time to it, and eventually they produced an advertisement, which ran in an Ontario water skiing magazine, featuring a line-drawing based on Athans's trademark image. The camp had deliberately altered their image so it would not be a direct reproduction of Athans's.

The court accepted that Mr Athans had rights in his persona, evidenced by the fact that he was able to obtain commercial endorsements based upon it. Yet, without any acknowledgment of shifting the reasoning in *Krouse*, the judge held the right was a property right. 'It is clear that Mr. Athans has a proprietary right in the exclusive marketing for gain of his personality, image and name, and that the law entitles him to protect that right, if it is invaded' (*Athans*, 1977: 434). It was also clear to the court that Athans himself was the 'author' of the property in his self. There was no discussion that anyone else might have any rights in the property of the persona. Interestingly, the court made its findings even while conceding that outside of the relatively small community of competitive water skiers, most people would not even recognize Athans.

What flows from this tenuous beginning is a series of cases involving a motley lot of quasi-celebrities and inconsistent and poorly reasoned legal decisions. The early tension in American law between privacy and publicity plays out in Canada – because of the conflicting findings in *Krouse* and *Athans* – in the uncertain position of the courts as to whether the right to one's persona is anchored in persona as an aspect of the human person or as a property interest. Tort is the law of civil injury. A tort occurs when a person acts in a way towards another that causes personal harm or injury or damage to property. It arises out of a duty imposed by society for us to take care not to injure others or their property by our actions. In the case of appropriation of personality, the tort means that someone used someone else's persona, without their consent, thereby causing financial damage, and perhaps emotional distress that can be compensated with money. Therefore, if the misappropriation of personality is construed as a tort against the person, the right vests in the individual, there must be fault on the part of the transgressor, damages must be suffered, it cannot be sold or licensed, and it ends with the death of the person. Five provinces have legislation recognizing personality rights, and all of them have framed them as personal, rather than property, rights.[42]

If, on the other hand, the persona is treated as property, then, as we saw in the American context, the rights associated with it change significantly. Property rights are alienable, assignable, and descendible, meaning that they can be broken up into various parts, they are or can be assigned to others through sale, licensing, and so on, and they continue after death (i.e., can be inherited). Significantly, there does not have to be any kind of express harm for the rights to accrue and be enforced; merely infringing on someone's property right is enough. Therefore, Canadian law was left with uncertainty about whether the persona anchored a personal right intimately associated with the person, necessarily tied to it, or whether the persona had become property, severable from its person, but necessarily connected through the labour of self-authorship.[43]

The fledgling Canadian right was strengthened and expanded again in the case of *Joseph* v. *Daniels* (1986) when the court found that the purpose of the appropriation of persona does not have to be commercial. The damage is done through the act of appropriation alone. Even more significantly, however, the British Columbia Supreme Court affirmed that the persona is constituted in its recognizability. In that case, the plaintiff, Joseph, was an amateur bodybuilder who had agreed to pose for a photographer for a series of black-and-white photographs featuring his torso and arms as he cradled a kitten. He refused to sign the waiver permitting the photographer, Daniels, to market the photograph. After the photograph won a design award, Daniels decided to market the image on posters and greeting cards. He apparently made a failed attempt to track down Joseph to obtain his permission. The court held:

> [t]he cause of action is proprietary in nature and the interest protected is that of the individual in the exclusive use of his own identity in so far as it is represented by his name, reputation, likeness or other value. For the defendant to be found liable he must be taking advantage of the name, reputation, likeness, or some other components of the plaintiff's individuality or personality which the viewer associates or identifies with the plaintiff. (*Joseph*, 1986: 549)

Thus, the nature of the elements of the persona that evokes the recognition of the person is of secondary importance to the fact of that recognition.

In the only case in Canada involving a 'celebrity' of any significant international stature, the immortality of the persona in Canada was asserted.[44] At the time of his death in 1982, Glenn Gould had been a famous classical pianist for many years. He was also notable for his desire to maintain his privacy and to retain control over anything associated with his name; he was in many respects, an anti-celebrity.[45] However, in 1956, before he had achieved even celebrity status, his agent was interested in getting him some further media attention and so arranged with a freelance writer to do a series of interviews and take a number of photographs for incorporation into a magazine article. The writer took approximately four hundred photographs and conducted a number of taped interviews. Forty years later, fourteen years after Gould's death, the writer, Jock Carroll, published *Glenn Gould: Some Portraits of the Artist as a Young Man* (1995), a coffee-table book featuring many of the interviews and photographs. The Gould Estate (which neither authorized the publication nor received any royalties) sued the author and the publishing company for, among other things, appropriation of personality.

While the decision on appeal ultimately turned on copyright law, the trial court did provide some insights into the law of appropriation of personality, holding that the right survived Gould's death and confirming a 'sales versus subject' distinction. Claiming to rely on American authority, the judge held that the fact that the book was a biographical text with broader social value overrode any interest the estate might have in controlling the personality of the subject. Gould, as the subject of the work, rather than merely a vehicle for its sale, was of interest to a broader public and therefore the right of publicity did not accrue. Justice Lederman held:

> it seems that the courts have drawn a 'sales vs. subject' distinction. Sales constitute commercial exploitation and invoke the tort of appropriation of personality. The identity of the celebrity is merely being used in some fashion. The activity cannot be said to be about the celebrity. This is in contrast to situations in which the celebrity is the actual subject of the work or enterprise, with biographies perhaps being the clearest example. These activities would not be within the ambit of the tort. To take a more concrete example, in endorsement situations, posters and board games, the essence of the activity is not the celebrity. It is the use of some attributes of the celebrity for another purpose. Biographies, other books, plays, and satirical skits are by their nature different. The subject of the activity

is the celebrity and the work is an attempt to provide some insights about that celebrity. (*Gould*, 1996: 527)

So while hierarchizing culture in terms of its level of engagement with its subject, Lederman also recognizes a broader public interest: '[t]here is a public interest in knowing more about one of Canada's geniuses' (ibid.).[46]

The public interest was also the factor preventing a posthumous property claim by Tim Horton's widow for revenues from his persona. In that case, an artist had created a commemorative print featuring an image of the late Tim Horton, the hockey star turned doughnut mogul. The print was used by Horton's business partner to advertise a children's charity he created to commemorate his deceased friend and business associate. Horton's wife was suing the charity because it did not obtain her consent to use the image. The court found that Horton had engaged in active self-promotion before his death, placing himself in the public eye. He had already licensed his image for use in multiple arenas; as a result, no inappropriate appropriation had taken place. Because a charity was involved, there was a larger public good again being served that would militate against unlimited property rights on the part of Horton's widow. Again, the court organized culture according to its relationship with the market and an undefined public interest.

> It is inescapable and uncontradicted that the predominant purpose of the portrait is charitable and commemorative. It is neither exploitative nor commercial. ... In my view, this is of as much public interest to the sports world as a book on Mr. Gould's life is to the music world. Any commercial purpose is incidental at best. Accordingly, the portrait falls into the 'protected category.' (*Horton*, 1997: 22–3)

Interestingly, the case which provides the most direct insights into Canadian courts' thinking about the relationship between person and persona did not even involve a Canadian celebrity. It is also the only case touching on appropriation of personality that has gone all the way to the Supreme Court of Canada.[47] *Aubry* v. *Les Éditions Vice-Versa Ltd.* (1998) featured a dispute between a young woman from Quebec, Pascale Aubry, and a small art magazine called *Les Éditions Vice-Versa*. The decision was ultimately decided upon the basis of the privacy provisions of the Quebec Civil Code, but Canada's highest court made some comments that suggest that, when given the opportunity, it will interpret the right of publicity broadly. Ms Aubry was awarded damages for invasion of privacy because she was recognizable in a photograph of her sitting on the steps of a building published without her consent in the magazine. Interestingly, Aubry was not a famous personality and the photograph was not only for commercial purposes.[48] There was very little evidence that there had been any negative consequences to the plaintiff because of the publication: she testified that a few of her friends laughed at her.

Despite such a minor infraction, the Court advocated a very strong right of publicity from within the right of privacy, one which summarily trumped the artist's right of freedom of expression. Linking the persona strongly to the possessive individualism of the person, the Supreme Court asserted, '[i]f the purpose of the right to privacy ... is to protect a sphere of individual autonomy, that right must include the ability to control the use made of one's image, since the right to one's image is based on the idea of individual autonomy, that is, on the control each person has over his or her identity' (*Aubry*, 1998: 14). Reminiscent of the assertions of Warren and Brandeis in 1890, the Court favourably quotes a legal authority: '[a] person surprised in his or her private life by a roving photographer is stripped of his or her transcendency and human dignity, since he or she is reduced to the status of a "spectacle" for others. ... This "indecency of the image" deprives those photographed of their most secret substance' (ibid.: 17). Clearly preferring a Hegelian to a Lockean characterization of the relationship between the person and persona, the Supreme Court suggests that the persona captures the essence of the identity of the person and that the person has, then, the corresponding rights in that identity and its communication. Reflecting a deep aversion to current notions of celebrity, the court does not seek to propertize the persona, but rather to link it more intimately, through identity, with the person.

A number of scholars have devoted energy to attempting to encapsulate where this motley lot of mediocre athletes, eccentric musicians, and purveyors of pastries leaves the state of the Canadian law (Singer, 1999; Flagg, 1999; Nest, 1999; Potvin, 1997a, 1997b; Abramovitch, 2000; Howell, 1986; 1989; 1998). This is, at some level, an impossible task and arguably not a very interesting one. What is intriguing about these cases and the commentaries on them is the ways in which they map onto, and into, a broader discourse on Canadian celebrity. First, of course, we see the recognition, albeit somewhat reluctantly, that we do have celebrity in Canada. At a minimum, the fact of publicity rights in Canada legitimates the fact of Canadian celebrity constituted in personality and with potential economic value. Yet seemingly inevitably, there is an assertion of sovereignty in the apparent reluctance of Canadian courts to embrace with enthusiasm a strong property right in the persona. This sovereignty is celebrated within the legal scholarship on the cases. Our reluctance to go as 'star-crazy' as the United States is cast as a sign of our moral and cultural superiority (e.g., Flagg, 1999). Indeed, Canada has witnessed nothing on the order of the Waits, Midler, and White cases. While some of this might be explained by the disproportionately sized entertainment industries, I do not think that the refusal to value the persona as valuable property, or the repeated attempt to limit the property right with other public policy considerations grounded in a wider discourse of merit, can be brushed aside as resulting only from the fact that Hollywood North is smaller and less lucrative. Rather, we see a repetition of the deep-seated trouble with persona as property, the self as commodity, that is present in our broader celebrity culture. Unlike the American context, where the courts and commentators alike seemed to hasten to provide a legitimating framework for a burgeoning industry in personality, Canadian courts and scholars have not acted similarly. There seems little interest on their part to play a role in supporting the cultural industries.

Related to this, our cases feature a disproportionate number of athletes – those celebrity figures constituted, as I noted previously, in an *a priori* discourse fusing merit and sovereignty. This preponderance of national athletes is also reflected in cases which are merely threatened and do not ultimately end up being resolved in court, including triathlete, Olympic gold medallist, notorious Gomery Inquiry witness, and recent fugitive from justice Myriam Bédard, and Canada's (eventual) Olympic gold medal figure skating darlings, Jamie Salé and David Pelletier.

While recognizability is clearly a (most-of-the-time) necessary aspect of the legal endorsement of the persona in Canada, visibility is problematic for Canadian celebrities. Writing about the 2004 Juno Awards, journalist Mike Ross noted, 'Dave Francey, who won the roots Juno last night, is among them, though I wouldn't be able to pick him out of a lineup if you held a gun to my head' (Ross, 2004: ES4). He goes on: '[t]his is the trouble with many Canadian celebrities. No one knows what they look like' (ibid.). Canadian courts have seemingly recognized the reduced visibility of Canadian celebrities. For example, the court acknowledged that George Athans would only be recognizable to a very small and very specific audience. Perhaps recognition in Canada is not as indebted to visibility as its American counterpart; it must draw upon a complex of name, image, and achievement. Recognition is also clearly not a generalized standard drawing upon a 'Canadian audience,' but rather, the recognizing audiences are constituted in special interests; they are CFL viewers, water-skiing aficionados, or classical music lovers.

Ultimately, I suggest, the sales versus subject distinction and the use of public interest considerations in the Canadian case law reflect a merit discourse, reproducing a high-low culture distinction. If the cultural product at issue is merely of the market, then we must protect the person from this marketization and the ownership rights are the tools granted them to do so. One thinks of the horrors of Glenn Gould T-shirts. If, however, the work is a high culture product, such as a biography where the public domain is enriched by our increased knowledge of the subject, then the persona is not being objectified. The person does not require protection because the referential effect is in operation, linking person to persona. Similarly, when there is a meritorious public interest pitted against the avarice of an individual who is not the author of the persona at issue, the claim of merit will always trump the financial claim. In other words, where the persona circulating gives the audience authentic insights into a meritorious person, it is not property. When, however, it is already a commodity, it cannot draw for its legitimacy on its intimacy with the person and therefore can be property. We have seen the reluctance of Canadian courts to propertize the person. The closer the persona is seen to be to the identity of the person, the less likely it is to be rendered in its commodity form.[49] The only legitimate activity of the persona, then, is to authenticate the person.

Prosthesis, Proxy, or Promiscuous

The underlying rationale for endorsing publicity rights in Canada is revealing. There is a visible tension, as yet unresolved, in the rationale of a Lockean labour theory of value and a more Hegelian approach where the persona, as property, serves as a completion of the self, as a fundamental instantiation, and catalyst, of identity. Canadian courts clearly see the meritorious persona, namely one that is not merely commodity, as an affirmation of the person, and a completely marketed persona as existing at a greater distance from the person. The meritorious persona provides affirmation and authentication for the person; yet at the same time, the commodity persona is a reflection of a person's labour and market relations. The labour rationale, entrenched and unquestioned in the United States, is not as popular in Canada. In reading the decisions, the labouring self is not the self being protected. Even in the case of Glenn Gould or Tim Horton, a strong labour discourse is absent.

And yet, we see at the Supreme Court of Canada most spectacularly, and elsewhere in the subordination of publicity rights to public policy concerns, a strong sense of the relationship between person and persona. If not already sullied by the market, then that relationship verges on the sacred. It cannot be owned. If already constituted in market relations, then the persona becomes profane, losing its claim for legitimacy based in its relationship with the person. It can be property with no loss to the person. In this way, somewhat ironically, the Canadian propertized persona is even more promiscuous than its American sibling because its authorship is less emphasized. As a creature completely of the market, it has a freedom to roam, to reproduce, and to rework culture. Rather than being interested in this activity, however, Canadian courts have rejected it as not particularly worthy. I would assert, however, meritorious or not (on the measure of a narrow cultural nationalist discourse), personae, like their Canadian celebrity counterparts, exist and are 'out there' working. They trouble and constitute the relationship between person and personae with their every gesture. The personae, as much as the persons, therefore, are worth watching.

On its surface, publicity law, in both Canada and the United States, recognizes that there is something we can call a persona, related to, but not fully determined by, the person. First and foremost, it is a publicly endorsed representation of the person, perhaps more accurately an evocation. But like the mirrors in a fun house, it does not promise a 'realist' portrayal. Personae skew the person. Further, this variable and volatile representation of the person is both commodified and propertized, with full (or in Canada, partial) sanction of the law. The law exacts a price for this concretization of the personae, however; and that is the fiction of the authentic relationship between person, as author or subject, and persona, as text or embodied personality. And it would seem that we want to believe. We want to propertize our public selves in order to self-affirm. However, at the same that this 'promiscuous personification of living property' reveals the ongoing investment in possessive individualism at the heart of our notion of the person, it also offers the resources to trouble it. Publicity law can be read against the grain as elevating the persona to a level of importance that exceeds that of the person. After all, the persona of publicity law is, by definition, multiply authored, contingently constituted in the ephemerality of recognition, potentially immortal, disembodied, and simultaneously subject and object of law.

7 Conclusion: Impersonations

Rosemary J. Coombe suggests, '[s]elf, society and identity are realized only through the expressive cultural activity that reworks those cultural forms that occupy the space of the social imaginary' (1992b: 78). The person, I have tried to suggest, is just such a cultural form. The person is, and has been, central to our social imaginary, and as I have demonstrated over the course of this book, we are continually troubling it, reworking it. This animated cultural activity is taking place, not only in the person's 'natural' home of the law, but in social sites as diverse as documentary cinema, celebrity discourse, online poker, genetic science, commemorative practices, science fiction, and corporate policy. Simultaneously a marker of legal-political status and sociocultural agency, the person is often synonymous with the rational individual, subject, or citizen. And yet, as we saw through the preceding stories, being a person is neither benign nor uncontested. 'We are not by nature persons. Becoming a person is the price we pay, and perhaps the reward we receive, for participation in certain forms of social life' (Poole, 1996: 52). Personality, rather than an outcome, then, is revealed as a process, as something we do, rather than something that we are. In doing personality, an array of social resources is available to us, accessible with varying degrees of ease, and in inevitable negotiation with society's interpretation of our personality type.

Law, however, trumps even capital and science as the favourite tool of those seeking personification. And thus, through tactics as diverse as constitutional references, commercial law, patents, contracts, and publicity rights, we saw various liminal beings re-produced in complicated relationships with the individuated abstraction of the Western, liberal person. Yet these personifications take place in ways that the law can neither fully capture nor contain. What begins as a quest for personhood, therefore, often ends up looking much more like an impersonation. In this brief conclusion, I will re-examine the ways in which my five stories of personification are also stories of impersonation. They make visible to us that, first, the person is an always incomplete normative project; second, the person acts as a social divining rod for certain shared cultural anxieties; and third, the person inevitably brings forth its double – the persona – allowing us to productively refocus our gaze towards it.

The corporation, as the quintessential artificial person, has long occupied, and arguably demanded the invention of, the category of the P1 person. Smug in its role as legal agent, it was not the corporation, itself, that sought re-personification. Rather, it was other persons – mostly human concerned with its heady combination of rights without corresponding social responsibilities and its seemingly unbridled power in late capitalism – that sought its redefinition. Attempts have been made, within popular discourse, corporate policy, and the law (both legislation and litigation), to responsibilize the corporation, to hold it accountable for the negative consequences of its actions similarly to other persons. In other words, attempts have been made to force the corporation from its comfortable P1 slot to the more difficult identity of a P3 moral agent ... without much success. This failure is in large part because the P1 person is as close as the law will come to recognizing the persona. Therefore, in addition to the potential injustices that might be produced in individual circumstances of 'immoral' corporate action, trying to hold the corporation as persona accountable, trying to figure it as a moral agent, reveals the person as a fundamentally amoral concept. Personality does not require moral agency to precede metaphysical agency. What does this say about us?

Women, as particularly sexed human beings, as P2 persons, sought, through challenging their categorization in the Canadian constitution, to enter the hallowed category of the P3 rational, responsible subject. The P3 person, with its accompanying guarantee of a place in the polis, is a powerful marker of status. In its enlightened act of recognition and, indeed, in the quest for it, the courts and the Famous Five alike participated in a legal-cultural fiction: that sex could be effaced by personification, or phrased differently, that the person was a gender-neutral identity formation. Instead, there is a threefold revealing that takes place in this attempted personification. First, it becomes apparent that our notions of personality are inextricably connected to our notion of the nation-state. 'Ideas of society, variously conceptualized, and the nature of the concept of the person are thus interdependent' (La Fontaine, 1985: 138). In this way, progressive personification reproduces, not the recognition of the gendered nature of the person, but the imagination of the enlightened nation. Second, we recognize that women (and men), as personae, are sexed beings and that sexing has a complex and undetermined relationship with the law. The law is premised on personification preceding any other forms of personality. Third, we see that persons, and their nobler subset, heroes, both operate as technologies of gender, revealing and reproducing the masculine nature of the person, to the exclusion of other ways of imagining subjects at law, and at large.

Clones, as the archetypical invented human, force us to realize the indebtedness of our legal categories of the person to another grand narrative, biological science. Clones could be P1 persons should any jurisdiction wish to engage in such social science fictional legislating. Yet at the same time, most of the entities in the P1 category do not look like 'us,' and as genetic reproductions, clones look a lot like us. P2 is a category that seems more appropriate for the clone; however, that encounter reveals the significance (or not) of traditional forms of reproduction and birth. P2 signals our residual desire for mystery in human reproduction. Finally, there is no reason to assume that clones will not be reasoning actors who could be required to take responsibility for their actions in the social, and therefore they are strong candidates for P3 personhood. However, with clones, those debates may be moot. Because of their necessary status as property, clones, as invented humans, might well be understood as animals and therefore as property, not persons. While this offends our current morality, as popular culture attests, naïve humanism, with its reliance on an untroubled, uncomplicated notion of the human being, no longer holds. There is no original anymore, or at least, we cannot distinguish it from the copy. Therefore, the clone as a copied person, as persona, makes apparent that the person can no longer be defined through species borders or along subject-object lines, if ever it could. Now that we can make the monster and it looks a lot like us, the person is a lot more complicated.

Mechanical kin to its posthuman cousin the clone, the bot, too, relies upon the prior trick of the informated subject. We have developed a specific technique by which to determine the difference between machine and man, a long-standing puzzle case, to contain the threat of machines that do the labour of the mind. The Imitation Game privileges the powerful trilogy of reason, communication, and deception in order to produce that difference, to mark that boundary. However, what happens when that test results in sameness, instead of difference? What begins first as a parlour trick in the 1700s, and then as legally endorsed fact in the 2000s, is that the machine can pass. It is impersonating us. The law has recently conceded, enthusiastically in practice, if reluctantly in its letter, that the bot is a P1 person, by virtue of the fact of our recognition of it as a contracting entity. However, the bot's personification turns on its intelligence defined in terms of reason, not a necessary requirement for P1 persons, but the very foundation of P3. But can the bot be a P3 person? Can it be a responsible moral agent? To date, the fears of its immorality stem from its capacity to mislead, and even lie to, consumers. However, we must remember that such dishonesty is required in its personification via the Imitation Game. As such, our concerns with deception are paradoxical at best, and, at worst, moot. Yet there is another problem with the bot's bid for P3 status, and that is its disembodiment. The bot, as posthuman person, reveals both the celebration of disembodiment, and the high level of investment we still have in our bodies, as conflicting desires manifest in law and culture. While the person is fundamentally constituted in an attempt to produce a Cartesian separation of mind and body, seemingly evidenced in allowing the bot to win the Imitation Game of the contract, at the same time, the residue of the embodied person, of the human, continues to haunt it. This explains our despondency at Kasparov's loss, and our rush from reason to emotion as the next horizon point of machine personhood.

Finally, at first glance, there is little doubt that celebrities comfortably inhabit the P3 category of personality, except, of course, for stars like Elvis, Mickey Mouse, Michael Jackson, or Christopher Reeve before his death, who are arguably much more powerfully figured as personae by reasons of death, animation, extreme bodily malleability, and the cyborgian management of physicality, respectively. Celebrities can be understood as persons in perpetual performance, as quintessential personae. They are signs without necessary referent. Unlike the personae produced by the encounter between liminal identity and technologies of personification in the other fringe cases I consider, the personae constituted in the relations of fame are recognized and endorsed by the law, not as persons, but as property. In this way, they are refused entry into the legal characterization of personality. Yet, rather than understanding personae as the property outcome of the pre-existing labouring celebrity subject, publicity law can be read as following Locke to his logical outcome, suggesting that the valuable result of this process is not in fact property, but rather self-proprietorship. The celebrity person as authentic self is produced in the circulation of the personae as the logical outcome of Macpherson's diagnosis of the possessive individual.

Doubly endorsed by law and commodity capitalism, these personae take on a value and significance that begins to overshadow their authors, however. Famous personae live far longer than, circulate more widely than, and can be re-inscribed in languages unknown to, their mediating persons. They are more valuable and slower to deteriorate. But at the same time that publicity law enables, and indeed naturalizes, this activity, it works to fetter the persona to the person in a relationship of authenticity and authorship. The persona, as its communicative identity would imply, is notoriously nimble, however. It resists containment within the strictures that law and capitalist property relations seek to place on it. And the cycle continues.

In addition to revealing the contingency, limitations, and potential of our notion of person, the personae produced in my five stories of liminal beings, my five fringe cases, figure deep-seated cultural apprehensions. Being a person in the twenty-first century is stressful. Molecular biology, capitalism, computing technology, neoliberalism, and law have, since the Second World War, been rewriting how we do subjectivity and how we understand our selves, up to and including our material substrate. These processes are contested, however. By contestation, I do not mean simple 'us' and 'them' or 'yes' and 'no' antagonisms, although certain forces work to frame the debates in those terms. Most of my cases do not involve a significant amount of controversy; this is because in most instances, the challenge to the person is already well underway – the personality debate that does take place in each serves as a moment of distillation in which we can finally discern the stakes of that shift. These cases, then, are moments of a working out, processes of sense-making whereby cultural anxiety is finally recognized, seemingly managed, and ultimately, not fully quieted by the coping strategies offered by law, science, government, philosophy, and popular culture.

The person has served as one of the cultural icons in which we have confidently located our trust and our identity. It has measured the ethical progress of nations, the enfranchisement of populations, and the boundaries of propriety by which we have organized society. The person is a notion we have assumed, rather than interrogated. No longer. It figures our shared cultural anxieties and we adopt a variety of strategies – from purification to juridification to romanticization – to manage our stress. In the case of the corporation, we see the concern with a simultaneously powerful, and yet seemingly amoral, being, one which causes significant amounts of social good as we reckon standards of living, but also increasing amounts of individual, social, and environmental harm. With the decline of recognized systems for the determination of moral questions, we worry that the person may not be a moral being, may not offer us the compass that we seek to tackle the difficult questions that emerge when well-trodden boundaries are transgressed. We worry that the abstract, individuated liberal subject around whom we have organized our democratic ideals and practices may not be, and may never have been, the identity-neutral category that we have pretended at past moments that it is. Further, our processes of expanding personification, lauded as by definition progressive, while expanding the polis, do not address the structural inequities upon which the polis is ordered and the person as a cultural form aiding in that work.

The messy complicatedness of our bodies has been an ongoing problem within modernity, which has arguably been a project, among other things, of purification and disembodiment. However, with the redefinition of our human essence in an informated language that is the basis for all other forms of organic life, and the corresponding unprecedented molecular manipulation of the bodies of humans and other creatures understood in that code, the repressed has returned in full force. We have relied upon the notion of the person to place our bodies and those of Other beings into hierarchical relations. Key to this has been the maxim that human beings are persons, animals are property. However, our kinship with animals and the instrumentalization of our bodies through genetic science has meant that we, too, are candidates for property. The law's tools for renegotiating these boundaries of propriety are blunt, and we recognize that. We worry, however, that there is nowhere else to turn for the answers we seek.

The Industrial Revolution forced us to recognize that human beings, as physical labourers, were replaceable, that we were obsolete by any measure of efficiency. With the advent of the 'Information Revolution' and modern computing in the Second World War, we had to face the unsettling fact that human beings, as mental labourers, were also replaceable, and were arguably obsolete by any measure of calculating intelligence. That machines could not only think, but pass as persons, posed a powerful fascination and fear borne out long before the twentieth century. This disquiet has, however, reached new levels in the twenty-first. In the past, humans have always held a trump card (be it embodiment, emotion, intelligence, or consciousness) to contain the machine in its proper place. In acceding without demur to the demands of information capitalism, however, we have granted the machine the status of legal person in e-commerce. In admitting its personality, we concede the permeability of another boundary – that between human being and technology. Yet this powerful cyborg subjectivity is premised, not only on the manipulability of the body, as with genetic science, but on the body's irrelevance. Our unease manifests in our feeble protestations of human attributes that have typically been disprivileged within formulations of the modern subject, including embodiment and emotion. It remains to be seen if the irony will be lost on us.

Finally, it is in and through the figure of the celebrity that I suggest we are working out a deep-seated crisis in authenticity. We are increasingly troubled by the fact that we cannot distinguish between the real person and the performance. This poses the inevitable question of whether or not there is a 'real' person, or whether there ever has been. The celebrity exposes our notion of the person as containing the fundamental tensions and doubled aspect of the Greek and Latin notions of person: our substantial existence as well as our social role enactment. The ephemeral link between person and persona, present, I have argued, in all of the fringe cases, is materialized and socially recognized in the case of the celebrity. We cling to publicity law's constructed connection between person and persona as our proof in the authenticity of the self and the performativity of representation. However, when the persona begins to outshine the person, this prefigures a predicament. It forces us to question the authenticity of the original, and thus all of the social ordering dependent upon that claim.

In addition to helping us challenge and question the privileged figure of the person, and revealing our shared apprehensions about the order of things, my examination of the five fringe cases requires us to recognize the person's increasingly powerful and ever more visible alter-ego, the persona. Thus, we saw that corporations, women, clones, bots, and celebrities are all involved in contests of personification. Yet the outcomes are often ambivalent. These liminal beings are always partially failed persons, because their existence challenges the boundaries and legitimacy of the very category itself. The technologies of personification were not designed with them in mind and, therefore, the 'fit' is only partial. Personae denaturalize the person, revealing its constructedness, and hence its normative power. Personae thrive in the border zones, simultaneously subject and object, sexed and gender-neutral, amoral and responsible, embodied and disembodied, real and artificial. And yet, personae are not the instantiation of an excess of postmodern abandon. They are actual entities negotiating the social spaces we all inhabit. They are us. They reveal, not a rejection of the person, even with all of its flaws, but a regretful nostalgia for its confidence and a hopeful glance to a more complicated future. We are simultaneously persons and personae, not either/or.

This recognition of our doubled identity as persons and personae requires us to recognize another set of social tactics, however, which I call impersonation. If personification is the means by which entities are constituted (or not) and circulate as recognizable persons within a legal-social framework of legitimation, then impersonation is the name I give to the process by which entities are constituted and circulate as personae. Impersonation describes how we all play at being persons. Impersonation is therefore about dodging in and through and behind the lines that separate the categories that seem to matter to us, all the more so now that they are at their least tenable – lines between natural and artificial; copy and original; men and women; human and animal; human and machine; subject and object. Acts of impersonation recognize the boundaries, acknowledge to whom they matter and why, and realize their stakes. They do not (and indeed could not) wish them away. '[I]t is difficult or even impossible to conceive of what it would be like if we abandoned the concept of a person' (Dennett, 1976: 175). At the same time, impersonators do not feel constrained to categorically inhabit one side of the boundary or the other as a determination of essence. Rather, impersonation is about our always fraught experience as persons, which becomes less stressful as soon as we release ourselves from the burden to personify.

Impersonation is premised upon an interest in the benefits that come with personification, but with an accompanying knowledge that most of us do not inhabit the category with complete ease. Impersonation embraces the permeability of the category of person, realizing that each time the person encounters a fringe case, a liminal being seeking entry or not, important social questions are posed. In working on those questions without expectation of resolution, we may realize that we can no longer answer such questions in categorical terms. Impersonation is above all, therefore, an epistemological practice, a way of working out personality at a time when a simple retreat into the person is no longer tenable. Through impersonation, norms are made visible, reproduced, and then possibly challenged. As I hope this book has demonstrated, it is becoming an increasingly unproductive, as well as uninteresting, question to inquire whether a particular entity is a person. Perhaps because, all along, we have been impersonating.

Notes

1. Introduction

1 An extremely broad-ranging and large study revealed that recovery from PVS is rare, and if it happens, usually takes place within three months of the trauma resulting in the condition. No medically verified recovery has ever been recorded for any patient after two years of PVS being established.

2 Ultimately the feeding tube was removed for the final time in 2005, having been removed and then reinserted twice before, in 2001 as a result of a legal appeal and in 2003 as a result of Governor Jeb Bush's actions.

3 For a very comprehensive timeline of events, particularly those legal and legislative, see the University of Miami, Ethics Program website: http://www6.miami.edu/ethics/schiavo/terri_schiavo_timeline.html.

4 In more detail he said, 'I urge all those who honor Terri Schiavo to continue to work to build a culture of life, where all Americans are welcomed and valued and protected, especially those who live at the mercy of others' (Bush in Bazinet, 2005: 17).

5 In March 2004, Pope John Paul II addresses the World Federation of Catholic Medical Associations and Pontifical Academy for Life Congress on 'Life-Sustaining Treatments and Vegetative State: Scientific Advances and Ethical Dilemmas.'

6 An ABC News poll found that 64 per cent of respondents supported removing Schiavo's feeding tube and 28 per cent did not. Fifty-four per cent of social conservatives supported removing the tube, and those who identified themselves as evangelical Christians were also split, with 46 per cent supporting removal and 44 per cent opposed. Further, 70 per

cent of Americans felt it was inappropriate for Congress to get involved (see Morrill, 2005: 5A).

7 Both the Schindlers and Michael Schiavo continue to advance their respective causes around Terri and to profit from her life and death. The Schindlers established the Terri Schindler Schiavo Foundation (www.terrisfight.org), a disability rights and right to life organization, and Michael Schiavo established TerriPAC (www.terripac.com) in order to support or oppose politicians based on their positions on the intervention into private lives. Mary and Robert Schindler, together with their son and daughter, Bobby Schindler and Suzanne Schindler Vitadamo, published, *A Life That Matters: The Legacy of Terri Schiavo – A Lesson for All of Us* (2006) and Michael Schiavo (with Michael Hirsh) published *Terri: The Truth* (2006).

8 Philip Kennicott (2005) refers to this phenomenon as '"Terri" speak' and suggests that Terri as a figure ultimately failed for the power brokers because the American public would not make the woman who lay in the hospice bed bear all the symbolic baggage and weight that was being heaped upon her.

9 Poole (1996) offers a compelling analysis tracing the initial distinction between the Greek and Roman persons through Hobbes, Locke, Kant, Hegel, and finally to Nietzsche.

10 Rorty, too, suggests four general questions: class differentiation ('what distinguishes the class of persons from their nearest neighbours, from baboons, robots, human corpses, corporations'); individual differentiation ('what are the criteria for the numerical distinctness of persons who have the same general description'); individual reidentification ('what are the criteria for reidentifying the same individual in different contexts, under different descriptions, or at different times'); and individual identification ('what sorts of characteristics identify a person as *essentially* the person she is, such that if those characteristics were changed, she would be a significantly different person') (1976b: 1–2).

11 Christopher Gill (1988) makes a distinction between personhood and personality. Those who use the concept of personhood, including a vast majority of ancient thinkers, are concerned with persons as a class. They try to develop the boundaries of that class through normative criteria such as self-consciousness, rationality, and legal and moral responsibility. The concept of personality is more recent, he asserts, and focuses on persons as individuals. These thinkers are concerned with the factors which distinguish individuals, emphasizing their individuality and

uniqueness. While the distinction is somewhat useful, I remain convinced that we are as concerned with person as we are with personality in the early twenty-first century.

12 In this, I am indebted, in part, to Charles Taylor, who suggests persons as 'self-interpreting beings': 'I become a person and remain one only as an interlocutor' (1976: 276).

13 While not linking this argument to the Greek notion of person, Davies and Naffine suggest that '[t]he legal person may technically be a bundle of rights and responsibilities, which vary from case to case, but a culturally-specific model of a natural person, with natural capacities, and even natural rights, frequently gives shape and meaning to the legal concept of the person' (2001: 182).

14 For an interesting discussion of fetuses and women as persons within a liberal, individualist framework see Ruhl (2002).

15 It seems an open question for Naffine between her 2003 and 2004 pieces whether a non-human entity with reason and a will could not fall within the P3 characterization, opening the door for computers, corporations, and others.

16 In addition to the reasons stated, I selected my particular liminal beings because they are mediated by the law and yet continue to act out in popular culture. Each case selected draws attention to current social issues where the narratives remain contested. These are narratives where personae are still visible and we have not yet fully wrapped up the liminal being in person's clothing ... even if we think that we have.

2. *Persona Ficta*

1 Each has also come under substantial criticism from legal scholars seeking consistency and reliability in the law (see Welling, 1991; Neyers, 2000; vanDuzer, 2003). Welling goes so far as to describe 'fiction' and 'realist' theories as 'opposing and equally preposterous' (79).

2 Neocleous goes on to argue that the corporation's personification is modelled on, and parallel to, that of the state (domination in union) and that it is a form of the personification of capital.

3 Allegedly we owe the notion of *persona ficta* to Pope Innocent IV (circa 1245); see the discussion in Neocleous (2003), chapter 3.

4 Offering a 'Turing Test' (see chapter 5), Maitland's formulation is classic: 'Not all the legal propositions that are true of a man will be true of a corporation. For example, it can neither marry nor be given in marriage; but

in a vast number of cases you can make a legal statement about x and y which will hold good whether these symbols stand for two men or for two corporations, or for a corporation and a man' (1911: 307).

It is interesting that voting and marriage are the markers of being a 'real' or 'natural' person. In one stroke then legal commentators mark women, Aboriginal peoples, and gays and lesbians as artificial persons, and as legal fictions, for much of Canadian (and indeed Western) history. More specifically, women in Canada were legally fictitious until 1918 federally and as late as 1940 in Quebec, federal inmates until 2002, Aboriginal peoples until as late as 1960, and gays and lesbians until 2005. More kin with corporations, according to the law, than with their *fellow* human beings. The corporation's lack of embodiment produces the same legal/social effects as certain subjects' excess of embodiment.

5 Central English Pluralists involved in this movement included F.W. Maitland (1900; 1905; 1911), John Figgis (1913; 1916), Ernest Barker (1915), Harold Laski (1915–16) and G.D.H. Cole (1920). See also D. Runciman (1997) and P.Q. Hirst (1989) for good discussions of the Pluralists and their theories of states and organizations.

6 It permits us to ask, as one feminist scholar does, for example: 'does a corporation have a sex?' (Corcoran, 1997).

7 Most provinces in Canada have similar provisions in their provincial corporate legislation. For a discussion of the provincial differences, see van-Duzer (2003), beginning at page 81.

8 The distinction between corporate and natural persons is clearer in Quebec. The *Quebec Civil Code* provides in Title V, Section 298 that 'legal persons are endowed with juridical personality.' At no time are corporations referred to as persons or given personality defined in relation to natural persons. They are specifically referred to as legal persons, distinct from persons and natural persons. While Section 301, for example, provides for full civil rights to legal persons (corporations), the reference point is not the natural person but the legal person in its own right.

9 At the same time, corporations have been found not to have freedom of religion, citizenship rights, or the right to life, liberty, and security of the person.

10 The two important acts of incorporation that year which established limited liability were: 'An Act to establish freedom of Banking in this Province, and for other purposes relative to Banks and Banking' and 'An Act to provide for the formation of Incorporated Joint Stock Companies, for Manufacturing, Mining, Mechanical or Chemical Purposes.'

11 Mr Justice Estey quoting Justice Cooke with approval in *Canadian Dredge and Dock Co. Ltd. v. R.* [1985], 1 S.C.R. 662 (SCC).

12 Direct liability in tort proceeds in a similar manner.

13 Here vanDuzer is referring to the decision in *Clarkson Co. v. Zhelka*, [1967] 2 O.R. 565 (H.C.J.).

14 However, there is an actual test that can be applied to determine the relationship of agency (see *Smith, Stone and Knight*, 1939).

15 Although it is not relevant to the argument being made in this chapter, it is interesting to note that the legislation applies, not only to corporations, but to all organizations, a much broader category of group entity.

16 Sethi (1997) identifies nine distinct definitions of CSR, for example; see also Karake-Shalhoub (1999).

17 In recent years we have seen a sustained popular inquiry into corporate responsibility through documentary films, including *Black Gold* (2006), *Wal-Mart: The High Cost of Low Price* (2005), *Supersize Me* (2004), *Who Killed the Electric Car* (2006), and *Just for Kicks* (2006), as well as the two under consideration here. These films, in different ways, all examine the role of corporations in contemporary America, and the function of law in attempting to make corporations accountable to people. As the *Economist* noted in 2005, popular culture has 'the corporate psycho in plain view' (2005c: 11).

18 The film follows on the heels of Enron's collapse and therefore much of the initial footage focuses on the responses to the bankruptcy announcement and revelations of fraud, as American business and political administrations struggle to contain the scandal.

19 See the discussion in Schane (1987) of the three cases that cumulatively produced this legal situation.

20 WorldCom's bankruptcy in 2002 is now the largest corporate bankrupty in American history, followed by Enron.

21 Skilling reportedly wanted to talk to the film's director, Alex Gibney, but his lawyers would not permit it.

22 In accordance with American law when a defendant cannot maintain an appeal, his sentence was voided on 17 October 2006.

23 WorldCom founder Bernard Ebbers received a twenty-five-year sentence, Tyco chairman Dennis Kozlowski got eight to twenty-five years, and John and Timothy Rigas of Adelphia received fifteen- and twenty-year sentences respectively.

24 Certainly, the subsequent scandals involving WorldCom, Tyco, Adelphia, and Global Crossing suggest that something bigger is going on than merely Jeffrey Skilling's greed and corruption.

3. 'Not a Sex Victory'

1 This was how Wilson was referred to at the time by a journalist in the *Ottawa Journal*, quoted in Dawson, 1994: 38. Prime Minister Mackenzie King referred to her as 'bilingual, a Liberal and a lady,' in direct contrast to Murphy, whom he described as 'a little too masculine and perhaps a bit too flamboyant' (in Brown 1988: 694).

2 While Dorland and Charland do not suggest the Famous Five are heroes, they note in their analysis that the Five have generally been figured as heroes (2002: 217) without problematizing the implications of that figuration.

3 In Manitoba and Alberta, the United Farmers formed in the early 1900s and were in power between the early 1920s and the early 1930s. Other parties in the three prairie provinces included, among others, the Dominion Labour Party (1918–20), the Communist Party (1921-present), the Independent Labour Party (1920–43), the Social Democratic Party of Canada (1911–20), the Socialist Party of Canada (1904–15), the Progressive Party (1920–35), the Provincial Rights Party (1905–12), and the United Farmers of Alberta (1909–35).

4 For an interesting discussion of this time and these movements see Valverde (1991) and Henderson (2003, 2005).

5 In 1896 when Wilfrid Laurier became prime minister, he returned to the system where provincial voters' lists determined the eligibility for the federal franchise.

6 Asian and Indo-Canadians were not enfranchised federally until 1947, and Aboriginal peoples, not until 1960.

7 Interestingly, Canadian women showed themselves not that interested as a larger group in voting or running for office, much to the chagrin of the leaders of the various women's movements of the day. We then see a doubled discourse: the first component aimed at the masculine establishment making the argument that even if women are not using the right, it did not detract from the 'correctness' of their having the option to do so. The second component focused on the women of Canada, urging them to use their freedom and take up their responsibility to make the nation a better, more moral place. These exhortations were frequent in the early 1900s in women's magazines; for example, see Robertson (1929).

8 As examples of prudential politics within the Canadian women's suffrage movement, they detail the mock parliaments staged by the suffragists and a significant essay by Sonia Leathes in 1914.

9   The significance of the Woman's Court as a particularly complex initiative within Canadian women's legal history is under-analysed, I suggest. Henderson (2003, 2005) is a notable exception in addressing the specificities of the court, although not from a legal history perspective.

10 For an interesting discussion of the tensions within elitist, maternal feminism, as well as the politics of national memory, as they played out in the case of Lizzie Cyr, see Bright (1998).

11 In *Hostetter*, at issue was the eligibility of a married woman to be elected as a county clerk in Missouri. Mr Hostetter had been appointed by the governor to fill a vacancy, yet in the subsequent election, a Mrs Wheeler received an overwhelming majority of votes. Mr Hostetter uncharitably refused to give up the position on the grounds that Mrs Wheeler was ineligible for election as a woman. The court held that while a variety of offices in state government were specifically limited to male citizens, some were not. Those that were not were governed by the general principle that words referred to in the masculine gender implied the feminine, and vice versa, unless otherwise specified. The court found for Mrs Wheeler. See Bourne and Eisenberg (1980) for a review of the British, American, and Canadian cases on women's political personhood.

12 See Henderson (2003).

13 According to Mander (1985: 118), this was a controversial manuscript which never found a publisher and was never completed.

14 For a discussion of the huge support for Murphy across the country, see Sanders (1945: 218–22).

15 In addition to Murphy's own personal ambition, the Senate was a desirable location because, at that time, it was more significant as a house and approved divorces, making it a key locus for affecting the social position of women.

16 See *Viscountess Rhondda's Claim* [1922], 2 A.C. 339 (H.L.).

17 The five were those of Prime Ministers Robert Borden, Arthur Meighen, R.B. Bennett, and Mackenzie King in two different terms.

18 While the capacity for Cabinet to request a reference on a point of constitutional clarification still exists in the *Supreme Court Act*, the specific provision enabling five concerned citizens to initiate such action no longer exists.

19 The 'tea party' itself has an interesting history as a prudential feminist practice. Suffragist meetings often took place as 'pink tea parties' to disguise their real purpose. Interestingly, for the launch of their spoken-word CD entitled *She Pushed from Behind: Emily Murphy in Story and Song*,

marking the seventy-fifth anniversary of the Persons Case, storyteller Ruth Stewart-Verger and singer-songwriter Teresa Healy opted to have a 'feminist tea party' at the National Library on Sunday, 22 August 2004 (which the author attended). The event reflected many of the tensions between first, second, and third wave feminisms, in no small part because of its structuring trope of the tea party.

20 She died on 1 September 1951 at the age of seventy-eight in Victoria, BC.

21 She ran as an independent and was elected alongside nursing sister Roberta MacAdams.

22 The *Dower Act* entitled women to a one-third share of their husband's property upon the dissolution of the marriage or the death of the husband.

23 Louise McKinney died in 1931 in Claresholme, Alberta at sixty-three years of age.

24 Henrietta Muir Edwards passed away at eighty-two years of age in 1930 in Fort McLeod, Alberta.

25 Irene Parlby died at the age of ninety-seven on 12 July 1965 in Alix, Alberta.

26 It is interesting to note that, on the original petition containing the three questions, there is a word blacked out after 'female' in the second question that might well have been 'persons,' adding credence to the deliberate attention the petitioners had paid to not using that loaded term.

27 In fact, as a longstanding matter of policy, the Supreme Court is supposed to refuse to hear the question if it is fundamentally political and without a substantial point of law.

28 Throughout the case, in the judgments as well as in the press, much was made of the language provisions of the *BNA Act* which enabled 'persons' to address the court during legal proceedings, in either French or English. If women were not persons, one witty commentator remarked, then Agnes McPhail should address her fellow members in either Gaelic or Iroquois, 'both being languages which have a good historical background in Canada' (Sandwell, 1928: 22).

29 For a good discussion of these precedents, see Stone, 1979.

30 Persons case lore suggests that his statement was in response to a question posed by Agnes McPhail; in fact, it was posed by Mr A.W. Neil, the Independent member from Comox-Alberni (Marchildon, 1981: 109).

31 The cost of the entire case to the federal government was $23,368.47 in legal fees, $21,000 of which was for the appeal to the JCPC (Benoit, n/d: 11).

32 The typical practice was for the court to merely verbally state the outcome and circulate copies of the judgment to the gallery.

33 Murphy wrote a somewhat piqued letter to the government expressing her frustration with the fact that religious creed was seemingly being used as a criterion for Senate appointments, contrary to the law. It was not until fifty years after the Persons Case that a woman was appointed to the Senate from Alberta; Prime Minister Joe Clark appointed Martha Beilish in 1979.

34 Notable instances of this include Mark Starowitz's seventeen-part series *Canada: A People's History* (2000) and the Canadian Heritage Minute initiative. The Persons Case is addressed in Episode 12, *Ordeal by Fire 1915–1929* originally aired 14 October 2001. Murphy and McClung each are subjects of a Heritage Minute.

35 Interestingly, this is the only statue of individuals not elected to Parliament on the grounds of Parliament Hill.

36 The Foundation also established an educational wing which offers material to elementary and secondary classrooms, and was integral in having a Sparks, Brownie, and Girl Guide crest established marking the Famous Five's achievement.

37 It is an intriguing question, for another day, whether or not Canada has a particular inability to embrace the notion of the national hero.

38 In particular, she argues that it cannot be divorced from the judgment in favour of Leillani Muir, awarding her damages from the Alberta government for her forcible sterilization, and the problematic response of the Alberta government to the situation (Kulba, 2002: 80–1).

39 Henderson (2003, 2005) also argues effectively for a more complex interpretation of the maternal feminism of Murphy.

40 One journalist felt this was appropriate. 'The new fifty will probably be printed anyway, and in some way it's a fitting bill for the Famous Five – being rarely seen by the riff-raff. The $50 certainly suits the group who wanted equality for all – so long as "all" meant rich, white and intelligent' (Platt, 2004).

41 It bears noting that that legislation was not repealed until 1972.

42 Pointedly, the historical record in which the authentic American heroines are constituted is never problematized.

43 See Andersen (1974) for an interesting and powerful perspective on the issue of the multicultural nature of the effects of the Persons Case as well as its far-reaching impact.

44 The Persons Case itself is evidence of this.

45 Every province has similar statutory provisions for interpreting gender in relation to personhood.

46 For a comprehensive review of the Canadian case law leading up to the same-sex marriage recognition legislation, see Wintermute (2004).

4. Invented Humans

1 Since Dolly, mice, cattle, pigs, goats, rabbits, cats, and horses have all been successfully cloned.

2 For an interesting discussion of the split between the public's views on animal cloning and human cloning see Robertson (1998: 1383–4).

3 See discussion of the media and governmental response to Richard Seed's claims in Gerlach and Hamilton (2005).

4 Canada's legislation is the *Assisted Human Reproduction Act*, 2002. There are two kinds of cloning which have generated different levels of controversy. The most controversial has been reproductive cloning, which involves the cloning of an embryo for the purpose of initiating a pregnancy. Therapeutic cloning, on the other hand, involves creating an embryo for research and disease treatment, with no intention to bring it to term. Stem cell research, for example, involves therapeutic cloning.

5 See the discussion of science fictional tropes in the representation of biotechnology more generally in Hamilton (2003).

6 For a more detailed discussion of the notion of social science fiction, see the special issue of *Science Fiction Studies* (July 2003) on the topic of the same name edited by Gerlach, Hamilton, and Latham. In particular, see Gerlach and Hamilton's 'Introduction: A History of Social Science Fiction,' 161–73 and Bogard's own addition, 178–9.

7 The others are copyright, trademark, industrial designs, integrated circuit topographies, trade secrets, publicity rights, and plant breeders' rights.

8 Canada has a one-year grace period during which the invention can be made public by the applicant or someone deriving their knowledge from the applicant, without penalty to the inventor, but this is not the case in other jurisdictions with similar patent regimes to Canada, notably the United States.

9 This applies to applications filed after 1989. The patent period is seventeen years for applications filed prior to that year.

10 See Merton, 1942 for the original propositions, and Shorett et al. (2003) for a consideration of how these values are, and should be, faring in current patenting practice.

11 See discussion at 131–3.

12 Biovalue is Catherine Waldby's rich notion which 'specifies the ways in which technics can intensify and multiply force and forms of vitality by ordering it as an economy, a calculable and hierarchical system of value' (2000: 33). Biovalue is generated whenever living entities can be instru-

mentalized in a manner that renders them useful as human products, from the medical to the industrial to the agricultural.

13 Carlos Novas and Nikolas Rose (2000) make this claim in interesting ways specifically in relation to biotechnology.

14 Irma van der Ploeg (2003) argues that late modernity is witnessing a shift in 'body ontologies.' Gerlach, Hamilton, Sullivan, and Walton take this further in the *Becoming Biosubjects* (forthcoming).

15 See the discussion in Gerlach and Hamilton (2005) and in Gerlach, Hamilton, Sullivan and Walton (forthcoming), particularly chapter 5.

16 For example, see Frow (1995), Boyle (1996), McLeod (2001), Andrews and Nelkin (2002), and Hyde (1997) for more socio-cultural analyses of the legal case.

17 Manifesting some of the alarmist media headlines that followed Dolly, Jeremy Rifkin and Dr Stuart Newman filed an ultimately unsuccessful patent for a social science fiction of their own: a chimera created from merging a human and animal embryo.

18 Some key texts in this debate include Singer (1975), Regan (1983); Regan and Singer (1989); Wise (2000); Singer (1985); Singer (1991); Sapontzis (1981); Francione (2004), which support animal rights. Some of those arguing against animal personality include Dennett (1976) and Posner (2004). Arguing against moral status for animals at all, see Carruthers (1992); Frey (1980); and Leahy (1994). On the overall terms of the debate, see Jasper and Nelkin (1992) or Black (2003).

19 See the interesting discussions of the shifting meanings of DNA in Fox Keller (2000); van Dijck (1998); Nelkin and Lindee (1995); Kay (2000).

20 In 2006, Justice Rothstein was appointed to the Supreme Court of Canada. Interestingly, he was the first judge to be subjected to a multi-party 'interview' by Members of Parliament before his appointment. His decision in the Oncomouse case was seen as one of the most significant of his time on the Federal Court of Appeal. His appointment also likely completes the shift in ideology within the Supreme Court towards the patentability of non-human higher life forms.

21 It reports to the unwieldy (and therefore often ineffective) Biotechnology Ministerial Coordinating Committee composed of the federal ministers of industry, agriculture and agri-food, health, environment, fisheries and oceans, natural resources, and international trade.

22 Studies focused on a variety of themes, including a history of the patent system in Canada, international comparisons, patenting genes, the use of animals in research, economic arguments, agricultural issues, human bio-logical materials, ethical issues, competition law issues, and human

rights issues. The consultations included a CEO/President Briefing in Ottawa on 29 September 2000 with sixteen participants, primarily involving representatives from the pharmaceutical, bio-pharmaceutical, and plant and animal biotechnologies industries; a non-governmental organization hearing on 23 November 2000 with seventeen participants; and a scientific researcher electronic forum in February of 2001 with thirteen participants. See the CBAC website for an archive of all the background material (http://www.cbac-cccb.ca/).

23 Von Tigerstrom's definitions of these terms are helpful. She noted, 'A transgenic animal is one that contains one or more genes from another species. A hybrid is a genetic cross between a male of one species and a female of another. A ... chimera is a mosaic, containing cells from more than one species. Unlike a hybrid which contains material from both species in every cell, the cells in a chimera remain distinct. There are various methods for producing such animals. No one has ever created a human/non-human chimera, but there is apparently no technical barrier to doing so' (2001a: 26, footnote 113).

24 Elsewhere I have analysed the conceptual preconditions manifested within the Oncomouse's legal battles that even enable the thinking of the higher life form as property (see Gerlach, et al., forthcoming). Here I focus on the implications of the invented human, in particular.

25 Macpherson's claim can be mapped onto Henry Maine's (1883) claim that during this same time period, we witness a shift from society organized around relations of status to one premised on contract.

26 Others have taken up and worked with the notion of possessive individualism, including MacFarlane (1978); Abercrombie et al. (1986), Pateman (1988); Butler (1993); Diprose (1994); Lury (1998).

27 Section 7 of the *Canadian Charter of Rights and Freedoms* provides: 'Everyone has the right to life, liberty and security of the person and the right not to be deprived thereof except in accordance with the principles of fundamental justice.'

28 The Thirteenth Amendment provides: 'Neither slavery nor involuntary servitude, except as a punishment for crime whereof the party shall have been duly convicted, shall exist within the United States, or any place subject to their jurisdiction.' This basis for dispossessing the individual is not without its critics, who argue that because patents do not confer positive ownership rights, but rather negative rights to limit forms of use, patenting is in no way a legal equivalent to slavery (von Tigerstrom, 2001a: 23–4; 2001b: 9).

29 Much of the legal discussion of clones focuses on their place in larger

debates about reproductive freedom; for example, Robertson (1998) and Foley (2002).

5. Machine Intelligence

1 For a more extended discussion of intelligent agents, please see UMBC Agent Web, University of Maryland Baltimore County, online: http://agents.umbc.edu and 'Agentlink,' European Network of Excellence for Agent Based Computing, online: http://www.agentlink.org. See also footnotes 13–16 in Kerr (2004) at 290.

2 I am going to use the term 'bot' throughout to refer to intelligent software agents for three reasons. First, it is a more general term; second it does not directly reference agency or intelligence (both contested notions); and third, it is reflective of a historical relationship with robots and other forms of quasi-autonomous technology.

3 Turing had worked on the Colossus calculating machine and had been central in cracking the German Enigma codes during the Second World War. He was key in the development of computer theory and a number of early computers on both sides of the Atlantic. A brilliant scholar, he led a tortured life in a repressive period of British history. He was prosecuted for gross indecency in 1952 as a result of his homosexuality, and escaped a prison sentence, but was placed on probation. His probation included the condition that he undergo a course of hormone treatment to 'cure' him of his condition. The drug treatment had terrible physical side effects, rendering him impotent and causing him to grow breasts. Two years later, he committed suicide by eating an apple which he had laced with cyanide. See the bibliography of Turing by Alan Hodges (1985) for more on Turing's life and career.

4 Hayles offers a powerful analysis of the ways in which information became disembodied in the post-war period, in part through the Turing Test, as well as noting the gendered implications of both Turing's original imitation game and the subsequent almost total elision of gender in subsequent treatments of the test.

5 Interestingly, computer designers have always worried that the public would find game-playing too fanciful or trivial a pastime for such powerful machines. From the 1950s onward, media reports frequently feature computer scientists reassuring the public that it will lead to the development of other more practical applications, frequently military, industrial, and pharmaceutical. Interestingly, Wolfgang von Kempelen, as we shall see, was a reluctant promoter of the Turk and described it as a mere

'bagatelle,' preferring to talk about his speaking machine and other inventions of greater social utility.

6 The terror comes, she notes later, from the fear that humans might be superseded altogether (283); the pleasure comes from the possibilities of rethinking what the human means outside some of the boxes that have constrained past thinking (285).

7 In mapping out the 'life' of the Turk, Tom Standage's 2002 book, *The Turk: The Life and Times of the Famous Eighteenth-Century Chess-Playing Machine*, was an invaluable resource, regularly confirming and expanding upon the primary material from which I was working.

8 James Cox, an English inventor, built an eight-foot-high mechanical elephant encrusted with precious jewels. Given how expensive they were to produce, automata in the 1700s tended to be the playthings of the wealthy, particularly royalty, often serving as gifts between rulers (Standage, 2002: 2–5).

9 Many of the inventors working on automata also had a number of more useful projects that they also developed. For example, Vaucanson was also trying to build a weaving machine that would replace human workers. While that project was never realized, Vaucanson was key to the European popularity of automata throughout the mid-eighteenth century.

10 Mark Sussman (1999) describes this as 'the reveal,' the part of the display of magic designed specifically to remove the possibility for the rational explanation; it enhances the believability of the experience and interpellates the audience. It parallels the later practice of opening up the cabinet containing the lovely assistant before she is sawn in half by the illusionist.

11 In chess, the player with the white pieces always gets to open the game with first move.

12 See the discussion of Knight's Tour in Standage (2002: 30).

13 In seeking to show both machine intelligence and the machine's capacity to speak, von Kempelen arguably was reproducing the Imitation Game many years before Turing.

14 Interestingly, many media reports of the match claimed, inaccurately, that the Turk had won, further contributing to its outlandish reputation.

15 Elements of it still circulate as truth and it was in the 1911 issue of the *Encyclopaedia Britannica.*

16 Speculation then, and since, is that Maelzel was sympathetic to Carroll and ordered the Turk to lose to such a dignified opponent.

17 Poe joined scores of others in writing an exposé of the Turk, but interestingly, his particular style of ratiocination in presenting the evidence in the essay 'Maelzel's Chess-Player' (1836) is read by scholars as a precur-

sor to the mysteries for which he was later to become much more famous.

18 One account published in the 1830s was likely by a former conspirator who had hit hard times and sold his story.

19 The English translation of the title of a promotional pamphlet published by a friend of von Kempelen's in 1783, for example, was *Inanimate Reason*. One of the most credible of the attempts to uncover the secret of the Turk was written by Robert Willis and published in 1821. In *An Attempt to Analyse the Automaton Chess Player ... With an Easy Method of Imitating the Movements of that Celebrated Figure*, he suggested that the machine itself could not play chess; 'this was the province of the intellect alone.'

20 The program was written by American computer programmer, Alex Bernstein, and it ran on an IBM 704 computer.

21 The bot from the University of Alberta Computer Poker Research Group, being significantly better than the rest, was asked to referee rather than play.

22 A number of commentators note the strengths and weaknesses of shopping bots, pointing out that they do not function in a neutral fashion, but privilege certain sellers.

23 Kerr and Bornfreund (forthcoming) dub these 'buddybots' when deployed in a marketing context and they discuss some of the problematic implications for their use in trust-based advertising, particularly that directed at children (see also Steeves and Kerr, forthcoming).

24 Examples of anthropomorphized bots include buddybots or chatterbots or vReps (see Kerr, 2004; Kerr and Bornfreund, forthcoming).

25 Commentators agree, however, that the validity of contracts is not the only legal issue with respect to bots and that many issues remain outstanding, among them other forms of liability, privacy, consumer protection, bot error, and security (Brazier et al. 2004: 6; Kerr, 2004; Kerr and Bornfreund, forthcoming; Steeves and Kerr, 2005).

26 See also examples in Chopra and White, 2004 and Kerr, 1999.

27 Wise, drawing upon Langdon Winner (1977), suggests that the anxiety around technological control ultimately can be productively understood through Hegel's understanding of master and slave (Wise, 1998: 418). Interestingly, the ideal and/or dominant form of agent relationship advocated by a number of scholars to resolve the relationship between bots and their operators is that of master and slave. This intriguing parallel merits further analysis.

28 The capacity for dissembling is linked to other moral panics: '[What if]

bots could be programmed to infiltrate people's homes and lives *en masse*, befriending children and teens, influencing lonely seniors, or harassing confused individuals until they finally agree to services that they otherwise would not have chosen? What if interactive bots ... [offer] porn or alcohol to children, [send] teens dangerous or illegal recipes, or [provide] misleading financial information to potential investors or competitor companies?' (Kerr, 2004: 312)

6. Celebrity Personae

1 The album was entitled *Sketches, Songs and Shoes*, and the band subsequently changed their name to The Vestibules.

2 What I prefer about Coombe's definition is its focus on recognizability as the criterion for propertization. Barbara Singer, for example, defines the persona 'to mean any unique aspect of the individual capable of appropriation by a third party' (1991: 3) While this definition is adequately broad, the aspect of the individual does not have to be unique, I suggest, and indeed, often is not, but rather is recognizable. It articulates a relationship between person and persona. Its ascription of uniqueness, I suggest, is an ideal quality that emerges after this first symbolic move, in the characterization of the person as author.

3 The notion that the right lies dormant was articulated by the court in *Lugosi* v. *Universal Pictures* (1979). In that case, the court held that while publicity rights did survive death, they did not accrue to Lugosi for his characterization of Dracula because that character was neither invented nor completely subsumed by his performance of it, no matter how culturally dominant it might be. Different results were found for characters originated by particular actors, such as Spanky McFarlane, Charlie Chaplin, and the Marx Brothers.

4 Both Gable and Wayne were posthumously reworked within gay culture – Wayne with lipstick and the caption 'It's such a bitch being butch' and Gable with a man substituted for Scarlett O'Hara in his arms – to the chagrin of their respective estates, who wanted to control the macho heterosexuality of the stars' personae.

5 See discussion of *Moore* v. *Regents of University of California* in chapter 4, 116–18.

6 See the discussion of Macpherson in chapter 4, 132–3.

7 She makes the important point that property designations precede determinations of value, as a policy choice, not the other way around.

8 See for example, the discussion in Hughes (1988–9).

9 Margaret Radin (1982) develops Hegel's thought in order to offer her theory of property for personhood. She argues that there are two types of property: fungible property and personal property. Fungible property is property which is not fundamental to our sense of self and therefore is properly exchanged in and through market relations. Personal property, on the other hand, is property that is integral to how we define and understand ourselves, and this property, she asserts, should not be exchanged. Radin's primary motivation was to develop a theory of property which offered a rationale against the complete commodification that she sees taking place, and which would therefore preclude the ownership of the human being. Contrary to the scholars of possessive individualism, she is attempting to develop her theory of property from a theory of the person.

10 See the discussion presented in Grieveson, 2002.

11 Susman, too, makes this claim distinguishing a previous 'culture of character' – and posits a shift to a 'culture of personality.' The culture of character focused on a series of internal traits – self-discipline, devotion to duty, etc. – as providing for the mastery over, and moral development of, the self. However, with the rise of mass consumer society at the end of the nineteenth century, self-sacrifice began to yield to the value of self-realization. Self-improvement now focused on the importance of developing a unique and individual personality, through various cultural activities – dress, gesture, consumption, etc. (Susman 1984: 271–85). Unlike Braudy, however, he does not anchor his claims in a close historical analysis of shifting notions of fame. Such a hard distinction is almost inevitably inflected with a moral valuation privileging the former period over the latter, is historically difficult to sustain, denies the many merit-based elements of current celebrity, and finally, does not allow us to take account of the significance of a discourse of meritorious celebrity in current celebrity.

12 Most scholars, including the 'revisionists,' concern themselves with the period of the 'rise of the star system' from approximately 1880 to 1930, with most disputes taking place about the respective agency of the stars, the audience, technologies, the studio heads, the publicity machine, and so on (Dyer, 1979/1998; de Cordova 1985; Ponce de Leon, 2002).

13 This is Kahn's phrase (1999: 215).

14 We can see how Warren and Brandeis characterize both the working class of journalists and the new media technology of photography as a threat to their comfort. Their notion of privacy was explicitly linked to appropriation of personality by William Prosser in his 1960 article 'Privacy.' He

broke privacy into four different types: intrusion upon one's private affairs; public disclosure of private facts; public portrayal that places the plaintiff in a (non-defamatory) 'false light'; and appropriation of personality.

15 An example of this was the case of a famous football player held to have surrendered his privacy in *O'Brien* v. *Pabst* in 1941.

16 Michael Madow somewhat cynically refers to this as a 'high-class form of special-interest pleading for the star image industry' (1993: 174).

17 He did suggest that non-famous individuals had property in their personae as well, but they stood much less chance of its being used and could not claim as much damages if it were.

18 Reflecting its original emergence from, and ongoing tensions with, the right to privacy, differing approaches were taken to the right in the two American centres of celebrity: Hollywood and New York. In California, the right of publicity was enshrined as a property right that was fully alienable and descendible. In New York, on the other hand, the right retains some of its privacy baggage and does not survive the death of the person.

19 This judicial and legislative activity resulted in what Mitchell Flagg refers to as a 'crazy quilt' of law (1999: 182).

20 *Grant* v. *Esquire Inc.* (1973); *Onassis* v. *Christian Dior-New York* (1985)

21 *Midler* v. *Ford Motor Co.* (1988). Not long before this case, Nancy Sinatra had lost her case regarding her song 'These Boots Were Made for Walkin'' (Sinatra, 1970).

22 *Waits* v. *Frito-Lay Inc.* (1992)

23 *Hoffman* v. *Capital Cities et al.* (1999) – see discussion in Gibeaut, 1999.

24 This claim is made effectively by Kahn, 1999.

25 *Carson* v. *Johnny Portable Toilets* (1983).

26 *Lugosi* v. *Universal Pictures* (1979)

27 See the discussion of this in Madow (1993).

28 Madow is taking particular exception to Armstrong (1991).

29 Stacey L. Dogan and Mark A. Lemley (2006) have argued that this tendency to a copyright incentives rationale has seen a recent upsurge in American courts.

30 Most recently, amendments to the *Lanham Act*, the American trademark legislation, have added an anti-dilution provision which protects famous trademarks from uses which blur the distinctiveness of the mark.

31 This is made literal in the most recent trends towards direct audience participation in the selection of celebrity through 'reality' contests such as *American Idol*, *Dancing with the Stars*, and so on. Arguably this is an inter-

esting next step in what Gamson refers to as the increasing democratization of celebrity over the latter half of the twentieth century.

32 The best work in the field on identity and intellectual property in
general, and publicity law in particular, is that of Rosemary Coombe,
1998; 1992a and 1992b.

33 There was discussion in the press about the suitability of Pickford for the
2004 Walk of Fame. She was inducted with Studio bosses Jack Warner
(Warner Brothers) and Louis B. Mayer (Metro Goldwyn Mayer) and
comedy producer Mack Sennett.

34 The other candidates featured elite athletes, scientists and inventors,
politicians, and humanitarians. In addition to Cherry, the top ten contenders were Frederick Banting, Alexander Graham Bell, Tommy
Douglas, Terry Fox, Wayne Gretzky, Sir John A. Macdonald, Lester B.
Pearson, David Suzuki, and Pierre Elliott Trudeau.

35 The assistant coach of the Phoenix Coyotes, Rick Tocchet, was accused of
being the chief financier of a multi-million-dollar sports gambling ring
that had, among its clients, Janet Gretzky, wife of Coyote head coach, the
NHL's all-time scoring leader, and Canada's darling, Wayne Gretzky. The
story broke just before Gretzky and the Canadian men's hockey team
were to leave for Turin to play in the 2006 Winter Olympics. Gretzky
denied any knowledge of, or role in, the affair. Canadians rallied around
Gretzky, refusing to believe that he could be involved in criminal activities. (See the discussion in O'Connor, 2006; Adami, 2006; Cole, 2006; Mac-
Gregor, 2006.)

36 Walton and van Luven in their textbook, *Pop Can: Popular Culture in
Canada* (1999), and Geoff Pevere and Greig Dymond in *Mondo Canuck: A
Canadian Pop Culture Odyssey* (1996) are two of the very few works which
take up Canadian popular culture. While offering tantalizing suggestions, the nature of those works is such that the aspects of celebrity and
its apparatuses remain understudied.

37 More specifically, I examined the Juno/Félix Awards; the national/Quebec
television awards, the Geminis/Gémaux; popular music competitions
Canadian Idol and *Star Académie*; the national film awards, the Genies; the
MuchMusic Awards, the hockey and baseball Halls of Fame, Canada's
Walk of Fame, the launch of new entertainment television channels, such
as *Star!* and their various new programs, new celebrity news magazines
such as the *Weekly Scoop* and others, literary awards, CBC's popular *The
Greatest Canadian*, popular press on all the events and on celebrity in
general, and so on.

38 The format change towards celebrity and entertainment industry news

and away from crime and commentary was 'an effort to win more female and minority readers' (Brent, 2004: FP01).

39 Interestingly, it, too, is democratic. For example, more than thirty thousand ballots were cast in 2000 and that figure more than doubled in 2002.

40 Results were revealed on 29 November 2004 and the winner was Tommy Douglas. This event was a curious blend of democratic techniques, cultural elitism, and cultural nationalist didacticism, as each contender had an 'advocate.' Advocates were Melissa Auf der Maur (rock musician) for David Suzuki; Charlotte Gray (author, historian, and professor) for Macdonald; Deborah Grey (federal politician) for Gretzky; Bret Hart (professional wrestler) for Don Cherry; Sook-Yin Lee (musician, writer, director, and broadcaster) for Fox; Rex Murphy (broadcaster and editorialist) for Trudeau; Evan Soloman (journalist, editor, author, and anchor) for Bell; George Stroumboulopoulos (media personality and broadcaster) for Douglas; and Mary Walsh (comedian and entertainer) for Banting. See the interesting discussion by Jubas (2006) of citizenship, gender, and this contest.

41 Both Adrienne Clarkson and Michaëlle Jean were former CBC/Radio Canada journalists turned political figure(head)s.

42 British Columbia, Saskatchewan, Manitoba, and Newfoundland and Labrador all protect personality in their privacy legislation, and Quebec's privacy provisions of the Civil Code extend to personality.

43 I am focusing on the most significant cases for my purposes and with respect to the law in general. There are several others that I will not be dealing with here including *Shaw* v. *Berman* (1997), *Baron Philippe de Rothschild S.A.* v. *Casa de Habana Inc.* (1987), *Racine* v. *CJRC Radio Capitale Ltée* (1977), *Heath* v. *West-Barron School of Television Canada Ltd.* (1981), *Dowell* v. *Mengen Institute* (1983), *Corlett-Lockyer* v. *Stephens* (1996). For a complete legal treatment of such cases, see: Flagg (1999), Abramovitch (2000), and Singer (1999).

44 According to some commentators, this case is seen to have rejuvenated publicity law in Canada (Nest, 1999: 14). Ultimately the Supreme Court refused to hear the appeal, however, depriving Canadians of the possibility of a clear resolution of the nature of publicity rights in Canada.

45 Gould was posthumously inducted onto Canada's Walk of Fame in 1998.

46 The case was appealed and the Ontario Court of Appeal declined to decide the case on the basis of publicity, preferring copyright. Leave to appeal to the Supreme Court of Canada was denied.

47 In general, this case is considered by legal commentators to be a weak and problematic decision from the Supreme Court of Canada. Because,

strictly speaking, it dealt with the privacy provisions of the Quebec Civil Code, there is a basis upon which the other provinces (which are common-law jurisdictions) can distinguish the decision. All eyes continue to await a Supreme Court decision directly on the issue of appropriation of personality or publicity rights, however.

48 There are other cases in Canada confirming publicity rights for the non-famous including *Dowell* v. *Mengen* (1983) and *Corlett-Lockyer* v. *Stephens* (1996).

49 One wonders whether the distinction is merely between the merit of different types of cultural products, biographies versus board games, or whether the merit of persons is also relevant. Would a biography of Pamela Anderson receive the same treatment as that of our eccentric classical pianist? Do we have the same public interest in knowing about our celebrities as we do our geniuses?

Bibliography

Books and Articles

Abercrombie, Nicholas, Stephen Hill, and Bryan S. Turner (1986). *Sovereign Individuals of Capitalism*. Boston: Allen and Unwin.

Abramovitch, Susan H. (2000). 'Misappropriation of Personality.' *Canadian Business Law Journal* 33(2): 230–46.

Ackerman, R., and R. Bauer (1976). *Corporate Social Performance: The Modern Dilemma*. Reston: Reston Publishing.

Acland, Charles (2003). *Screen Traffic: Movies, Multiplexes, and Global Culture*. Durham: Duke University Press.

Adam, Alison (1998). *Artificial Knowing: Gender and the Thinking Machine*. New York: Routledge.

Adami, Hugh (2006). 'Allegations Swirl around Hockey Great: Gretzky Says He Has Not Placed Bets for His Wife.' *Times-Colonist*, 10 February 2006: A3.

Alberta Women's Secretariat (1991). *The Famous Five*. Edmonton.

Andersen, Margret, ed. (1974). *Mother Was Not a Person*. Montreal: Black Rose Books.

Anderton, Paula (1997). 'IBM Takes on Kasparov in Chess Re-Match.' *Computing Canada*, 28 April: 13.

Andrews, Lori, and Dorothy Nelkin (2002). 'Propriety and Property: The Tissue Market Meets the Courts' in *Who Owns Life?* (David Magnus, Arthur Caplan and Glenn McGee, eds.), 197–222. Amherst, NY: Prometheus Books.

Ansen, David (2005). 'Asking Why: A New Documentary Takes a Shocking Behind-the-Scenes Look at the Enron Debacle.' 20 April. http://www.msnbc.msn.com/id/7563967/wite/newsweek/.

Aoki, Keith (1993). 'Authors, Inventors and Trademark Owners: Private Intellectual Property and the Public Domain.' *The Columbia VLA Journal of Law and the Arts* 18: 1–173.

Armstrong, Jr., George M. (1991). 'The Reification of Celebrity: Persona as Property.' *Louisiana Law Review* 51: 443–68.

Arthur, Kate (2005). '"South Park" Echoes the Schiavo Case.' *New York Times*, 2 April: 8.

Asendorf, Christoph (1993). *Batteries of Life: On the History of Things and Their Perception in Modernity* (transl. Don Reneau). Berkeley: University of California Press.

Atkins, Peter (1987). 'Purposeless People' in *Persons and Personality: A Contemporary Inquiry* (Arthur Peacocke and Grant Gillet, eds.), 12–32. Oxford: Basil Blackwell.

Aubry, Jack (2000). 'Famous Five to Grace $50 Bills.' *Ottawa Citizen*, 4 June: A4.

Australian, The (1997). 'Clones from Human Bodies.' *Australian*, 28 February: 7.

Bacchi, Carol Lee (1983). *Liberation Deferred? The Ideas of the English-Canadian Suffragists, 1877–1918*. Toronto: University of Toronto Press.

Bakan, Joel (2004). *The Corporation: The Pathological Pursuit of Profit and Power*. London: Penguin.

Barker, Ernest (1915). *Political Thought in England 1848 to 1914*. London: Thomas Butterworth.

– (1917). *Political Thought in England from Herbert Spencer to Today*. Cambridge: Cambridge University Press.

– (1950/1919). 'Introduction to Gierke *Natural Law and the Theory of Society*' (transl. Ernest Barker). Cambridge: Cambridge University Press.

Bateson, Mary Catherine (1991). *Our Own Metaphor: A Personal Account of a Conference on the Effects of Conscious Purpose on Human Adaptation* (1972). Washington, DC: Smithsonian Institution Press.

Battaglia, Debbora (1995). 'Fear of Selfing in the American Cultural Imaginary or "You are Never Alone with a Clone."' *American Anthropologist*, New Series 97(4): 672–8.

– (2001). 'Multiplicities: An Anthropologist's Thoughts on Replicants and Clones in Popular Film.' *Critical Inquiry* 27(3): 493–514.

Bauder, Don (2001), 'Enron Debacle Could Be Steppingstone to Reform.' *San Diego Union-Tribune*, 2 December: H2.

Bazinet, Kenneth R. (2005). 'Bush Seeks to Build "Culture of Life" in Wake of Terri Schiavo's Death.' *Daily News*, 1 April: 17.

Beck, Ulrich (1992). *Risk Society: Towards a New Modernity*. London: Sage.

Benoit, Monique (n/d). *The 'Persons' Case*. Ottawa: National Archives of Canada.

Benjamin, Walter (1969/1950). 'Theses on the Philosophy of History' in *Illuminations*, transl. Harry Zohn (Hannah Arendt, ed.), 253–64. New York: Schocken Books.

– (1955/1968). 'The Work of Art in the Age of Mechanical Reproduction' in *Illuminations*, transl. Harry Zohn (Hannah Arendt, ed.), 217–251. New York: Schocken Books.

– (1983–4). 'Theoretics of Knowledge, Theory of Progress' (Transl. Leigh Hafrey and Richard Sieburth). *Philosophical Forum* 15(1–2): 1–40.

Black, Jason Edward (2003). 'Extending the Rights of Personhood, Voice, and Life to Sensate Others: A Homology of Right to Life and Animal Rights Rhetoric.' *Communication Quarterly* 51(3): 312–31.

Bloomfield, Brian P., and Theo Vurdubakis (1997). 'The Revenge of the Object? On Artificial Intelligence as a Cultural Enterprise.' *Social Analysis* 41(1): 29–45.

Bogard, William (1996). *The Simulation of Surveillance: Hypercontrol in Telematic Societies*. Cambridge: Cambridge University Press.

– (2003). 'Symposium on Social Science Fiction' (with Tom Moylan, Arthur and Marilouise Kroker, and Carl Freedman). *Science Fiction Studies* 30(2), July: 174–9.

Boorstin, Daniel (1961). *The Image: A Guide to Pseudo-Events in America*. New York: Vintage.

Boston Herald (2001). 'Editorial: The Lessons of Enron.' *Boston Herald*, 2 December: O38.

Bourgeois, Warren (1995). *Persons: What Philosophers Say about You*. Waterloo, Ont: Wilfrid Laurier University Press.

Bourne, P., and J. Eisenberg (1980). 'The Emergence of Women as Full Legal Persons' – Legal Education Project. Toronto: OISE (Ontario Institute for Studies in Education).

Bowen, H.R. (1953). *The Social Responsibilities of the Businessman*. New York: Harper and Row.

Bower, Lisa C., David Theo Goldberg, and Michael Musheno, eds. (2001). *Between Law and Culture: Relocating Legal Studies*. Minneapolis: University of Minnesota Press.

Boyle, James (1996). *Shamans, Software and Spleens: Law and the Construction of the Information Society*. Cambridge, MA: Harvard University Press.

Braudy, Leo (1986). *The Frenzy of Renown: Fame and Its History*. New York: Oxford University Press.

Braun, Liz (2005). 'Enron Documentary Will Make You Sick.' *Toronto Sun*, 29 April.

Brazier, Frances, Anja Oskamp, Corien Prins, Maurice Schellekens, and Niek Wijngaards (2004). 'Law-Abiding and Integrity on the Internet: A Case for Agents.' *Artificial Intelligence and Law* 12: 5–37.

Brent, Paul (2004). 'Toronto Sun Out to Copy British Tabs: But No Page Three Pin-Ups.' *Financial Post*, 21 February: FP01.

Bright, David (1998). 'The Other Woman: Lizzie Cyr and the Origins of the "Person Case."' *Canadian Journal of Law and Society* 13(2): 99–115.

Brown, Craig, ed. (1988). *Histoire générale du Canada*. Montreal: Boréal.

Brown, Jeff (2001). 'Accounting Rules Must Share Blame for Enron Collapse.' *Philadelphia Inquirer*, 2 December: E01.

Brunker, Mike (2004). 'Are Poker "Bots" Raking Online Pots?' *MSNBC.com* 21 September: http://www.msnbc.msn.com/id/6002298/.

Butler, Judith (1993). *Bodies That Matter: On the Discursive Limits of "Sex."'* New York: Routledge.

Calgary Herald (2004). Comment in *Calgary Herald*, 29 August: A15.

Canada, Government of (2003). *Capitalizing on Corporate Social Responsibility*. Ottawa, Canada.

Canadian Annual Review (1928–9). *Canadian Annual Review*. Toronto: University of Toronto Press.

Canadian Biotechnology Advisory Committee (2001a). *Biotechnological Intellectual Property and the Patenting of Higher Life Forms – Consultation Document 2001*. Ottawa: Canadian Biotechnology Advisory Committee.

– (2001b). *Interim Report on Biotechnology and Intellectual Property*. Ottawa: Canadian Biotechnology Advisory Committee.

– (2002). *Patenting of Higher Life Forms*. Ottawa: Canadian Biotechnology Advisory Committee.

Canadian Business for Social Responsibility (2004). 'Welcome to Canada's Leading Voice on Corporate Social Responsibility (CSR).' http://www.cbsr.ca.

Carroll, Archie B. (1979). 'A Three-Dimensional Conceptual Model of Corporate Social Performance.' *Academy of Management Review* 4: 497–505.

Carroll, Charles M. (1975). *The Great Chess Automaton*. New York: Dover Publications.

Carroll, Jock (1995). *Glenn Gould: Some Portraits of the Artist as a Young Man*. Toronto: Stoddard.

Carruthers, M., Steven Collins, and Steven Lukes, eds. (1985). *The Category of the Person: Anthropology, Philosophy, History*. Cambridge: Cambridge University Press.

Carruthers, P. (1992). *The Animal Issue: Moral Theory in Practice*. Cambridge: Cambridge University Press.

Cassell, Andrew (2001). 'Divergent Lessons in Enron Collapse.' *Philadelphia Inquirer*, 7 December: C01.

Cernetig, Miro (2003). 'Where a Lobsterman Can Become a Star.' *Toronto Star*, 26 April: E04.

Chilliwack Progress, The (2006). '"Persons Day" to Be Marked by Women, Wit and Wisdom.' *Chilliwack Progress*, 13 October: A12.

Chopra, Samir, and Laurence White (2004). 'Artificial Agents – Personhood in Law and Philosophy' in *Proceedings of the 16th European Conference on Artificial Intelligence, ECAI 2004*, 635–9. Amsterdam: IOS Press.

Clark, Andrew (1997). 'Deep Sixed.' *Financial Post*, 17 May: 26.

Cleverdon, Catherine L. (1974). *The Woman Suffrage Movement in Canada*. Toronto: University of Toronto Press.

Cole, Cam (2006). 'No One Has to Tell Gretzky What to Do.' *Ottawa Citizen*, 10 February: F2.

Cole, G.D.H. (1920). *The Social Theory*. London: Methuen.

Collins, Steven (1985). 'Categories, Concepts, or Predicaments? Remarks on Mauss's Use of Philosophical Terminology' in *The Category of the Person: Anthropology, Philosophy and History* (Michael Carrithers, Steven Collins, and Steven Lukes, eds.), 46–82. Cambridge: Cambridge University Press.

Colvin, Jonathan (2000). 'I Wish to Clone Myself.' *National Post*, 7 February: A18.

Coombe, Rosemary J. (1992a). 'Author/izing the Celebrity: Publicity Rights, Postmodern Politics, and Unauthorized Genders.' *Cardozo Arts and Entertainment Law Journal* 10: 365–95.

– (1992b). 'The Celebrity Image and Cultural Identity: Publicity Rights and the Subaltern Politics of Gender.' *Discourse* 14.3: 59–88.

– (1996). 'Authorial Cartographies: Mapping Proprietary Borders in a Less-Than-Brave New World.' *Stanford Law Review* 48: 1357–67.

– (1998). *The Cultural Life of Intellectual Properties*. Durham: Duke University Press.

Coombe, Rosemary J., and Andrew Herman (2001). 'Culture Wars on the Net: Intellectual Property and Corporate Propriety in Digital Environments.' *South Atlantic Quarterly* 100(4): 919–47.

Corcoran, Suzanne (1997). 'Does a Corporation Have a Sex?' in *Sexing the Subject of Law* (Ngaire Naffine and Rosemary J. Owens, eds.), 215–32. London: Sweet and Maxwell.

Cordero, Steven M. (2006). 'Cocaine-Cola, The Velvet Elvis, and Anti-Barbie:

Defending the Trademark and Publicity Rights to Cultural Icons.' *Fordham Intellectual Property, Media and Entertainment Law Journal* 8: 599–654.

Cormack, Barbara Villy (1969). *Perennials and Politics: The Life Story of Hon. Irene Parlby, LL.D.* Sherwood Park, Alberta: Professional Printing.

Cortinas, Marty (2005). 'Who Says Robots Can't Bluff?' *WiredNews* 28 July. http://www.wired.com/news/culture/0,1284,68223,00.html.

Daily Mail (1998). 'Human Organs Next Says Dr. Dolly.' *Daily Mail*, 12 January: 7.

Dalby, Paul (2003). 'Star Treatment.' *Toronto Star*, 8 March: R01.

Davies, Margaret (1994). 'Feminist Appropriations: Law, Property and Personality.' *Social and Legal Studies* 3: 365–91.

– (1997). 'Taking the Inside Out: Sex and Gender in the Legal Subject' in *Sexing the Subject of Law* (Ngaire Naffine and Rosemary J. Owens, eds.), 25–46. North Ryde, New South Wales: LBC, Sweet and Maxwell.

– (1999). 'Queer Property, Queery Persons: Self-Ownership and Beyond.' *Social and Legal Studies* 8(3): 327–52.

Davies, Margaret, and Ngaire Naffine (2001). *Are Persons Property? Legal Debates about Property and Personality.* Aldershot: Ashgate.

Dawson, Bret (1997). 'The Intelligence of Machines.' *Quill and Quire* (August): 19.

Dawson, T. Brettel (1994). *Relating to Law: A Chronology of Women and Law in Canada* (2nd ed.). North York: Captus Press.

de Cordova, Richard (1985). 'The Emergence of the Star System in America.' *Wide Angle* 6(4): 4–13.

– (1990). *Picture Personalities: The Emergence of the Star System in America.* Urbana: University of Illinois Press.

DeCoste, F.C. (2003). 'Forum: Bill C-10 and the Place of Animals in Canadian Law: Animals and Political Community, Preliminary Reflections Prompted by Bill C-10.' *Alberta Law Review* 40: 1057–70.

De George, Richard T. (1996). 'The Myth of Corporate Social Responsibility: Ethics and International Business' in *Is the Good Corporation Dead? Social Responsibility in a Global Economy* (John W. Houck and Oliver F. Williams, eds.), 17–36. London: Rowman and Littlefield.

Dennett, Daniel (1976). 'Conditions of Personhood' in *The Identities of Persons* (Amélie Oksenberg Rorty, ed.), 175–96. Berkeley: University of California Press.

Dewey, John (1926). 'The Historic Background of Corporate Legal Personality.' *Yale Law Journal* 35(6): 655–73.

Deziel, Shanda (2004). 'Sex, Sue and Celebrity: How a Canadian Granny Became the Darling of *Letterman* and the American Media.' *Maclean's*, 17 May: 30–6.

Diprose, Rosalyn (1994). *The Bodies of Women: Ethics, Embodiment, and Sexual Difference*. London: Routledge.

Dogan, Stacey L., and Mark A. Lemley (2006). 'What the Right of Publicity Can Learn from Trademark Law.' *Stanford Law Review* 58: 1161–1220.

Dorland, Michael (1996). *The Cultural Industries in Canada: Problems, Policies and Prospects*. Toronto: J. Lorimer and Co.

– (1998). *So Close to the State/s: The Emergence of Canadian Feature Film Policy*. Toronto: University of Toronto Press.

Dorland, Michael, and Maurice Charland (2002). *Law, Rhetoric and Irony in the Formation of Canadian Civil Culture*. Toronto: University of Toronto Press.

Dorland, Michael, and Priscilla Walton (1999). 'Untangling Karla's Web: Post-National Arguments, Cross-Border Crimes, and the Investigation of Canadian Culture' in *Pop Can: Popular Culture in Canada* (Lynn van Luven and Priscilla Walton, eds.), 195–206. Scarborough: Prentice-Hall.

Dranoff, Linda Silver (1977). *Women in Canadian Law*. Toronto: Fitzhenry and Whiteside.

Drucker, Susan J., and Robert S. Cathcart, eds. (1997). *American Heroes in a Media Age*. Creskill, NJ: Hampton Press.

Drucker, Susan J., and Robert S. Cathcart (1994). 'The Hero as a Communication Phenomenon' in *American Heroes in a Media Age* (Susan J. Drucker and Robert S. Cathcart, eds.), 1–11. Creskill, NJ: Hampton Press.

Dyer, Richard (1979/1998). *Stars*. London: British Film Institute.

Economist, The (1997). 'Fool's Mate.' *Economist*, 3 May: 18.

– (2001). 'The Amazing Distingetrating Firm – Enron.' *Economist*, 8 December.

– (1999). 'The Automaton' (cover story). *Economist*, 31 December, 108–9.

– (2003). 'Not So Smart.' *Economist*, 1 February: 11.

– (2005a). 'The Good Company: Capitalism and Ethics.' *Economist*, 22 January: 9.

– (2005b). 'The Union of Concerned Executives.' *Economist*, 22 January: 8.

– (2005c). 'The World According to CSR.' *Economist*, 22 January: 11.

– (2005d). 'The Good Company: Leaders.' *Economist*, 22 January: 11.

– (2005e). 'The Ethics of Business.' *Economist*, 22 January: 17, 20.

Edwards, L.R. (1984). *Psyche as Hero*. Middletown, CT: Wesleyan University Press.

Edwards, Henrietta Muir (1908). *Legal Status of Canadian Women*. Calgary: National Council of Women of Canada.

– (1921). *Legal Status of Women in Alberta*, 2nd ed. Macleod [s.n.].

Eells, Richard (1956). *Corporation Giving in a Free Society*. New York: Harper and Brothers.

European Network for Excellence for Agent Based Computing. http://agentlink.org, see 'Agent Link.'

Ewart, Bradley (1980). *Chess: Man vs. Machine*. London, Tantivy.

Famous Five Foundation.
http://www.acs.ucalgary.ca/~gpopcont/BASIC/famous5.html.

Fayer, Joan M. (1994). 'Are Heroes Always Men?' in *American Heroes in a Media Age* (Susan J. Drucker and Robert S. Cathcart, eds.), 24–35. Cresskill, NJ: Hampton Press.

Figgis, John Neville (1913). *Churches in the Modern State*. London: Longman's Green.

– (1916). 'The Law of Associations, Corporate and Unincorporate.' *English Historical Review* 31(121): 175–7.

Fisher, M. (1911). *The Collected Papers of Frederick William Maitland*. Cambridge: Cambridge University Press.

'Five Judges of Canada's Supreme Court Hear When Woman Is Not a "Person."' 14 March 1928, from scrapbook Emily Murphy 1913–33 (Accession I232, vol 24, page 2) MG 28.

Flagg, Mitchell A. (1999). 'Star Crazy: Keeping the Right of Publicity Out of Canadian Law.' *Intellectual Property Journal* 13: 179–236.

Foley, Elizabeth Price (2002). 'Human Cloning and the Right to Reproduce.' *Albany Law Review* 65: 625–48.

Foucault, Michel (2003). *'Society Must Be Defended': Lectures at the Collège de France 1975–6* (Mauro Bertani and Alessandro Fontana, eds.). New York: Picador.

Fox Keller, Evelyn (2000). *The Century of the Gene*. Cambridge, MA: Harvard University Press.

Francione, Gary L. (1995). *Animals, Property and the Law*. Philadelphia: Temple University Press.

– (1996). *Rain without Thunder: The Ideology of the Animal Rights Movement*. Philadelphia: Temple University Press.

– (2004). 'Animals – Property or Persons?' in *Animal Rights: Current Debates and New Directions* (Cass R. Sunstein and Martha C. Nussbaum, eds.), 108–42. Oxford: Oxford University Press.

Frederick, W.C., J.E. Post, and K. Davis (1992). *Business and Society: Corporate Strategy, Public Policy, Ethics* (7th ed.). New York: McGraw Hill.

Freeman, R.E. (1984). *Business Management: A Stakeholder Approach*. Boston: Ballinger.

French, Peter (1979). 'The Corporation as a Moral Person.' *American Philosophical Quarterly* 16(3): 207–15.

Frey, R.G. (1980). *Interests and Rights: The Case against Animals*. Oxford: Clarendon Press.

Fridman, Gerald Hewy Louis (1986). *The Law of Contract in Canada*. Toronto: Carswell.

Friedman, Milton (1962). *Capitalism and Freedom*. Chicago: University of Chicago Press.

Frow, John (1995). 'Elvis' Fame: The Commodity Form and the Form of the Person.' *Cardozo Studies in Law and Literature* 7(2): 131–71.

Gaines, Jane M. (1991). *Contested Culture: The Image, the Voice, and the Law*. Chapel Hill: University of North Carolina Press.

– (1993). 'Bette Midler and the Piracy of Identity' in *Music and Copyright* (Simon Frith, ed.), 86–98. Edinburgh: Edinburgh University Press.

– (1995). 'Reincarnation as the Ring on Liz Taylor's Finger: Andy Warhol and the Right of Publicity' in *Identities, Politics, and Rights* (Austin Sara and Thomas R. Kearns, eds.), 131. Ann Arbor: University of Michigan Press.

Gamson, Joshua (1992). 'The Assembly Line of Greatness: Celebrity in Twentieth-Century America.' *Critical Studies in Mass Communication* 9(1): 1–24.

– (1994). *Claims to Fame: Celebrity in Contemporary America*. Berkeley: University of California Press.

Garver, Eugene (1987). *Machiavelli and the History of Prudence*. Madison: University of Wisconsin Press.

Gavin, Tom (1977). *King Kill*. London: Cape.

Geewax, Marilyn (2001). 'Congress Eager to Explore Decline and Fall of Enron.' *Atlantic Journal-Constitution*, 6 December: 3E.

Gelertner, David (1997). 'How Hard Is Chess?' *Time*, 19 May: 42–3.

Gerlach, Neil, and Sheryl N. Hamilton (2003). 'Introduction: A History of Social Science Fiction.' *Science Fiction Studies* 30(2), July: 161–73.

– (2005). 'From Mad Scientist to Bad Scientist: Richard Seed as Biogovernmental Event.' *Communication Theory* 15: 78–99.

Gerlach, Neil, Sheryl N. Hamilton, and Rob Latham, eds. (2003). *Science Fiction Studies* 30(2), July.

Gerlach, Neil, Sheryl N. Hamilton, Rebecca Sullivan, and Priscilla L. Walton (forthcoming). *Becoming Biosubjects: Public Cultures of Biotechnology in Canada*. Toronto: University of Toronto Press.

Gibeaut, John (1999). 'Image Conscious.' *American Bar Association Journal*, June: 46–50.

Giddens, Anthony (1991). *Modernity and Self-Identity: Self and Society in the Late Modern Age*. Cambridge: Polity Press.

Gierke, Otto Friedrich von (1902). *Political Theories of the Middle Ages* (transl. F.W. Maitland). Cambridge: Cambridge University Press.

Gill, Christopher (1988). 'Personhood and Personality: The Four-*Personae* Theory in Cicero, *De Officiis I*.' *Oxford Studies in Ancient Philosophy* 6: 169–99.

– (1990). *The Person and the Human Mind*. Oxford: Clarendon Press.

Gledhill, Christine (1991). 'Signs of Melodrama' in *Stardom: Industry of Desire* (Christine Gledhill, ed.), 207–29. New York: Routledge.

Globe. (1929). 'Woman, as Person, May Sit in Senate, Says Privy Council.' *Globe*, 18 October: 6.

Gold, Marta (1998). 'No Bluffing – Computer Poker Is in the Works.' *Edmonton Journal*, 6 July: B1.

Goodenough, Oliver R. (1992). 'The Price of Fame: The Development of the Right of Publicity in the United States.' *European Intellectual Property Review* Part I, 14(2): 58–9.

Goodnough, Abby (2005). 'Schiavo Dies, Ending Bitter Case over Feeding Tube.' *New York Times*, 1 April: 1.

Gray, John Chipman (1909). *The Nature and Sources of the Law*. New York: Macmillan Company.

Greenall, David (2004). *The National Corporate Social Responsibility Report: Managing Risks, Leveraging Opportunities*. Ottawa: Conference Board of Canada.

Grier, David Alan, and Dan Campbell (2004). '"Echec": The Deutsches Museum Reconstructs the Chess-Playing Turk.' *IEEE Annals of the History of Computing* 26(2), April–June: 84–5.

Grieveson, Lee (2002). 'Stars and Audiences in Early American Cinema' in *Screening the Past*. Melbourne, Australia: La Trobe University Press. http://www.latrobe.edu.au/screeningthepast/classics/c10902/lgc114c.htm#fn1

Gruen, Lori (1991). 'Animals' in *A Companion to Ethics* (Peter Singer, ed.), 343–53. Oxford: Blackwell.

Gulko, Boris (1997). 'Is Chess Finished?' *Commentary*, July: 45–7.

Guly, Christopher (1998). 'Deep Blue Turns Its Computing Talents to Worldly Pursuits.' *Financial Post*, 31 December: D3.

Gumpert, Gary (1997). 'Heroes: A Communication Perspective' in *American Heroes in a Media Age* (Susan Drucker and Robert Cathcart, eds.), 15–23. Creskill, NJ: Hampton Press.

Guterl, Fred (1996). 'Silicon Gambit.' *Discover*, 17 June: 49–56.

Haemmerli, Alice (1999). 'Whose Who? The Case for a Kantian Right of Publicity.' *Duke Law Journal* 49(2): 383–492.

Hamilton, Sheryl N. (2002). 'The Last Chess Game: Computers, Media Events, and the Production of Spectacular Intelligence.' *Canadian Review of American Studies* 30(3): 339–60.

– (2003), 'Traces of the Future: Biotechnology, Science Fiction and the Media.' *Science Fiction Studies* 30(2): 267–82.

Hannaford, Nigel (2004). 'Should the Famous Five Be on the $50?' *Calgary Herald*, 22 August: A13.

Hanson, Mark J. (2002). 'Patenting Genes and Life: Improper Commodification' in *Who Owns Life?* (David Magnus, Arthur Caplan, Glenn McGee, eds.), 161–74. Amherst, NY: Prometheus Books.

Haraway, Donna J. (1991). *Simians, Cyborgs and Women: The Reinvention of Nature*. New York: Routledge.

– (1997). *Modest_Witness@Second_Millennium. FemaleMan©_Meets_Onco-Mouse™: Feminism and Technoscience*. New York and London: Routledge.

Harford, Tim (2006). 'The Poker Machine.' *Financial Times Week-End Magazine*, 6 May: 16.

Harré, Rom (1987). 'Persons and Selves' in *Persons and Personality: A Contemporary Inquiry* (Arthur Peacocke and Grant Gillet, eds.), 99–115. Oxford: Basil Blackwell.

Harris, Neil (1973). *Humbug: The Art of P.T. Barnum*. Chicago: University of Chicago Press.

– (1990). *Cultural Excursions: Marketing Appetites and Cultural Tastes in Modern America*. Chicago: University of Chicago Press.

Harris Poll. 2005 (15 April). http://harrisinteractive.com/harris_poll/index.asp?PID=558.

Harvard Law Review Association (2001). 'Note: What We Talk about When We Talk about Persons: The Language of a Legal Fiction.' *Harvard Law Review* 114: 1745–68.

Hasbrouck, Amy (2003). 'Worthy of Living?' *Gazette*, 27 October: A27.

Hassell, Greg (2001). 'The Fall of Enron: The Culture.' *The Houston Chronicle*, 9 December: A1.

Hayles, N. Katherine (1999). *How We Became Posthuman: Virtual Bodies in Cybernetics, Literature, and Informatics*. Chicago: University of Chicago Press.

– (2005), 'Computing the Human.' *Theory, Culture and Society* 22(1): 131–51.

Hearne, Alison (2004). 'XX.' *Toronto Star*, 19 April.

Hegel, G.W.F. (1821/1967). *Philosophy of Right* (T.M. Knox transl.). Oxford: Oxford University Press.

Henderson, Jennifer (2003). *Settler Feminism and Race Making in Canada*. Toronto: University of Toronto Press.

– (2005). 'How Janey Canuck Became a Person.' *Topia: Canadian Journal of Cultural Studies* 13: 73–87.

Hill, H.P. National Archives of Canada, Cairine Wilson Fonds, MG 27 III, C. 6, vol. 8 speech at a banquet honouring Senator Cairine Wilson.

Hilzenrath, David S. (2001a). 'After Enron, New Doubts about Auditors.' *Washington Post*, 5 December: A01.

– (2001b). 'Accountants Urged to Do Better Job.' *Washington Post*, 7 December: E01.

Hirst, Paul Q. (1989). *The Pluralist Theory of the State: Selected Writings of G.D.H. Cole, J.N. Figgis, and H.J. Laski*. London: Routledge.

Historica Foundation (1992). http://www.histori.ca/minutes/minute.do?id=10205.

Hobbes, Thomas (1968). *Leviathan* (ed. with introduction by C.B. Macpherson). Harmondsworth: Penguin.

Hodges, Alan (1985). *Alan Turing: The Enigma*. London: Vintage.

Hopkins, Michael (2003). *The Planetary Bargain: Corporate Social Responsibility Matters*. London: Earthscan.

Howell, Robert G. (1986). 'The Common Law of Appropriation of Personality Tort.' *Intellectual Property Journal* 2: 149–200.

– (1989). 'Is There an Historical Basis for the Appropriation of Personality Tort?' *Intellectual Property Journal* 4: 263–300.

– (1998). 'Publicity Rights in the Common Law Provinces of Canada.' *Loyola of Los Angeles Entertainment Law Journal* 18: 487–508.

Howes, David (1993). 'Inverted Precedents: Legal Reasoning as "Mythologic."' *Journal of Legal Pluralism* 33: 213–29.

Hughes, Justin (1988–9). 'The Philosophy of Intellectual Property.' *Georgetown Law Journal* 77: 287–366.

Hunter, Ian (2005). 'Person' in *New Keywords: A Revised Vocabulary of Culture and Society* (Tony Bennett, Lawrence Grossberg, and Meaghan Morris, eds.), 254–6. Malden, MA: Blackwell Publishing.

Hyde, Alan (1997). *Bodies of Law*. Princeton: Princeton University Press.

Ince, M. (1994). 'The Limitations of Imitations.' *Times Higher Education Supplement*, 22 April: 15.

Ivanovich, David (2001). 'Warning Lights Flashed before Collapse of Enron: Management, Board of Directors and Auditors Share the Blame.' *San Antonion Express-News*, 2 December: 27A.

Jasper, James, and Dorothy Nelkin (1992). *The Animal Rights Crusade: The Growth of a Moral Protest*. New York: Free Press.

Jaszi, Peter (1991). 'Toward a Theory of Copyright: The Metamorphosis of "Authorship."' *Duke Law Journal* 413: 455–502

Jubas, Kaela (2006). 'Theorizing Gender in Contemporary Canadian Citizenship: Lessons from the CBC's Greatest Canadian Contest.' *Canadian Journal of Education* 29(2): 563–83.

Kahn, Jonathan (1999). 'Bringing Dignity Back to Light: Publicity Rights and the Eclipse of the Tort of Appropriation of Identity.' *Cardozo Journal of Arts and Entertainment Law* 17: 213–72.

Kang, Young-Chul, and Donna J. Wood (1995). 'Before-Profit Social Responsibility: Turning the Economic Paradigm Upside Down.' *International Association for Business and Society 1995 Proceedings*, June: 408–18.

Kant, Emmanuel (1930). *Lectures on Ethics* (transl. Louis Infield). London: Methuen and Co.

Karake-Shalhoub, Zeinab A. (1999). *Organizational Downsizing, Discrimination, and Corporate Social Responsibility*. London: Quorum Books.

Kasparov, Garry (1996). 'The Day That I Sensed a New Kind of Intelligence.' *Time*, 1 April: 57.

–(1997). 'IBM Owes Mankind a Rematch.' *Time*, 26 May: 38–9.

Kay, Lily E. (2000). *Who Wrote the Book of Life: A History of the Genetic Code*. Stanford, CA: Stanford University Press.

Kelsen, Hans (1945). *General Theory of Law and State*. New York: Russell and Russell.

Kelso, Louis O., and Mortimer J. Adler (1958). *The Capitalist Manifesto*. New York: Random House.

Kennicott, Philip (2005). 'Symbol of Emptiness: Terri Schiavo Was a Woman, Not an Idea.' *Washington Post*, 1 April: C01.

Kerr, Ian R. (1999). 'Spirits in the Material World: Intelligent Agents as Intermediaries in Electronic Commerce.' *Dalhousie Law Journal* 22: 189–249.

– (2004). 'Bots, Babes and the Californication of Commerce.' *University of Ottawa Law and Technology Journal* 1: 285–324.

Kerr, Ian R., and Marcus Bornfreund (forthcoming). 'Buddy Bots: How Turing's Fast Friends Are Under-Mining Consumer Privacy' in *Presence: Teleoperators and Virtual Environments* http://www.iankerr.ca/content/blogcategory/39/78/

Kirby, Terry (2005). 'Poker Playing Robots? Surely Not.' *Independent (London)*, 6 July. http://www.news.independent-co.uk/world/science_technology/article297242.ece.

Kolata, Gina (1998). 'Human Cloning: The Race Is On Since Dolly the Sheep Appeared on the Scene.' *Globe and Mail*, 18 December: A17.

Krantz, Michael (1997). 'Deeper in Thought.' *Time*, 10 March: 76–7.

Krauthammer, Charles (1996). 'Deep Blue Funk.' *Time*, 26 February: 50–1.

Kulba, Tracy (2002). 'Citizens, Consumers, Critique-al Subjects: Rethinking the "Statue Controversy" and Emily Murphy's *The Black Candle* (1922).' *Tessera* 31: 74–89.

Lacey, Nicola (2001a). 'In Search of the Responsible Subject: History, Philosophy and Social Sciences in Criminal Law Theory.' *Modern Law Review* 64(3): 350–71.

– (2001b). 'Responsibility and Modernity in Criminal Law.' *Journal of Philosophy* 9(3): 249–76.

La Fontaine, J.S. (1985). 'Person and Individual: Some Anthropological Reflections' in *The Category of the Person: Anthropology, Philosophy and History* (Michael Carrithers, Steven Collins, and Steven Lukes, eds.), 123–40. Cambridge: Cambridge University Press.

Lahey, Kathleen A. (1998). 'Legal "Persons" and the *Charter of Rights*: Gender, Race, and Sexuality in Canada.' *Canadian Bar Review* 77: 402–27.

– (1999), *Are We Persons Yet? Law and Sexuality in Canada*. Toronto: University of Toronto Press.

Lakritz, Naomi (2004). 'Should the Famous Famous Five Be on the $50?' *Calgary Herald*, 22 August: A13.

Lange, David (1981). 'Recognizing the Public Domain.' *Law and Contemporary Problems* 44(4): 147–78.

LaSalle, Mick (2004). 'The Corporation.' *San Francisco Chronicle*, 4 June: http://www.sfgate.com/cgi-bin/article.cgi?f=/c/a/2004/06/04/DDG316VU3K1.DTL#corporation.

Lashinsky, Adam (2001). 'Bankrupt Analysis.' *New York Times*, 30 November: A27.

Laski, Harold (1915). 'The Personality of the State.' *Nation*, 22 July: 11.

– (1915–16). 'The Personality of Private Associations.' *Harvard Law Review* 19: 404.

Law Reform Commission of Canada (1976). *Criminal Responsibility for Group Action*. Ottawa: Law Reform Commission of Canada.

Leahy, M.P.T. (1994). *Against Liberation – Putting Animals in Perspective*. London: Routledge.

Leathes, Sonia (1914). 'Votes for Women.' *University Magazine* 23: 68–78.

Lehmann, Megan (2004). 'We All Owe Our Souls to the Company Store' in *New York Post*, 30 June: New York Pulse 49.

Leonard, Andrew (1997). *Bots: The Origin of New Species*. New York: Penguin.

Lester, L.G., S.A. Convers, B.A. Stone, S.E. Kohler, and S.T. Barlow (1997), 'Animated Pedagogical Agents and Problem-Solving Effectiveness: A Large-Scale Empirical Evaluation' in *Proceedings of the Eighth World Conference on Artificial Intelligence in Education*. Washington, DC: JOS Press, 23–30.

Létourneau, Lyne (2003). 'Toward Animal Liberation? The New Anti-Cruelty Provisions in Canada and Their Impact on the Status of Animals.' *Alberta Law Review* 40: 1041–55.

Levitt, Theodore (1958). 'The Dangers of Social Responsibility.' *Harvard Business Review*, September–October: 41–50.

Levy, Stephen (1996). 'Tangled Up in Deep Blue.' *Newsweek*, 26 February: 51.

- (1997a). 'Big Blue's Hand of God.' *Newsweek*, 19 May: 72.
- (1997b). 'Garry Sings the Blues.' *Newsweek*, 26 May: 84.
- (1997c). 'Man vs. Machine.' *Newsweek*, 5 May: 51–6.

Lewis, Michael (2001). 'Three Lessons from Enron's Failure'. *Toronto Star*, 5 December: E06.

L'Heureux-Dubé, Claire (2000). 'The Legacy of the "Persons Case": Cultivating the Living Tree's Equality Leaves.' *Saskatchewan Law Review* 63(1): 389–401.

Liu, Gabriel (2000). 'The Darker Side of Our Feminist Heroines: The Gang of Five Did Well in Bringing Legal "Personhood" to Women. But Do We Want Racists on Our Money?' *Vancouver Sun*, 21 September: A23.

Livingston, J.A. (1958). *The American Stockholder*. Philadelphia: Lippincott.

Locke, John (1980). *Second Treatise of Government* (C.B. Macpherson, ed.). Indianapolis: Hackett Publishing Co.

- (1984). *An Essay Concerning Human Understanding*. Oxford: Clarendon Press, II , XXVII.

Lury, Celia (1998). *Prosthetic Culture: Photography, Memory and Identity*. London: Routledge.

MacGregor, Roy (2006). 'Distractions Aside, It's Time for Canada to Get Down to Hockey.' *Globe and Mail*, 15 February: O1.

Maclean, Una (1962). 'The Famous Five.' *Alberta Historical Review* 10(2): 1–4.

Maclean's (1999). 'The Persons Case.' *Maclean's*, 1 July: 28–9.

MacFarlane, Alan (1978). *The Origins of English Individualism: The Family, Property and Social Transition*. Oxford: Blackwell.

Machen, A.W. (1911). 'Corporate Personality.' *Harvard Law Review* 25: 253.

Macpherson, C.B. (1974). *The Political Theory of Possessive Individualism: Hobbes to Locke*. Oxford: Oxford University Press.

Macpherson, Darcy L. (2004). 'Extending Corporate Criminal Liability? Some Thoughts on Bill c-45.' *Manitoba Law Journal* 30: 253–84.

Madow, Michael (1993). 'Private Ownership of Public Image: Popular Culture and Publicity Rights.' *California Law Review* 81(1): 125–240.

Magder, Ted (1993). *Canada's Hollywood: The Canadian State and Feature Films*. Toronto: University of Toronto Press.

- (1998). *Franchising the Candy Store: Split-Run Magazines and a New International Regime for Trade in Culture*. Orono: University of Maine.

Maine, Henry Sumner, Sir (1883). *Ancient Law: Its Connection with the Early History of Society, and Its Relation to Modern Ideas*. London: Murray.

Maitland, Frederick William (1900). 'Introduction to Gierke's Political Theories of the Middle Ages' in *Political Theories of the Middle Ages*. Cambridge: Cambridge University Press.

– (1905). 'Moral Personality and Legal Personality.' *Journal of Comparative Law* 6: 192.

– (1911/1981). 'Moral Personality and Legal Personality' in *The Collected Papers of Frederick William Maitland*, vol 3 (H.A.L. Fisher, ed.), 304–20. Buffalo, NY: William S. Hein and Company.

Mander, Christine (1985). *Emily Murphy: Rebel*. Toronto: Simon and Pierre.

Manning, Rita C. (1984). 'Corporate Responsibility and Corporate Personhood.' *Journal of Business Ethics* 3: 77–84.

Marchildon, Rudy G. (1981). 'The "Persons" Controversy: The Legal Aspects of the Fight for Women Senators.' *Atlantis: A Women's Studies Journal* 6(2): 99–113.

Marshall, P. David (1997). *Celebrity and Power: Fame in Contemporary Culture*. Minneapolis: University of Minnesota Press.

Mauss, Marcel (1985). 'A Category of the Human Mind: The Notion of Person; The Notion of Self' in *The Category of the Person: Anthropology, Philosophy, History* (Michael Carrithers, Steven Collins, and Steven Lukes, eds.), 1–25. Cambridge: Cambridge University Press.

May, Howard (2001). 'Crusading Women Land on New $50 Bill.' *Calgary Herald*, 26 January: A1FRO.

Mazlish, Bruce (1993). *The Fourth Discontinuity: The Co-Evolution of Humans and Machines*. New Haven: Yale University Press.

McCall, Catherine (1990). *Concepts of Person: An Analysis of Concepts of Person, Self and Human Being*. Aldershot: Avebury.

McCallum, Sandra K., and A. Anne McLellan (1980). 'The Persons' Case: A Beginning – Not the End' in *Women As Persons*, 76–9. Edmonton: CRIAW.

McCarthy, J. Thomas (1987/1999). *The Rights of Publicity and Privacy*. West Group.

– (1995). 'The Human Persona as Commercial Property: The Right of Publicity.' *Columbia-VLA Journal of Law and the Arts* 19(3–4): 129–48.

McClanahan, E. Thomas (1998). 'What Follows Dolly? Cloning Humans Should Not Be the Next Scientific Step.' *Kansas City Star*, 8 January: C6.

McClung, Nellie (1945). *The Stream Runs Fast: My Own Story*. Toronto: Thomas Allen.

McCorduck, Pamela (1979). *Machines Who Think: A Personal Inquiry into the History and Prospects of Artificial Intelligence*. San Francisco: Freeman.

McKay, John (2004). 'Quartet of Hollywood Legends Joins Canada's 2004 Walk of Fame Inductees.' *Canadian Press Newswire*, 30 March.

McLean, Janet (1999). 'Personality and Public Law Doctrine.' *University of Toronto Law Journal* 49: 123–49.

Mclean, Bethany, and Peter Elkind (2003). *The Smartest Guys in the Room: The Amazing Rise and Scandalous Fall of Enron*. New York: Portfolio.

McLeod, Kembrew (2001). *Owning Culture: Authorship, Ownership, and Intellectual Property Law*. New York: Peter Lang.

McLuhan, Marshall (1957). 'Sight, Sound, and the Fury' in *Mass Culture: The Popular Arts in America* (Bernard Rosenberg and David M. White, eds.), 489–95. Glencoe, Ill.: Free Press.

McRae, Earl (2002). 'Rompin' Ronnie Deserves Honour.' *Ottawa Sun*, 1 August: 7.

Merton, Robert K. (1942). 'A Note on Science and Technology in a Democratic Order.' *Journal of Legal and Political Sociology* 2: 115–26.

Michaux, Scott (2004). 'Turning/Leaf/In a Distinctively Canadian Fashion, Mike Weir Rose from Struggling Athlete to Superstar.' *August Chronicle*, 4 April: M07.

Milner, Brian (2001). 'Enron Is Paying Dearly for Uncontrolled Growth.' *Globe and Mail*, 1 December: B2.

Minkus, P.A. (1960). *Philosophy of the Person*. Oxford: Basil Blackwell.

Mitchell, Robert (2004). '$ell: Body Wastes, Information, and Commodification' in *Data Made Flesh: Embodying Information* (Robert Mitchell and Phillip Thurtle, eds.), 121–36. New York and London: Routledge.

Monmaney, Terence (1997). 'Identical Twins: Human Cloning Wouldn't Take Away Individuality.' *Los Angeles Times*, 9 March: 12.

Morrill, Jim (2005). 'Polls Show Complexity beyond Party Politics.' *Charlotte Observer*, 22 March: 5A.

Morris, Wesley (2004). 'The Corporation Takes Stock of Big Business.' *Boston Globe*, 16 July.

Moysa, Marilyn (1997). 'Dolly Cloner Was Asked to Clone Dead Teenagers.' *Edmonton Journal*, 18 October: D16.

Murphy, Emily F. (n/d). *Pruning the Family Tree*. Unpublished manuscript.

– (1919). 'Woman on the Bench: My Experiences as a Magistrate of the Woman's Court.' *Maclean's Magazine* 23(11): 34–6, 81.

– (1922). *The Black Candle*. Toronto: T. Allen.

Naffine, Ngaire (2003). 'Who Are Law's Persons? From Cheshire Cats to Responsible Subjects.' *Modern Law Review* 66: 346–67.

– (2004). 'Our Legal Lives as Men, Women and Persons.' *Legal Studies* 21(4): 621–42.

NSERC (Natural Sciences and Engineering Research Council of Canada) (2003). 'The Inscrutable, Digital Winner.' http://www.nserc.ca/news/features/schaeffer_e.htm

National Archives (RG 13, vol. 2525, p. 71, Box Misc.).

Nature (1999). 'New Zealand Bill Aims to Give Apes Same Rights as Humans.' *Nature* 397: 554–5.

Nedelsky, Jennifer (1990). 'Law, Boundaries and the Bounded Self.' *Representations* 30: 162–89.

Nelkin, Dorothy, and M. Susan Lindee (1995). *The DNA Mystique: The Gene as Cultural Icon*. New York: Freeman.

Neocleous, Mark (2003). *Imagining the State*. Philadelphia: Open University Press.

Nest, Conrad (1999). 'From "ABBA" to Gould: A Closer Look at the Development of Personality Rights in Canada.' *5 Appeal: Review of Current Law and Law Reform*: 12–17.

Newbury, Michael (1994). 'Eaten Alive: Slavery and Celebrity in Antebellum America.' *ELH* 61(1): 159–87.

Neyers, Jason W. (2000). 'Canadian Corporate Law, Veil-Piercing, and the Private Law Model.' *University of Toronto Law Journal* 50: 173–240.

Nimmer, Melville B. (1954), 'The Right of Publicity.' *Law and Contemporary Problems* 19: 203–23.

Normey, Robert J. (1993). 'Taking It Personally: The Persons Case.' *Law Now* 33: 11–13.

Novas, Carlos, and Nikolas Rose (2000). 'Genetic Risk and the Birth of the Somatic Individual.' *Economy and Society* 29(4): 485–513.

O'Connor, Joe (2006). 'Gretzky's Assistant Faces Betting Charges.' *National Post*, 8 February: A1.

OECD (2001). *Corporate Responsibility: Private Initiatives and Public Goals*. Paris: OECD.

OED (1989). 'Celebrity' in *Oxford English Dictionary*, 2nd edition, 10 vols., 2: 1019. New York: Oxford University Press.

O'Hara, Mary (1997). *The Logic of Human Personality: An Onto-Logical Account*. New Jersey: Humanities Press.

O'Hehir, Andrew (2005). 'Enron: The Smartest Guys in the Room.' *Salon.Com*, 21 April, 2005.

Olive, David (2003). 'Convergence Gets Personal at Quebecor.' *Toronto Star*, 12 September: E01.

O'Sullivan, Michael (2004). 'The Corporation Pays High Dividends.' *Washington Post*, 16 July: WE39.

Ottawa Evening Citizen. (1929). 'Privy Council Rules That Women Eligible to Become Members of the Canadian Senate.' *Ottawa Evening Citizen*, 18 October: 1.

Parfit, Derek (1984). *Reasons and Persons*. Oxford: Clarendon Press.

Pateman, Carole (1988). *The Sexual Contract*. Cambridge: Polity Press.

Peacocke, Arthur, and Grant Gillett (1987). 'Introduction' in *Persons and Per-*

sonality: A Contemporary Inquiry (Arthur Peacocke and Grant Gillet, eds.), 1–11. Oxford: Basil Blackwell.

Peacocke, Arthur, and Grant Gillett, eds. (1987). *Persons and Personality: A Contemporary Inquiry.* Oxford: Basil Blackwell.

Peterson, I. (1997). 'Computer Triumphs over Human Champion.' *Science News*, 17 May: 300.

Pevere, Geoff (2004). 'Big Biz Takes a Direct Hit.' *Toronto Star*, 16 January: B01.

Pevere, Geoff, and Greig Dymond (1996). *Mondo Canuck: A Canadian Pop Culture Odyssey.* Scarborough, Ont.: Prentice Hall.

Platt, Michael (2004). ' "Famous Five" Aren't Worth a Plug Nickel.' *Calgary Sun*, 19 August: 15.

Poe, Edgar Allan (1836). 'Maelzel's Chess-Player.' *Southern Literary Messenger* 2: 318–26.

Ponce de Leon, Charles (2002). *Self-Exposure: Human-Interest Journalism and the Emergence of Celebrity in America, 1890–1940.* Chapel Hill: University of North Carolina Press.

Poole, Ross (1996). 'On Being a Person.' *Australasian Journal of Philosophy* 74(1): 38–56.

Posner, Richard A. (2004). 'Animal Rights: Legal, Philosophical and Pragmatic Perspectives' in *Animal Rights: Current Debates and New Directions* (Cass R. Sunstein and Martha C. Nussbaum, eds.), 51–77. Oxford: Oxford University Press.

Pottage, Alain (1998). 'The Inscription of Life in Law: Genes, Patents, and Bio-politics' in *Law and Human Genetics: Regulating a Revolution* (Roger Brownsword, W.R. Cornish, and Margaret Llewelyn, eds.), 148–73. Oxford: Hart Publishing.

Potvin, Louise (1997a). 'Protection against the Use of One's Likeness in Quebec Civil Law, Canadian Common Law and Constitutional Law (Part I).' *Intellectual Property Journal* 11: 203–28.

– (1997b). 'Protection against the Use of One's Likeness in Quebec Civil Law, Canadian Common Law and Constitutional Law (Part II).' *Intellectual Property Journal* 11: 295–320.

Price (RG 133, letter from Elizabeth B. Price to the Hon. C.J. Doherty, 18 June, 1921).

Privy Council (19 October 1927, IH/5, P.C. 2034).

Prosser, William L. (1960). 'Privacy.' *California Law Review* 48: 383–423.

Quaid, Jennifer A. (1998). 'The Assessment of Corporate Criminal Liability on the Basis of Corporate Identity: An Analysis.' *McGill Law Journal* 43: 67–114.

Rabinow, Paul (1996). 'Severing the Ties: Fragmentation and Dignity in Late

Modernity' in *Essays on the Anthropology of Reason*, 129–52. Princeton: Princeton University Press.

Raboy, Marc (1990). *Missed Opportunities: The Story of Canada's Broadcast Policy*. Montreal and Kingston: Queen's University Press.

Radford, Tim (1997). 'Human Clones in Two Years.' *Guardian*, 7 March: 1.

Radin, Margaret (1982). 'Property for Personhood.' *Stanford Law Review* 34: 957–1015.

Regan, Tom (1983). *The Case for Animal Rights*. Berkeley: University of California Press.

– (1996). 'Animal Rights and Welfare' in *The Encyclopedia of Philosophy Supplement*, 27–8. New York: Macmillan Reference.

Regan, Tom, and Peter Singer, eds. (1989). *Animal Rights and Human Obligations*. Englewood Cliffs: Prentice-Hall.

Regina Morning Leader. (1929). 'So a Woman's a Person.' *Regina Morning Leader*, 18 October: 1.

Robbins, Michael (1996). *Conceiving Personality*. New Haven: Yale University Press.

Robertson, C.B. (1929). 'The Challenge of Freedom.' *Chatelaine Magazine*, 2(11), November: 10, 67.

Robertson, John A. (1998). 'Liberty, Identity, and Human Cloning.' *Texas Law Review* 76: 1371–1456.

Robinson, George (2004). '21st Century Pharaoh.' *Jewish Week*, 2 July: http://www.thejewishweek.com.

Rorty, Amélie Oksenberg, ed. (1976a). *The Identities of Persons*. Berkeley: University of California Press.

– (1976b). 'Introduction' in *The Identities of Persons* (Amélie Oksenberg Rorty, ed.), 1–15. Berkeley: University of California Press.

– (1976c). 'A Literary Postscript: Characters, Persons, Selves, Individuals' in *The Identities of Persons* (Amélie Oksenberg Rorty, ed.), 301–23. Berkeley: University of California Press.

– (1990). 'Persons and *Personae*' in *The Person and the Human Mind* (Christopher Gill, ed.), 21–38. Oxford: Clarendon Press.

Ross, Mike (2004). 'Seeing Stars.' *Edmonton Sun*, 4 April: ES4.

Ruhl, Lealle (2002). 'Disarticulating Liberal Subjectivities: Abortion and Fetal Protection.' *Feminist Studies* 28(1): 37–60.

Runciman, D. (1997). *Pluralism and the Personality of the State*. Cambridge: Cambridge University Press.

Sanders, Byrne Hope (1945). *Emily Murphy, Crusader. 'Janey Canuck.'* Toronto: Macmillan.

Sandwell, B.K. (1928). 'These Impersonal Women!' *Chatelaine Magazine*, 1(4), June: 22, 40.

San Francisco Chronicle (2001). 'Editorial.' *The San Francisco Chronicle*, 30 November: A28.

Sapontzis, Steven F. (1981). 'A Critique of Personhood.' *Ethics* 91(4): 607–18.

– (1984). 'The Evolution of Animals in Moral Philosophy.' *Between the Species* 3(2): 61–5.

Sarat, Austin, and Jonathan Simon, eds. (2003). *Cultural Analysis, Cultural Studies, and the Law: Moving beyond Legal Realism*. Durham: Duke University Press.

Sarat, Austin, and Thomas R. Kearns, eds. (1994). *Law in the Domains of Culture*. Ann Arbor: University of Michigan Press.

– (1999), *Cultural Pluralism, Identity Politics, and the Law*. Ann Arbor: University of Michigan Press.

Schaffer, Simon (1994). 'Babbage's Intelligence: Calculating Engines and the Factory System.' *Critical Inquiry* 21(1): 203–27.

– (1996). 'Babbage's Dancer and the Impresarios of Mechanism' in *Cultural Babbage: Technology, Time and Invention* (Francis Spuford and Jenny Uglow, eds.). London: Faber and Faber.

Schager, Nick (2005). 'Enron the Smartest Guys in the Room.' *Slant Magazine*, http://www.slantmagazine.com/film/film_review.asp?ID=1543.

Schane, Sanford A. (1987). 'The Corporation Is a Person: The Language of a Legal Fiction.' *Tulane Law Review* 61: 563–609.

Schiavo, Michael, with Michael Hirsh (2006). *Terri: The Truth*. New York: Dutton Adult.

Schickel, Richard (1962). *The Stars*. New York: Bonanza.

– (1985). *Intimate Strangers: The Culture of Celebrity*. Garden City, NY: Doubleday.

Schindler, Mary, and Robert Schindler (with Bobby Schindler and Suzanne Schindler Vitadamo) (2006). *A Life That Matters: The Legacy of Terri Schiavo – A Lesson for All of Us*. Lebanon, IN: Warner Books.

Schwartz, Hillel (1996). *The Culture of the Copy: Striking Likenesses, Unreasonable Facsimiles*. New York: Zone Books.

Schwartz, John (2005). 'The Schiavo Case: The Medical Situation'. *New York Times*, 25 March: 14.

Seltzer, Mark (1993). 'Serial Killers (1).' *differences: A Journal of Feminist Cultural Studies* 5.1: 92–128.

Serenko, Alexander, and Brian Detlor (2004). 'Intelligent Agents as Innovations.' *AI & Society* 18: 364–81.

Sethi, Suresh P. (1997). 'Dimensions of Corporate Social Performance: An Analytical Framework' in *Managing Corporate Social Responsibility* (A. Caroll, ed.), 69–75. Boston: Little, Brown and Co.

Shamir, Ronen (2004). 'Between Self-Regulation and the Alien Tort Claims

Act: On the Contested Concept of Corporate Social Responsibility.' *Law and Society Review* 38(4): 635–64.

Shannon, Claude E. (1950). 'A Chess-Playing Machine.' *Scientific American*, February: 11–15.

Sheckley, Robert (1968). 'Fool's Mate' in *The Metal Smile: 12 Battles of Wits between Man and Machine* (Damon Knight, ed.) (originally published in 1953), 16–31. New York: Belmont Books.

Shoemaker, Sidney. (1990). 'First-Person Access.' *Philosophical Perspectives* 4: 187–214.

Shorett, Peter, Paul Rabinow, and Paul R. Billings (2003). 'The Changing Norms of the Life Sciences.' *Nature* (February) 21: 123–5.

Singer, Barbara (1991). 'The Right of Publicity: Star Vehicle or Shooting Star?' *Cardozo Arts and Entertainment Law Journal* 10(1): 1–49.

Singer, Eric M. (1999). 'The Development of the Common Law Tort of Appropriation of Personality in Canada.' *Canadian Intellectual Property Review* 15: 66–80.

Singer, Peter (1975). *Animal Liberation*. New York: Avon Books.

Singer, Peter, et al. (1991). *A Companion to Ethics*. Oxford: Blackwell Reference.

Singer, Peter, ed. (1985). *In Defence of Animals*. Oxford: Blackwell.

Singer, Peter, and Tom Regan, eds. (1989). *Animal Rights and Human Obligations*. Englewood Cliffs: Prentice-Hall.

Sinha, Vandana (2005). 'Enron Documentary Film Hits Select Theatres.' *Business Journalism.org*, 21 April. http://www.business.journalism.oeg/pages/biz/2005/04/enron_documentary_film_hits_se/

Smart, Ninian (1972). 'Creation, Persons and the Meaning of Life' in *Six Approaches to the Person* (Ralph Ruddock, ed.), 13–36. Boston: Routledge and Kegan Paul.

Smith, Timothy (1981). 'The Ethical Responsibilities of Multinational Companies' in *Corporations and Their Critics* (Bradshaw Vogel, ed.), 77–86. New York: McGraw-Hill.

Le Soleil. (1929). 'Decision accueillie avec joie partout.' *Le Soleil*, 18 October, 1.

Spence, James (1998). 'Lifting the Corporate Veil.' *Advocate's Society Journal* 17.4: 19–20.

Spendlove, Paul (2001). 'The Dirt on Gossip Columns.' *UBC Journalism Review, Thunderbird Online Magazine* 3(4). http://www.journalism.ubc.ca/thunderbird/archives/2001.04.gossip.html.

Stafford, Barbara Maria (1993). 'Conjuring: How the Virtuoso Romantic Learned from the Enlightened Charlatan.' *Art Journal* 52: 22–30.

– (1994). *Artful Science: Enlightenment Education and the Eclipse of Visual Education*. Cambridge, MA: MIT Press.

Standage, Tom (2002). *The Turk: The Life and Times of the Famous Eighteenth-Century Chess-Playing Machine*. New York: Berkeley Publishing Group.
– (2003). 'Interview with Tom Standage at WNYC.' On DVD of *The Chess Player* (1927).
Steeves, Valerie, and Ian R. Kerr (2005). 'Virtual Playgrounds and Buddybots: A Data-Minefield for Tweens.' *Canadian Journal of Law and Technology*: 1–17.
Stone, Olive M. (1979). 'Canadian Women as Legal Persons: The Jubilee of *Edwards* v. *Attorney General for Canada*.' *Alberta Law Review* 17(3): 331–71.
Strate, Lance (1997). 'The Wrinkle Theory: The Deconsecration of a Hero' in *American Heroes in a Media Age* (Susan Drucker and Robert Cathcart, eds.), chapter 5. Creskill, NJ: Hampton Press.
Stratos Inc. (in collaboration with Alan Willis and Associates) (2003). *Building Confidence: Corporate Sustainability Reporting in Canada*. Toronto: Stratos.
Strauss, Stephen (1998). 'Alberta Team Teaches Computer to Put On Poker Face.' *Globe and Mail*, 13 October: A8.
Strawson, P.F. (1959). *Individuals*. London: Methuen.
Susman, Warren (1984). *Culture as History: The Transformation of American Society in the Twentieth Century*. New York: Pantheon.
Sussman, Mark (1999). 'Performing the Intelligent Machine: Deception and Enchantment in the Life of the Automaton Chess Player.' *Drama Review* 43.3: 81–96.
Swade, Doron (2002). *The Difference Engine: Charles Babbage and the Quest to Build the First Computer*. London: Penguin Books.
Swineburne, Richard (1987). 'The Structure of the Soul' in *Persons and Personaltiy: A Contemporary Inquiry* (Arthur Peacocke and Grant Gillet, eds.), 33–55. Oxford: Basil Blackwell.
Taylor, Charles (1976). 'Responsibility for Self' in *The Identities of Persons* (Amélie Oksenberg Rorty, ed.), 281–99. Berkeley: University of California Press.
– (1985). 'The Person' in *The Category of the Person: Anthropology, Philosophy, History* (Michael Carruthers, Steven Collins, and Steven Lukes, eds.), 257–81. Cambridge: Cambridge University Press.
Teichmann, Jenny (1985). 'The Definition of Person.' *Philosophy* 60(231): 175–85.
Terdiman, Daniel (2004). 'Beware of Bots Bearing Messages.' *WiredNews*, 10 September. http://www.wired.com/news/culture/0,1284,64888,00.html.
Tilley, Steve (2004a). 'Mulroney Rolls Out Red Carpet.' *Edmonton Sun*, 31 March: 39.
– (2004b). 'Going for the Gold: Ticket Is Route to Idol Glory.' *Edmonton Sun*, 21 April: 38.

Toronto Daily Star (1928a). 'Liberal Women to Ask Change in Act Wording.' *Toronto Daily Star*, 24 April: 1.

– (1928b). 'Act of Confederation Denies Women Right to Sit in Upper House.' *Toronto Daily Star*, 24 April: 1, 10.

– (1928c). 'Will Not Appeal Senate Judgment Is Ottawa's View.' *Toronto Daily Star*, 24 April: 1.

– (1929). 'Women Are Eligible for Upper Chamber Privy Council Rules.' *Toronto Daily Star*, 18 October: 1.

Toronto Star (2001). 'The Bitter Taste of Roast Enron.' *Toronto Star*, 1 December: D01.

Tur, Richard (1987). 'The "Person" in Law' in *Persons and Personality: A Contemporary Inquiry* (Arthur Peacocke and Grant Gillett, eds.), 116–29. Oxford: Basil Blackwell.

Turing, Alan (1950). 'Computing Machinery and Intelligence.' *Mind* 59(236): 433–60.

Turner, Lyn (2001). 'Lessons for Auditors in Enron's Collapse.' *New York Times*, 2 December: BU5.

UMBC Agent Web, University of Maryland, Baltimore County. http://www.agents.umbc.edu.

Valverde, Mariana (1991). *The Age of Light, Soap and Water: The Age of Moral Reform in English Canada, 1885–1925*. Toronto: McClelland and Stewart.

Vancouver Province (2004). 'In Other Words: Move Over, Queen Elizabeth.' *Vancouver Province*, 20 October: A24.

van der Ploeg, Irma (2003). 'Biometrics and the Body as Information: Normative Issues of the Socio-Technical Coding of the Body' in *Surveillance as Social Sorting: Privacy, Risk and Digital Discrimination* (David Lyon, ed.), 57–73. New York: Routledge.

van Dijk, Josée (1998). *Imagenation: Popular Images of Genetics*. New York: New York University Press.

vanDuzer, J. Anthony (2003). *The Law of Partnerships and Corporations* (2nd ed.). Toronto: Irwin Law.

Vaver, David (1981). 'What's Mine Is Not Yours: Commercial Appropriation of Personality under the Privacy Acts of British Columbia, Manitoba and Saskatchewan.' *University of British Columbia Law Review* 15: 241–340.

Velamuri, S.R., and R. Edward Freeman (2006). 'A New Approach to CSR: Company Stakeholder Responsibility' in *Corporate Social Responsibility: Reconciling Aspiration with Application* (Andrew Kakaadse and Mette Morsing, eds.), 9–23. New York: Palgrave MacMillan.

Viera, John David (1988). 'Images as Property' in *Image Ethics: The Moral Rights of Subjects in Photographs, Film, and Television* (Larry Gross, John

Stuart Katz, and Jay Ruby, eds.), 135–62. New York: Oxford University Press.

Vipond, Mary (1989). *The Mass Media in Canada*. Toronto: James Horner.

Volmers, Eric (2004). 'New Look for Junos.' *Toronto Star* 20: C1.

Von Tigerstrom, Barbara (2001a). 'Human Rights Issues in Patenting of Higher Life Forms: The Role of the Canadian Charter of Rights and Freedoms.' http://www.cbac-cccb.ca/epic/site/cbac-cccb.nsf/en/ah00391e.html.

– (2001b). 'Human Rights Issues Related to the Patenting of Human Biological Material.' http://www.cbac-cccb.ca/epic/site/cbac-cccb.nsf/en/ah00402e.html.

Wagner, Christian, and Efraim Turban (2002). 'Are Intelligent E-Commerce Agents Partners or Predators?' *Communications of the ACTM* 45(5): 84–90.

Waldby, Catherine (2000). *The Visible Human Project: Informatic Bodies and Posthuman Medicine*. London: Routledge.

Wall Street Journal Online/Harris Interactive Health Care Poll (2005). 'Harris Poll.' University of Miami, Ethics Program. http://www6.miami.edu/ethics/schiavo/terri_schiavo_timeline.html.

Walton, Priscilla L., and Lynn van Luven, eds. (1999). *Pop Can: Popular Culture in Canada*. Scarborough, Ont.: Prentice-Hall.

Warren, Samuel, and Louis Brandeis (1890). 'The Right to Privacy.' *Harvard Law Review* 4: 193–220.

Wartick, S.L., and Cochran, P.L. (1985). 'The Evolution of the Corporate Social Performance Model.' *Academy of Management Review* 10: 758–69.

Wayner, Peter (2003). 'The New Card Shark: Online Parlors and Speedy Computer Programs Change Poker.' *New York Times*, 10 July: G1.

Welling, Bruce (1991). *Corporate Law in Canada: The Governing Principles* (2nd edition). Toronto: Butterworths.

Wells, Celia (1993). *Corporations and Criminal Responsibility*. Oxford: Clarendon Press.

Wettig, Steffen, and Eberhard Zehendner (2004). 'A Legal Analysis of Human and Electronic Agents.' *Artificial Intelligence and Law* 12: 111–35.

White, Anne (n/d). 'The Persons Case: A Struggle for Legal Definition and Personhood' in *Alberta History*, 2–9. Calgary: Historical Society of Alberta.

Wiener, Norbert (1948). *Cybernetics; or Control and Communication in the Animal and the Machine*. New York: Wiley.

Wiggins, David (1987). 'The Person As ... ' in *Persons and Personality: A Contemporary Inquiry* (Arthur Peacocke and Grant Gillett, eds.), 56–74. New York: Basil Blackwell.

Williams, Rob (2004). 'A Geek God: Nardwuar Trades Celebrity Stalking for Ripple Rocking.' *Winnipeg Sun*, 13 May: W15.

Willis, Robert (1821). *An Attempt to Analyse the Automaton Chess Player of Mr. von Kempelen*. London: Booth.

Wilmington, Michael (2004). 'The Corporation.' *Chicago Tribune*, 15 July.

Windisch, Charles Gottliebe de (1784). *Inanimate Reason; or a Circumstantial Account of That Astonishing Piece of Mechanism, M. de Kempelen's Chess-Player*. London: S. Bladon.

Winner, Langdon (1977). *Autonomous Technology: Technics-Out-Of-Control as a Theme in Political Thought*. Cambridge, MA: MIT Press.

– (1996). 'It Plays Like God.' *Technology Review*, May/June: 68.

Winter, Jessica (2006). 'Film Review: Enron: The Smartest Guys in the Room.' *Time Out*, 26 April. http://www.timeout.com/film/82628.html.

Wintermute, Robert (2004). 'Sexual Orientation and the Charter: The Achievement of Formal Legal Equality (1985–2005) and Its Limits.' *McGill Law Journal* 49: 1143–80.

Wise, J. Macgregor (1998). 'Intelligent Agency.' *Cultural Studies* 12(3): 410–28.

Wise, Steven M. (2000). *Rattling the Cage*. Massachusetts: Perseus Publishing.

Wood, Donna J. (1991a). 'Corporate Social Performance Revisited.' *Academy of Management Review* 16: 591–718.

– (1991b). 'Social Issues in Management: Research and Theory in Corporate Social Performance.' *Journal of Management* 17: 383–406.

Woodmansee, Martha, and Peter Jaszi, eds. (1994). *The Construction of Authorship: Textual Appropriation in Law and Literature*. Durham and London: Duke University Press.

Woodmansee, Martha, and Peter Jaszi (1994). 'Introduction' in *The Construction of Authorship: Textual Appropriation in Law and Literature* (Martha Woodmansee and Peter Jaszi, eds.), 1–13. Durham and London: Duke University Press.

World Bank Group (2004).'CSR.' http://www.world.bank.org/

Wright, Frances (2004a). 'Famous Five Are Priceless.' *Calgary Sun*, 18 September: 15.

– (2004b). 'A Chance to Salute Pioneer Feminists.' *Calgary Herald*, 11 October: A8.

Wright, Robert (1996). 'Can Machines Think?' *Time* (South Pacific), 1 April: 50–8.

Yedlin, Deborah (2004). 'To Some, It's the Infamous Five.' *Globe and Mail*, 19 October: A23.

Zdenek, Sean (2003). 'Artificial Intelligence as a Discursive Practice: The Case of Embodied Software Agent Systems.' *AI & Society* 17: 340–63.

Canadian Cases Cited

Athans v. *Canadian Adventure Camps Ltd.* (1977), 17 O.R. (2d) 425, 34 C.P.R. (2d) 126, 80 D.L.R. (3d) 583 (Ont. H.C.)

Aubry v. *Les Éditions Vice-Versa Inc.*, [1998] S.C.R. 591 (S.C.C.)

Baron Philippe de Rothschild S.A. v. *Casa de Habana Inc.* (1987), 19 C.P.R. (3d) 114, 17 C.I.P.R. 185 (Ont. H.C.J.)

Big Bend Hotel v. *Security Mutual Casualty Co.* (1980), 19 B.C.L.R. 102 (B.C.S.C.)

Clarkson Co. v. *Zhelka*, [1967] 2 O.R. 565 (H.C.J.)

Corlett-Lockyer v. *Stephens*, [1996] B.C.J. No. 857 (B.C. Prov. Ct.)

De Salaberry Realities Ltd. v. *M.N.R.* (1974), 46 D.L. R. (3d) 100 (Fed. T.D.)

Dowell v. *Mengen Institute et al.* (1983), 72 C.P.R. (2d) 238 (Ont. H.C.J.)

Edwards v. *Canada (A.G.)* [1928], S.C.R. 276, [1928], 4 D.L.R. 98 (S.C.C.)

Gould v. *Stoddart Publishing Co.*(1996) 30 O.R. (3d) 520, 74 C.P.R. (3d) 206 (Ont. Ct. Gen. Div.)

Gould v. *Stoddart Publishing Co.* (1998), 39 O.R. (3d) 545, 161 D.L.R. (4th) 321 (Ont. C.A.)

Harvard College v. *Canada (Commissioner for Patents)* (Patent Appeal Board)

Harvard College v. *Canada (Commissioner for Patents)* [1998], 3 F.C. 510, 79 C.P.R. (3d) 98, 146 F.T.R. 279, 3 F.C. 510, [1998] F.C.J. 510 (F.C.T.D.)

Harvard College v. *Canada (Commissioner for Patents)* (2000), 189 D.R.L. (4th) 385, 7 C.P,.R. (4th) 1, [2000]4 F.C. 528, 4 F.C. 528, [2000] F.C.J. No. 213 (F.C.A)

Harvard College v. *Canada (Commissioner for Patents)*, (2002) S.C.C. 76, 219 D.L.R. (4th) 577, [2002] 4 S.C.R. 45, 21 C.P.R. (4th) 417, 296 N.R. 1, 235 F.T.R. 214 (S.C.C.)

Heath v. *West-Barron School of Television Canada Ltd.* (1981), 34 O.R. (2d) 126, 62 C.P.R. (2d) 92 (Ont. H.C.J.)

Horton v. *Tim Donut Ltd.* (1997), 45 B.L.R. (2d) 7, 75 C.P.R. (3d) 451, [1997] O.J. No. 390 (Q.L.) (Gen. Div.), aff'd 104 O.A.C. 234, 75 C.P.R. (3d) 467 (Ont. C.A.)

Joseph v. *Daniels* (1986), 11 C.P.R. (3d) 544, 4 B.C.L.R. (2d) 239 (B.C.S.C.).

Kosmopoulos v. *Constitution Insurance Co. of Canada*, [1987] 1 S.C.R. 2 (S.C.C.)

Krouse v. *Chrysler Canada Ltd.* (1973), 1 O.R. (2d) 225, 13 C.P.R. (2d) 28, 40 D.L.R. (3d) 15 (Ont. C.A.)

Monsanto Canada Inc. v. *Schmeiser*, (2004) S.C.C. 34, 239 D.L.R. (4th) 271, 320 N.R. 201, [2004] 1 S.C.R. 902, 31 C.P.R. (4th) 161 (S.C.C.)

Pioneer Hi-Bred v. *Commissioner of Patents* (1987), 11 C.I.P.R. 165, 14 C.P.R. (3d) 491, 77 N.R. 137, [1987] 3 F.C. 8 (F.C.A.)

Pioneer Hi-Bred v. *Commissioner of Patents* (1989), 25 C.P.R. (3d) 257 (S.C.C.)

Racine v. *CJRC Radio Capitale Ltée* (1977), 17 O.R. (2d) 370, 80 D.L.R. (3d) 441 (Ont. Co. Ct.)

Re: Application for Patent of Abitibi Co. (1982), 62 C.P.R. (2d) 81 (Patent Appeal Board)

Reference re Matter of the Meaning of the Word 'Persons' in s. 24, B.N.A. Act, [1928] S.C.R. 276 (S.C.C.)

Reference re Same-Sex Marriage [2004], 3 S.C.R. (S.C.C.)

R. v. *Canadian Dredge & Dock Co.,* [1985] S.C.J. No. 28, [1985] 1 S.C.R. 662 (S.C.C.)

R. v. *Cyr (Waters)* [1917], 3 W.W.R. 849 (Alta S.C. (A.D.))

R. v. *Safety-Kleen Canada Inc.* (1997), 32 O.R. (3d) 493 (Ont. C.A.)

R. v. *Waterloo Mercury Sales Ltd.* (1974), 49 D.L.R. (3d) 131 (Alta. Dist. Ct.)

R. v. *Wholesale Travel Group,* [1991] 3 S.C.R. 154, 7 C.P.R. (2d) 36 (S.C.C.).

Shaw v. *Berman* (1997), 144 D.L.R. (4th) 484, 72 C.P.R. (3d) 9 (Ont. Ct. Gen. Div.), aff'd 167 D.L.R. (4th) 576, 1150 A.C. (198), (Ont. C.A.)

Transamerica Life Insurance Company of Canada v. *Canada Life Assurance Company,* [1997] O.J. No. 3754 (Ont. C.A.)

Vancouver Rape Relief Society v. *Nixon et al.* 2003. B.C.S.C. 1936 (B.C.S.C.)

British Cases Cited

Edwards v. *A.-G. Canada,* [1930], A.C. 124, [1929] 3 W.W.R. 479 (J.C.P.C.)

Macaura v. *Northern Assurance Co.,* [1925] A.C. 619 (H.L.)

Salomon v. *Salomon & Co.,* [1897] AC 22 (H.L.)

Smith, Stone and Knight Ltd. v. *Birmingham Corp.,* [1939] 4 All. E.R. 116 (K.B.)

Viscountess Rhonda's Claim, [1922] 2 A.C. 339 (H.L.)

U.S. Cases Cited

Carson v. *Johnny Portable Toilets, Inc.* 698 F. 2d 831 (6th Cir. 1983).

Dartmouth College v. *Woodword* (1819) 17 U.S. (4 Wheat.) 518 (U.S.S.C.)

Diamond v. *Chakrabarty* 447 U.S. 303 (1980)

Edison v. *Edison Polyform Mfg. Co.* 67A 392 (N.J. 1907).

Grant v. *Esquire Inc.* 367 F. Supp. 876 (S.D. N.Y. 1973)

Hoffman v. *Capital Cities/ABC Inc., et al.* (1999), 33 F. Supp 2d 867, 27 Media L. Rep. 1527 (U.S.D.C. CA).

Haelan Laboratories, Inc. v. *Topps Chewing Gum, Inc.* (1953), 202 F.2d 866 (2d Cir. 1953), cert. denied, 346 US 816, 74 S. Ct. 26, 98 L. Ed. 343 (1953).

Lugosi v. *Universal Pictures* 25 Cal. 3d 813, 160 Cal. Rptr. 323, 603 P. 2d 425 (1979)

Midler v. *Ford Motor Co.* 849 F.2d 460 (9th Cir. 1988)

Moore v. *Regents of University of California* (1990), 51 Cal. 3d 120, 793 P. 2d 479 (U.S.S.C.).

O'Brien v. *Pabst Sales Co.* 124 F 2d. 167 (5th Cir. 1941)

Onassis v. *Christian Dior-New York Inc.*, 122 Misc. 2d 603, 472 N.Y. S. 2d 254 (S. Ct. N.Y.Co. 1984), aff'd 110 A.D. 2d 1095, 488 N.Y.S. 2d 943 (1st Dept. 1985)

Santa Clara County v. *Southern Pacific Railroad* 1886 (U.S.S.C.)

Sinatra v. *Goodyear Tire and Rubber Co.*, 435 F.2d 711 (1970)

State of Missouri ex. rel. Crow v. *Hostetter* (1898) 38 L.R.A.

Waits v. *Frito-Lay, Inc.* 978 F.2d 1093 (9th Cir. 1992)

White v. *Samsung Electronics America, Inc.*, 971 F.2d 1395 (9th Cir. 1992)

Canadian Legislation Cited

An Act to Amend the Criminal Code, 2nd Sess., 37th Parl. 2003 (Royal Assent, 7 November 2003), S.C. 2003, c. 21.

Assisted Human Reproduction Act, R.S.C. 2002

British North America Act, 1867

Canada Business Corporations Act, R.S. 1985, c. C-44.

Canadian Charter of Rights and Freedoms

Civil Code of Québec R.S.Q. Chapter C-1991.

Criminal Code, R.S. c. C-34.

Interpretation Act

Patent Act R.S.C. c. P-4.

Privacy Act R.S.B.C. 1996, c.373

The Privacy Act R.S.S. 1978, c. P-24

The Privacy Act C.C.S.M. c. P125

Privacy Act R.S.N.L. 1990, c. P-22

Supreme Court Act R.S. 1985, c. S-26.

Uniform Electronic Commerce Act, Annotated Version at http://www.ulcc.cca/en/poam2/index.cfm?sec=1999&sub=1999ia

Uniform Electronic Commerce Act (1999)

American Legislation Cited

The Lanham Act 15 U.S.C.A.

Uniform Electronic Transaction Act

Uniform Computer Information Transaction Act (1999)

Filmography

Artificial Intelligence: AI (2001), Dir.: Steven Spielberg (2 hrs. 26 mins.).

Black Gold (2006), Dir: Mark Francis and Nick Francis (1 hr. 18 mins.).

The Boys from Brazil (1978), Dir: Franklin J. Schaffner (2 hrs. 3 mins.).

Canada: A People's History #12 (2001), Dir.: Jacqueline Corkery.

The Chess Player (1927), Dir: Raymond Bernard (b/w, silent, 2 hrs. 15 mins.).

Colossus: The Forbin Project (1970), Dir: Joseph Sargent (1 hr. 40 mins.).

The Corporation (2004), Dir: Mark Achbar and Jennifer Abbott (2 hr. 25 mins.).

Desk Set (1957), Dir.: Walter Lang (b/w) (103 mins.).

Enron: The Smartest Guys in the Room (2005), Dir: Alex Gibney (1 hr. 50 mins).

Fahrenheit 9/11 (2004), Dir: Michael Moore (2 hrs. 2 mins.).

Game Over: Kasparov and the Machine (2003), Dir: Vikram Jayanti (1 hr. 25 mins).

The Island (2005), Dir: Michael Bay (2 hrs. 16 mins.).

Johnny Mnemonic (1995), Dir.: Robert Longo (96 mins.).

Just for Kicks (2006), Dir: Thibaut de Longeville and Lisa Leone (81 mins.).

La peau blanche (2004), Dir.: Danial Roby (1 hr. 32 mins.).

Multiplicity (1996), Dir: Harold Ramis (1 hr. 57 mins.)

Porky's (1982), Dir.: Bob Clark (1 hr. 34 mins.).

Resident Evil – Apocalypse (2004), Dir.: Alexander Witt (1 hr. 34 mins.).

The 6th Day (2000), Dir: Roger Spottiswoode (2 hrs. 3 mins.).

Supersize Me (2004), Dir: Morgan Spurlock (1 hr. 40 mins.).

2001: A Space Odyssey, Dir: Stanley Kubrick (2 hrs. 21 mins.).

Wal-Mart: The High Cost of Low Price (2005), Dir.: Robert Greenwald (98 mins).

War Games (1983), Dir. John Badham (1 hr. 54 mins.).

Who Killed the Electric Car? (2006), Dir: Chris Paine (92 mins.).

Other Media

Stewart-Verger, Ruth, and Teresa Healy (2004), *She Pushed from Behind: Emily Murphy in Story and Song*, Ottawa: Library and Archives of Canada.

Index